English G Neue Ausgabe

D1931975

Band A 2

für das 6. Schuljahr
an Gymnasien

Cornelsen

English G · Neue Ausgabe
Band A2

Im Auftrage des Verlages herausgegeben und erarbeitet von
Prof. Hellmut Schwarz, Mannheim · Carl Taylor M.A., München · Prof. Franz Vettel, Heppenheim

in Zusammenarbeit mit der Fremdsprachenredaktion
Michael R. Ferguson M.A. und Cedric J. Sherratt B.A. (Projektleitung),
Susanne Döpper, Margaret Kersten, Hartmut Tschepe *sowie* Irene Gagel

unter Mitarbeit von
StD Udo J. Hennig, Neuwied · StD Erich Fleischhack, Ebern/Unterfranken ·
Prof. Dr. Liesel Hermes, Karlsruhe · Prof. Dr. Günter Nold, Frankfurt am Main/PH Ludwigsburg ·
Martin Rosenthal, Berlin, *sowie* David W. Bygott, Oxford, und Karen Carlson-Kreibohm, Berlin

Beratende Mitwirkung
John Eastwood M.A., Street, Somerset · StD Dr. Jens-Peter Green, Vechta ·
StD Adolf Menzel, München · MR Burkhart Nather, Mülheim (Ruhr) ·
StD Dr. Peter Potansky, Holzkirchen · Prof. Dieter Vater, Weinheim

Grafik
Robert Broomfield, Tunbridge Wells,
sowie Gabriele Heinisch, Berlin

Layout
Peter Richter und Bernd Lenzner

Bildquellen
s. Verzeichnis auf S. 183

1. Auflage – 3. Druck 1988
Alle Drucke dieser Auflage können, weil untereinander unverändert, im Unterricht nebeneinander benutzt werden.

Bestellnummer 51099 – broschiert
50777 – gebunden

© 1986 Cornelsen Verlag GmbH & Co., Berlin

Das Werk und seine Teile sind urheberrechtlich geschützt. Jede Verwertung in anderen als den gesetzlich zugelassenen Fällen bedarf deshalb der vorherigen schriftlichen Einwilligung des Verlages.

Satz Adolph Fürst & Sohn, Berlin
Repro O.R.T. OffsetReproTechnik, Berlin
Druck Cornelsen Druck, Berlin
Weiterverarbeitung Fritzsche-Ludwig, Berlin

ISBN 3-464-05109-9 – broschiert
3-464-05077-7 – gebunden

Vertrieb Cornelsen Verlagsgesellschaft, Bielefeld

Contents

Unit	Page	Parts of the unit	Main speech functions/themes	Structures
	5	**Introduction**: Dave and his friends; Hatfield		
1		Revision Unit		
	8	**Acquisition**: A visit to a farm	Sagen, was jemand tun oder nicht tun will; über das Leben auf einem Bauernhof sprechen	**Revision:** simple present and present progressive · Word order with adverbials of place and time · Writing a letter
	10	**Text**: **Cows or bulls?**		
	11	**Exercises**		
2	17	Acquisition: All about BMX	Über den BMX-Sport sprechen; über einen Radunfall berichten; etwas zugeben oder abstreiten	Simple past in positive sentences, negative sentences and questions: *was/were*, regular verbs + a few irregular forms *(fell, overtook, rode, said)* · **Revision:** plurals; *your, his, its, their;* a mixed bag
	21	Text: **The race**		
	22	Exercises		
	27	Look at Britain: Traffic and vehicles		
	28	Summary		
3	30	Acquisition: British meals and food Song: This is the way you wash your face	Über einen Ausflug berichten; über Mahlzeiten sprechen; sagen und fragen, was jemand braucht oder nicht braucht	Simple past: more irregular verbs · Word order in questions with question words · Possessive form of plural nouns: *the Kings' house, her friends' magazines* · *some, any* and their compounds · **Revision:** British money; on the phone
	34	Text: **Spaghetti trees**		
	35	Exercises		
	40	Summary		
	42 ○	Extra Reading: **The film star**		
4	44	Acquisition: Health and the body Song: One finger, one thumb	Über Körperteile und Krankheiten sprechen; Vergleiche anstellen; fragen, wem etwas gehört; nach bestimmten Personen oder Sachen fragen; sagen, was jemand nicht tun darf oder nicht zu tun braucht; nach einer Meinung fragen; eine Meinung äußern	Comparison of adjectives: *fast – faster – fastest, exciting – more exciting – most exciting* · Sentences with comparisons: *faster than, (not) as fast as* · Questions with *whose, which* · *mustn't, needn't* · Prop-word *one/ones* · *both* · **Revision:** simple present or present progressive
	47	Text: **McPherson's virus?**		
	48	Exercises		
	54	Summary		
5	56	Acquisition: Sport	Über Sport sprechen und sagen, ob man Sport mag oder nicht mag; sagen, wie jemand ist und wie jemand etwas tut; sagen, was jemand vorhat; sagen, was man mag, nicht mag oder lieber mag	Adverbs of manner: usage, formation, word order, comparison · *Going to*-future · **Revision:** simple past; a mixed bag
	60	Text: **Sport for everybody**		
	61	Exercises		
	67	Look at Britain: A sports centre		
	68	Summary		
	70 ○	Extra Reading: **The big match**		

○ = wahlfrei

Unit	Page	Parts of the unit	Main speech functions/themes	Structures
6	71	Acquisition: A school trip	Mitteilen, was geschehen ist und was jemand getan hat; jemanden einladen	Present perfect in positive sentences, negative sentences and questions: regular verbs + certain irregular verbs, word order, position of adverbs of time · **Revision:** a mixed bag: present progressive, *there is/are,* prepositions; mixed tenses
	74	Text: **The old woman**		
	76 ○	Some British folk songs		
	77	Exercises		
	83	Look at Britain: Norwich		
	84	Summary		
7	86	Acquisition: Clothes	Über Kleidung sprechen; sagen, was jemand getan hat und wann jemand es getan hat	Present perfect and simple past: further practice and contrast · **Revision:** a mixed bag; *her, his, their, she's, he's, they're*; comparisons; mixed tenses
	89	Text: **The red stamp**		
	90	Exercises		
	97	Summary		
8	98	Acquisition: A visit to the zoo Song: The animals went in two by two	Über Tiere sprechen; über einen Zoobesuch sprechen; sagen, wem etwas gehört; Vorhersagen machen und Vermutungen über die Zukunft äußern	Possessive pronouns: *mine, yours,* etc. · *Will*-future · Sequence of tenses in main clause and subordinate clause with *when* · **Revision:** *do – does*; adjective or adverb; mixed tenses
	102	Text: **Lions and tigers**		
	104	Exercises		
	110	Look at Britain: Adverts		
	111	Summary		
	112 ○	Extra Reading: **The world after the year 2000**		
9	114	Acquisition: Summer holidays; Cornwall	Über Ferien sprechen: Pläne äußern und Vorhersagen machen; sagen, was gerade vor sich ging, als etwas anderes geschah; sagen, was jemand (nicht) tun durfte/konnte; sagen, was jemand tun mußte oder nicht zu tun brauchte	*Going to*-future and *will*-future in contrast · Past progressive · Past tense modals: *was/wasn't allowed to, could/couldn't, had to/didn't have to* · **Revision:** word order; simple present or present progressive; simple past; present perfect or simple past
	118	Text: **The wreckers**		
	120	Exercises		
	124	Summary		
10	126	Acquisition: New York, Florida	Sagen, was unter bestimmten Bedingungen geschehen wird; berichten, was andere gesagt oder geschrieben haben	[Conditional sentences with the simple present and the *will*-future] · [Reported speech with the introductory verb in the present tense] **Revision:** word order
	130	Text: **The Prince of the Sun and the Princess of the Sea**		[ ] = je nach Bundesland fakultativ
	131	Exercises		
	135	Summary		
	136 ○	A game: Lucky hands		

138 The English alphabet · English sounds · Grammatical terms
139 Names
140 Vocabulary (Beachte die Hinweise auf S. 140)
167 Alphabetical list of words (Books 1 + 2)
181 Irregular verbs
185 ○ Useful classroom phrases

Dave and his friends

1

Hallo!
Do you still know me?
I'm Dave King, of course.
And these are some of my friends from Hatfield.

I hope you still know Kevin Connor.
He has got two sisters – Carol and Tina. The Connors live in a flat. They've got a nice white rabbit. Its name is Blacky. Blacky eats *everything:* not only his food, but magazines, papers and sometimes the furniture, too.

And this is Sandra Bell. She and her mother live in Woodside, a small village near Hatfield. Sandra has got a dog, too. His name is Wag. Wag always barks when you come to the house, but he soon runs away.

Do you remember Liz Dean? She has got a brother – Peter. The Deans don't live in a flat, they live in a house. Liz and Peter have got a dog. His name is Peanut. Peanut doesn't eat tables or chairs. But you must take him for a walk every day, or he does other things.

2 This year we're all in class 2F. And Mr Hill still teaches English in our class. We think this is great. But he says it's terrible.

And you?

What can you say about your friends, your pets and your new class?

3 Kevin and I go to school together. We usually walk. My sister Sally goes by bus. She's lazy. Liz and Sandra often go by bike. It's all right for Liz, because she lives near Park School. But Sandra's home is about three miles from Hatfield. And that can be a problem when it rains.

And you?

How do you go to school in the morning?

4 We all like sports, but we've got other hobbies, too. I play football and I make models. I go to the model club every week. We usually meet after school on Thursdays. And I play the guitar and learn the piano.

Kevin likes football, too. And he goes to the photo club. They meet on Fridays and take photos together. Sometimes the photos are very funny.

Liz collects coins. And she plays table-tennis and hockey. Sandra learns the guitar. She's very good. When she plays, Wag sits on the floor and sings with her.

And you?

What are your hobbies?
What's your favourite sport?

5 Dave and his friends live in Hatfield. There is a new town and an old town. New Hatfield is not very interesting. The pedestrian precinct in the town centre is usually quiet. There are no cars or buses. But there are lots of shops and cafés. The children sometimes meet in the precinct after school or on Saturday afternoons.

◁ *Flats in New Hatfield*

▽ *The Hatfield swimming-pool*

△ *The precinct*

◁ *An old church*

An old house ▷

And, of course, there is Hatfield House. That is a very big old house with an interesting history. It is very popular with tourists. The house has got beautiful gardens and it is in a nice big park. The children often go to Hatfield House on their bikes and play in the park.

Revision Unit 1 A

1 Dave's Uncle Ernie and Aunt Mary live in the country. They live in a small village, Little Missenden. It is about 30 miles from Hatfield. Little Missenden has got a beautiful old church. In the summer you can walk through the woods and fields. Or you can climb the hills. There is a nice little river and a lake, too.

2 Aunt Mary and Uncle Ernie are farmers. They have got 90 cows on their farm. There are some bulls and horses on the farm, too. And they have got a few pigs and a few chickens. → Ex 2, 3

3

Mr and Mrs King want to visit Uncle Ernie and Aunt Mary next weekend. They want to drive to Little Missenden in their car. Sally wants to go, too.

Mr King wants to . . . .
Mrs King wants to . . . .
Sally . . . .
She . . . , too.

4 But Dave does not want to go. He does not think farms are interesting.

Mrs King: Why don't you want to come?
Dave: Farms are so boring. And they're smelly and dirty. Pooh!
Mrs King: Well, where do you want to go?
Dave: Let's go to the coast.
Sally: It's boring there, too. You just sit on the beach and look at the sea. And that's often dirty and smelly, too.
Mr King: Listen, young man. You can come with us, or you can stay at home and feed *our* animals. → Ex 4-7

5 It is Saturday and the Kings are on Bluebell Farm in Little Missenden.

What is happening here?

Uncle Ernie and Mr King are standing near the car.
Sally is riding a horse.
Dave . . . .
Aunt Mary and Mrs King . . . .

Aunt Mary . . . the cat.
A dog . . . .
Another dog . . . into the house.
Some chickens . . . across the field.

→ Ex 8

6 Uncle Ernie and Aunt Mary milk the cows every morning and every afternoon. It is five o'clock in the afternoon now. They are milking the cows and Sally is helping them.

Sally: Do the cows go into the fields in the winter, too?
Aunt Mary: No, they don't. It's too cold and there's not enough grass for them. They stay in the cowshed.
Sally: Oh, poor things.
Uncle Ernie: Why? It's warm in the cowshed. And our cows are lucky. On some farms the cows must stay in the cowshed all the winter *and* all the summer.
Sally: What? That's terrible.
Uncle Ernie: You're right. But people want cheap food. They don't want to know how the animals live.

→ Ex 9

7 The days are very long for Aunt Mary and Uncle Ernie. They get up at half past five. First they milk the cows. Then they have breakfast. Then Uncle Ernie works in the fields till lunch time. Aunt Mary usually feeds the animals. At five o'clock they milk the cows again. They do this every day – on Saturdays and Sundays, too. They sometimes watch TV in the evening when they are not too tired. They usually go to bed before ten o'clock.

→ Ex 10-12

Cows or bulls?

Sally and Dave are walking through the fields on the farm. It is a nice warm day and the sun is shining.

Dave: Would you like to live in the country?
Sally: Oh, yes. I'd like to live on a farm. You can ride horses. You can feed the animals. I think it's great. And you?
Dave: I don't think so. Farms are dirty and smelly. And what do people do in the evening?
Sally: What do people do in Hatfield? They watch TV.

Dave: Hey, Sally. Can you ride a cow?
Sally: Why don't we try it?
Dave: OK. Great. We can play cowboys.
Sally: Dave, wait! Those aren't cows. They're bulls!
Dave: Oh, no! . . . Help!

Mrs King: Well, Dave. Do you still think farms are boring?
Dave: No, I don't. Sometimes they can be exciting.
Sally: Yes, they can be very exciting when a bull is running after you.
Uncle Ernie: Well, you're young enough. You can run.
Aunt Mary: And how do *you* like it here in the country, Sally?
Sally: I think it's great. There are lots of beautiful places – the woods, the lake, the old church in the village. I like the animals, too. And your food is fantastic, Aunt Mary.
Dave: Yes, I like these cakes. Country food is super.
Aunt Mary: Oh, thank you, Dave. But these cakes are from the supermarket.

And you?

Where would you like to live? In the town or in the country? Can you say why?

→ Ex 1, 13

1 *Look at "Cows or bulls?" on page 10 again. Then complete this text.*

Sally and Dave are walking . . . the . . . on their uncle's and . . . farm. It is a nice . . . day and the sun is . . . . Sally would . . . to live on a farm. There you can ride . . . and feed the . . . . Dave thinks farms are . . . and . . . . There are some animals in the field. They are not . . . , they are . . . , and they are coming after Dave and Sally.
Later Dave says that farms can be . . . , and Sally thinks it is . . . in the . . . . There are lots of . . . places near the farm. Dave likes country . . . . But Aunt Mary's . . . are from the . . . .

R **Revision: be** („sein")

2 a *Ask your partner questions with "be".*

1. . . . you from . . . ?	– Yes, .../No, ...
2. Where . . . your flat/your house?	– Our flat/house . . . in . . . (Street).
3. How old . . . you?	– I . . . .
4. . . . you lively or quiet?	– I think I . . . .
5. What . . . your favourite colour?	– . . . .

Can you make some more questions like these?

b *Now make a text from your partner's answers and read your text to the other pupils. Ask who can guess your partner's name. – Remember: You use long forms in a text.*

My partner . . . from . . . . Her/His . . . in . . . . She/He . . . and she/he thinks she/he . . . . Her/His favourite colour . . . . There . . . people in her/his family: . . . .

R **Revision: simple present** (Ex 3-7)

3 **What are their hobbies?** *Remember the "-s" in the third person singular.*

1. Liz and Kevin . . . photos. *Go on.*

4 **Dave, Liz, Sandra and Kevin at Park School** *Complete the text.*

Dave, Liz and Kevin (live) in Hatfield, but Sandra (not live) there; she (live) in Woodside. The children (go) to Park School. All the pupils (wear) school uniforms at Park School. Dave and Kevin (walk) to school every morning. Liz and Sandra (not walk); they usually (go) by bike.
School in Britain (not start) at eight o'clock, it (start) at quarter to nine or nine o'clock.
Lessons (finish) at four o'clock. So lots of children (eat) lunch at school – Liz and Sandra, too. Dave (not eat) lunch at school, and Kevin (go) home for lunch, too.
Lots of children (not leave) school at four o'clock. They (meet) their friends at a school club.
On Thursdays Dave often (go) to the model club and (make) models; but he (not go) every Thursday. Liz and Sandra sometimes (play) table-tennis on Wednesdays, and Kevin (stay) for the stamp club on Tuesdays.
Some children at Park School (not go) to the school clubs; they (not like) them.

5 At a party

Remember: You make negative sentences with "don't" and, in the third person singular, with "doesn't".

1\.
Would you like another lemonade? – Sorry, I <u>don't drink</u> (not drink) lemonade. Can I have orange juice, please?

2\.
Let's listen to "The Pets". We all like their songs. – Well, Fred and Tom (not like) them. They think they're boring.

3\.
You must eat one of these sweets. – You're lucky. I (not eat) sweets. Now you can have two.

4\.
Do you want to take this cassette home? – Oh, that's very nice of you, but I (not listen) to pop songs at home.

5\.
Mary is very quiet tonight. – She talks lots at school, but she (not talk) much at parties.

6\.
Carol and Tina are very happy tonight. – That's right. They (not argue) when other people are there.

6 *Ask your friends (and your teacher) questions with question words. Remember: You make questions with "do" and, in the third person singular, with "does".*

a

When	do	you	get up in the morning?
What	does	Christoph	do after school?
Where		Julia	collect?
Why		Katja and Thomas	meet your/his/her/ their friends?
		...	go at weekends?
			like dogs?

b *Here are some other verbs for questions:*

visit
clean
do your homework
listen to
live
hate
read
watch TV

Example: When do you get up in the morning, Claudia? – At half past six usually.

7a Town or country? *Complete the dialogue.*

Jane: Mike is in London again today.
Kate: ... he (like) it there?
Jane: Yes, he (go) there every weekend. He (like) big towns.
Kate: Well, I must say I (not like) them. I (hate) them.
Jane: Why ... you (hate) them?
Kate: They're so loud and dirty. ... you (not agree) with me?
Jane: Well, no. I (not think) so. I (find) them fantastic. Of course they're dirty, but –
Kate: So why ... you (like) them? And why ... Mike (go) to London every weekend?
Jane: Look, on a nice day Mike (go) to Hyde Park. When it (rain), he (go) to museums or to the shops. You can do so many different things.
Kate: All right, but you only (see) the nice things. There are other things, too: lots of cars in the streets, and people (live) in small flats or expensive houses. No, I (think) towns are only good for one or two days. I (not agree) with you and Mike.

b *Now write and play a dialogue about a village or the country.*

R Revision: present progressive

Remember: *You make the present progressive with a form of the verb "be" + -ing form.*
Example: Dave **is** work**ing** in the garden.
Be careful how you spell some -ing forms: sit/sit**ting**, com**e**/com**ing**.

8

Ask your partner about the pictures. She/He must answer your questions.

In picture number 1, is Mr King driving the car? – No, he isn't.
Are the Kings driving to Little Missenden? – Yes, they are.
Go on.

Make two groups in your class. One group must ask questions and the other group must answer them.

What's Uncle Ernie doing in picture number 3? – He's sitting in the living-room and listening to the radio.
Go on. (You can use phrases like "Let me see, . . . ," "Can't you see . . . ?" or ". . . , of course.")

R Revision: simple present or present progressive? (Ex 9-11)

Remember: *simple present:* every day, always, usually, often, sometimes, never
present progressive: at the moment, now

9

	1	2	3	4
Now:				
Every day?	yes	no	no	yes
When?	after school	on Saturdays	at the weekends	in the evening

Look at the pictures and make dialogues with a partner.

What's Dave doing in picture number 1? – He's playing the guitar, of course.
Does he play the guitar every day? – Yes, he does.
Oh, when does he play the guitar? – (He plays the guitar) after school. *Go on.*

○

How can you leave the room with two legs[1] and come back with six? – Bring a chair with you.
Why does the Statue of Liberty stand in New York harbour[2]? – Because she can't sit down.

[1]leg *Bein* [2]harbour ['hɑːbə] *Hafen*

10 On Bluebell Farm *Use the words in ( ) and make new sentences.*

Examples: The Kings are in their car on the road to Little Missenden. (drive)
The Kings are driving to Little Missenden.

Every summer the Kings are on Bluebell Farm. (visit)
Every summer the Kings visit Bluebell Farm.

1. It is six o'clock in the morning. Aunt Mary and Uncle Ernie are in the kitchen. (have breakfast)
2. Every morning Uncle Ernie is in the fields till lunch time. (work)
3. Aunt Mary and Uncle Ernie are usually in bed before ten o'clock. (go to)
4. It is evening now. There is a good programme on TV and Uncle Ernie is in the living-room. (watch)
5. On nice days their dogs are often in the little river near the farm. (swim)
6. It is Sunday evening. Uncle Ernie is in the kitchen. (dry dishes)
7. Aunt Mary is with her friend, Mrs Carter, now. (talk to)
8. She is at Mrs Carter's house every Sunday. (visit)

11 *Look at the questions and answers, use the right forms of the verbs and practise with a partner.*

1. Why . . . Uncle Ernie and Aunt Mary (get up) at half past five in the morning? – Because they must milk the cows.
2. . . . Aunt Mary and Uncle Ernie (milk) the cows in the morning and in the afternoon? – Yes, they . . . .
3. What . . . Uncle Ernie (do) this morning? – He (work) in the fields.
4. . . . Mr and Mrs King (cook) the lunch for Aunt Mary and Uncle Ernie? – Yes, they are.
5. . . . Sally (ride) across the fields? – No, that's Dave.
6. . . . Uncle Ernie's dogs (stay) outside day and night? – No, sometimes they're in the house.

R 12 Revision: word order with adverbials of place and time

a **Tony's and Kate's day**

Finish the sentences. Use the words in the box. Remember: adverbials of place come before adverbials of time (place before time!).

Tony and Kate leave . . . . Tony arrives . . . . He works there. Kate arrives . . . . She is a teacher. . . . Kate starts work . . . . Tony is . . . , too. They are . . . . they sometimes meet some friends . . . . They do not go . . . .

b *Now write about your day.*

13 Revision: a letter to a friend

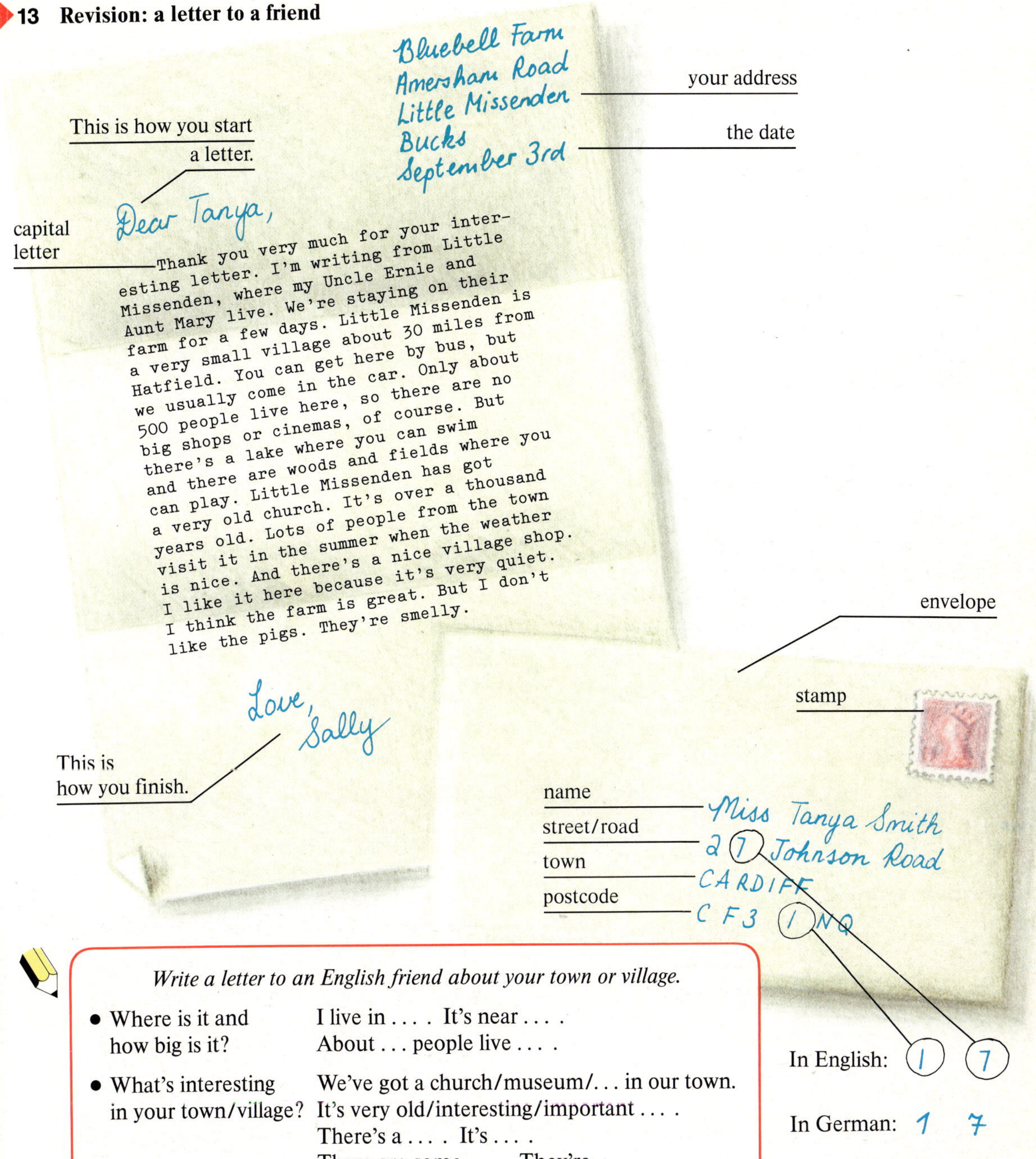
Bluebell Farm
Amersham Road
Little Missenden
Bucks
September 3rd

Dear Tanya,

Thank you very much for your interesting letter. I'm writing from Little Missenden, where my Uncle Ernie and Aunt Mary live. We're staying on their farm for a few days. Little Missenden is a very small village about 30 miles from Hatfield. You can get here by bus, but we usually come in the car. Only about 500 people live here, so there are no big shops or cinemas, of course. But there's a lake where you can swim and there are woods and fields where you can play. Little Missenden has got a very old church. It's over a thousand years old. Lots of people from the town visit it in the summer when the weather is nice. And there's a nice village shop. I like it here because it's very quiet. I think the farm is great. But I don't like the pigs. They're smelly.

Love,
Sally

Write a letter to an English friend about your town or village.

• Where is it and how big is it?	I live in . . . . It's near . . . . About . . . people live . . . .
• What's interesting in your town/village?	We've got a church/museum/. . . in our town. It's very old/interesting/important . . . . There's a . . . . It's . . . . There are some . . . . They're . . . .
• What do you like in your town/village?	I like the . . . . I think it's/they're nice/big/ . . .
• What don't you like?	I don't like the . . . because it's/they're terrible/dirty/smelly/noisy/. . .

14 WORDS WORDS WORDS

a **What is the "fourth man"?**

1. right – wrong
   cheap – ?
2. summer – winter
   town – ?
3. new – old
   quiet – ?
4. upstairs – downstairs
   inside – ?
5. he – she
   bull – ?
6. birds – sing
   dogs – ?

b **What can you do with your new words?**

You can: ride, milk, run, swim, climb, walk, learn, write, clean, go, play, stand, drink, wash, tell, visit, help

cold orange juice. him the way. a farmer. a horse. to church on Sundays. the piano. a long letter. across the fields. pupils. a cow. along the beach. a hill. in a lake. a museum. a dirty bike. on a chair. your father's car.

Examples: You can ride a horse.
You can ride across the fields.

c *Find the right English words for the wrong words in ( ).*
Be careful. One German word can sometimes be two different words in English,
e.g. Tasche: 1. bag (= Tragetasche), 2. pocket (= Tasche an einem Kleidungsstück).

1. Uncle Ernie and Aunt Mary must do lots of different *(works)* on their farm.
2. So they *(stand up)* at half past five every day.
3. Aunt Mary is Uncle Ernie's *(woman)* and Uncle Ernie is Aunt Mary's *(man).*
4. They often *(make)* the housework together but Aunt Mary usually cooks the meals.
5. Uncle Ernie is often late for lunch because he never looks at his *(clock).*
6. They do not often *(see)* television because they have not got much time.
7. Aunt Mary and Uncle Ernie like their work on the farm and they like Little Missenden: they are very *(lucky)* in the country.
8. They do not want to live in the town where there are no woods or *(seas).*

15 How much can you remember?

1. They live in a flat and they have got a rabbit. Who are they?
2. Their dog's name is Peanut.
3. He teaches class 2F English.
4. Does Sandra live in Hatfield?
5. Where does Kevin go on Fridays?
6. What are Liz's ['lɪzɪz] favourite sports?
7. He sits on the floor and sings.
8. It is very popular with tourists. What is it?
9. Is Sally's aunt a teacher?
10. What is the name of the village where Uncle Ernie and Aunt Mary live?
11. Is there a supermarket in the village?
12. What do Sally and Dave want to ride: a horse, a cow, or a bull?

BMX

:cycle Motocross

t of boys and girls
ritain and Germany
got BMX bikes.
se bikes are very
ılar because you can
them over fields
through woods.
can fly through the
r do tricks with
1X bike. And you can
great races.

e clothes

You can wear old clothes, of course – jeans and a pullover, for example. But some BMX fans wear special clothes, usually in blue, red and yellow. They protect the rider. And everybody must wear a helmet. Riders often fall off their bikes, so without one it can be dangerous.

And you?

Have you got a bike?
Have you got a BMX bike?
How many of your friends have got BMX bikes?
Do you or your friends wear special BMX clothes?

3 The bike

BMX bikes are different from other bikes. They are very strong. They have got small wheels and big tyres. They have got low saddles and high handlebars, and of course they must have good brakes. But many have not got a bell or lights, and without them you cannot ride a BMX bike in the streets.

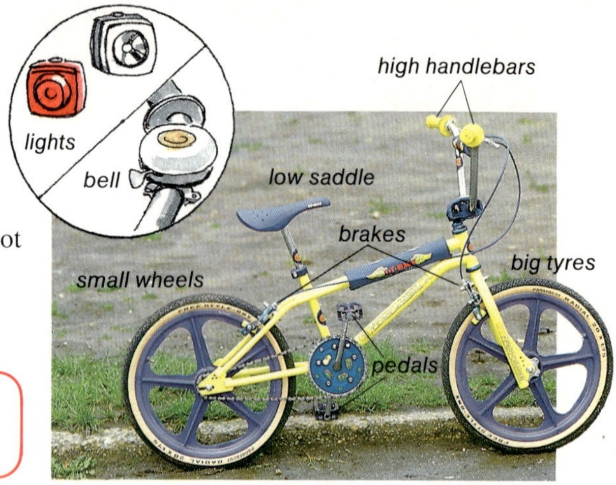

And you?

What have you got on your bike?

4 The track

In some towns there are special BMX tracks. But where there is no track, young people often make one. There are sometimes good places in the woods. Small hills, bends and even mud make the races exciting.

And you?

Is there a BMX track near your home/town/village?

5 In Hatfield there **is** no special BMX track.
So the young people use a field near Woodside for their races.

Races between schools **are** very popular. Last Saturday there **was** a race meeting between different classes from Park School and Grove School. Sandra was in the Park School team for class 2F. Her friend Janet was in the 2B team for Grove School. Andy and Tim **were** in the 2B team, too. Kevin and Dave were in the 2F team with Sandra. Mr Hill and his dog Sebastian were there, too. Mr Hill was the starter.

6 The race meeting was a week ago. – *Here are some questions about it.*

When **was** the race meeting?	– (It was) on Saturday.
Where . . . the race meeting?	– . . .
How many riders **were** in the race between 2F and 2B?	– (There were) . . . .
How many boys . . . in the 2F team?	– . . .
How many girls . . . in the race?	– . . .
Who was in the Park School team?	– Sandra, . . . (were . . .).
Who . . . the riders in the Grove School team?	– . . .

7

Was Mr Hill there, too?	– **Yes, he was.**
Was he in the race?	– **No, he wasn't.** He was the starter.
. . . Sandra in the 2F team?	– . . .
. . . Tim in the 2F team, too?	– . . .
Were Andy and Janet in the 2B team?	– **Yes, they were.**
. . . Dave and Kevin in the 2B team, too?	– **No, they weren't.**
. . . Sandra and Kevin in the 2F team?	– . . .
. . . Andy and Tim in the 2F team, too?	– . . .

→ S 2 · Ex 3, 4

Ask a partner.

Where were you yesterday/on Saturday?

Were you	at home at a friend's house at a bike race . . .	at the weekend? last night? a week ago? . . . ?

8 The race was at two o'clock. But first there were a lot of things to do.

Tim **prepared** his bike for the race.
Andy cleaned his wheels.
Sandra checked her brakes.
Liz helped her.
Kevin and Dave looked at the track.
Janet fetched some oil.

→ S 1, 3a, c · Ex 5

9 The riders prepared their bikes for the race. – *Ask questions.*

Did Sandra **check** her brakes?	– **Yes, she did.**
Did Dave help her?	– **No, he didn't.**
Did Kevin and Dave look at the track?	– Yes, they did.
Did Andy clean . . . ?	– Yes, ...
Did . . . ?	– . . .

What did Andy **clean**?	– His wheels.	What **did** Sandra **do**?	– She checked her brakes.
What did Kevin and Dave look at?	– . . .	What . . . Tim do?	– He prepared his bike for the race.
What did Janet . . . ?	– . . .	. . . Liz . . . ?	– . . .

→ S 3d · Ex 6, 7

10 Some of the riders **wanted** to practise before the race. They wanted to ride round the track.
"Be careful, Dave," Sandra shouted. "Don't fall off. We need you. Remember – you're our best rider."

→ S 3b

11 Janet, Dave and Andy **rode** towards the first bend.

Andy was in front of Dave. Dave wanted to overtake him, but Andy was in the way.

Dave **overtook** Andy after the bend.

Janet was next to Andy. There was a lot of mud on the track. Dave braked suddenly and ...

Janet and Andy crashed into Dave. They all **fell** off their bikes.

→ S 4a · Ex 8

12 After the accident the two teams started to argue.

Kevin:	Andy, you crashed into Janet.	–	*Andy:*	I **didn't crash** into Janet.
Janet:	Dave overtook Andy too soon.	–	*Kevin:*	Dave didn't overtake Andy too soon.
Sandra:	Janet wanted to crash into Dave.	–	*Janet:*	I ....
Tim:	Dave's wheel touched Andy's wheel.	–	*Sandra:*	Dave's wheel ....
Kevin:	Janet braked on the mud.	–	*Tim:*	Janet ....
Mr Hill:	Don't argue all the time.			

→ S 3e, 4b · Ex 9-11

13 Dave tried to walk.
"Oh," he said. "My foot."
Mr Hill looked at Dave's foot. "Well, I'm sorry, Dave, but you can't start with the others. You're out of the team now. Sandra and Kevin, you must look for a new rider. You know you must start against Grove School in five minutes."

The race

After his accident Dave King was out of the team for class 2F. Sandra and Kevin needed a new rider.

"What can we do now?" Sandra said. "Dave was our best rider." They walked to their bikes.

"Why not give me Dave's bike?" Liz said. "I can ride for him."

"Two girls in our team?" said Kevin.

Sandra said, "Why not?"

They asked Mr Hill, the starter, and he said, "OK, Liz can ride for Dave."

Everybody shouted when Park School's 2F started against 2B from Grove School. Kevin tried to overtake the others, but the girls were soon in front of him.

"Liz," he shouted, "I can't overtake you. You're in the way."

But Liz was not in the way. She was too fast for Kevin.

They rode into the first bend and over a small hill. Tim fell off his bike. Kevin overtook Andy and Sandra. Liz and Janet were still in front of him. There was now mud in Kevin's face. Liz and Janet rode round the next bend without a problem, but Kevin was too fast. He braked, but he did not fall off his bike. Sandra now overtook Kevin. Kevin and Andy rode after the girls. They rode towards the second hill.

And suddenly Sebastian, Mr Hill's dog, was on the track with them. He was next to Andy. "Go away," Andy shouted. But Sebastian did not leave the track. Before the hill there was a lot of mud. The girls rode through the mud. Sebastian jumped over it. And Andy crashed into Kevin. The two boys fell into the mud.

"Did you do that?" Kevin shouted.

"It wasn't me!" Andy shouted, "It was the dog."

It was too late for the boys. The three girls and Sebastian were on their way to the finish line. And then they were over it. Janet was first, Sebastian was second, Sandra and Liz were third. The boys never finished.

→ Ex 1, 2, 12

1 *Look at "The race" on page 21 again and complete these sentences.*

1. Sandra, Kevin and Liz rode for . . . .
2. In the Grove School team there were . . . .
3. After the first hill Tim . . . .
4. Kevin braked, but . . . .
5. Suddenly Sebastian . . . .
6. Kevin and Andy . . . .
7. Andy shouted, ". . .".
8. It was too late . . . .
9. The three girls and Sebastian . . . .
10. Tim, Andy and Kevin . . . .

2 Helen's unlucky day – Friday 13th!
Look at the pictures and write what happened. The words on the right can help you.

1. Helen – hospital / broken foot
2. accident – last Friday / way home from school / farmer with some cows / on their way – cowshed / overtake – dangerous bend / Suddenly – car – in front / farmer – shout – "Be careful!" / Helen – try to brake – lots of mud / Helen – crash – tree / fall off – bike
3. driver – very sorry / carry – Helen to his car / farmer – telephone – police and hospital / Some minutes later – doctor and ambulance / Two ambulance men – Helen to ambulance

Helen is in hospital. She has got a broken foot. Her accident happened . . . *Now you go on.*

3 An interesting Saturday for Liz
Complete this dialogue between Sandra and Liz and put Liz's answers in the right order.

Sandra:
1. Where were you on Saturday, Liz?
2. Oh. When . . . you there?
3. And why . . . you in New Hatfield?
4. Oh super! . . . he in one of the big shops?
5. Well, where . . . he then?
6. What . . . his name?
7. That's a good name for a magician. . . . his tricks good?
8. . . . Kevin there, too?

Liz:
– Well some . . . fantastic, but others . . . too good.
– Merlin.
– Oh, he . . . in the pedestrian precinct.
– Because there . . . a magician there.
– In New Hatfield.
– No, he . . . .
– Of course he . . . . He wants to do some tricks at Dave's birthday party.
– It . . . about 3.30, I think.

4a **Pam's photos**

Pam: And here's a photo of my sister Kate. We were in Germany last year.
Sue: Oh, that's interesting. Where ... you? In Bonn?
Pam: No, we .... We ... near Koblenz. Our pen-friends Katrin and Simone live there.
Sue: ... you there in the summer?
Pam: Yes, we .... Kate ... there for four weeks, but I .... I ... there for only three weeks.
Sue: ... it nice?
Pam: It ... fantastic.

b *Be careful here: You must use past and present tenses.*

Sue: And your parents? Where ... they last year? In Germany, too?
Pam: No, they .... My father ... in hospital for a long time, so they ... here in Hatfield all the time.
Sue: That's not so nice. He ... all right now, I hope.
Pam: Yes, he .... He ... ill from June till September last year, but now he ... OK again. – Oh look, here ... an old photo of us all. That ... in the autumn of 1980. We ... all at Hatfield House.

5 BMX BMX BMX

Sandra, Dave and Kevin often arrive one hour before the race. Sandra and Kevin usually check the brakes for the Park School team. Kevin sometimes fetches oil for their bikes. Dave often looks at the track for the team. Mr Hill is usually at the races. His dog Sebastian barks at race meetings all the time. After the races the children often play with Sebastian.

The race last Saturday
Sandra, Dave and Kevin arrived one hour before the race. Sandra and Kevin ... the brakes for the team. Kevin ... oil for their bikes. And Dave ... at the track. Mr Hill ... at the race. His dog Sebastian ... all the time. After the race the children ... .

6 Questions and answers
Make two groups in your class. Then ask and answer questions. Here is some help:

Did	you Andreas Bettina your teacher ...	write ... read ... go to ... play	yesterday? last week? last summer? ...?

Example: Sabine, did you write a letter to your pen-friend last week? – No, I didn't.

7 What did you say? "Woggle"? *Complete the questions and practise with a partner.*

You:	*Your partner:*	*You:*
1. Dr K. Nickel cooked a meal for Merlin last *woggle.*	– When did he cook it?	– Last Sunday.
2. Merlin cleaned his *woggle* last week.	– What did he . . . ?	– His library.
3. Dr K. Nickel answered *woggle* letters yesterday.	– How many letters . . . ?	– Twenty.
4. They watched TV in the *woggle* last night.	– Where . . . ?	– In the living-room.
5. Dr K. Nickel practised the guitar this *woggle.*	–When . . . ?	– This morning.

8 A terrible weekend for Sally *Be careful: Sometimes you must use the present tense and sometimes the past tense.*

Sally:
We (be) in Little Missenden last Saturday. It (rain) all the morning. But it (stop) at lunch time. I (ride) across the fields in the afternoon. Then, I don't know why, my horse (stop) and I (fall) into the mud. Five minutes later the horse (arrive) at the farm without me. I (arrive) there twenty minutes later. I – wet – dirty. Everybody (laugh). I – not very happy. My father (explain): "We – happy that you – here. But Dave – in the fields. He (try) to find you!"

9 All about pocket-money *Find the right answers for the five sentences on the left. Work with a partner.*

Your partner: Jenny gets pocket-money every Saturday.

You: Not every Saturday. She <u>didn't get</u> pocket-money last week, for example. *Go on.*

1. Jenny gets pocket-money every Saturday.
2. On Mondays Susan always asks her parents for pocket-money.
3. Your brothers spend all their pocket-money every month.
4. Mike only buys sweets with his pocket-money.
5. They sell records and cassettes in the village shop.

a) That's not right. She (not ask) her parents for pocket-money yesterday because she has still got enough from last week. 2

b) Records and cassettes? Well, I was there last week and they (not sell) them then. 5

c) Not every Saturday. She (not get) pocket-money last week, for example. 1

d) But yesterday he (not buy) sweets because they were too expensive in the little shop near the school. 4

e) I don't think you're right. They (not spend) it last month. They're saving for new bikes. 3

10 Jane's birthday *Complete the text with these verbs:*

not agree   be (2×)   not eat   not go   help (2×)   like   want

Mike plays football at the youth club every Friday afternoon. But last Friday he . . . to the club because it . . . his sister Jane's birthday. He . . . her to prepare the food for her birthday party. Mike . . . to make the cake, but Jane . . . . So Mike . . . his mother with the sandwiches. And his sandwiches . . . great! All the guests . . . Mike's sandwiches. Only Jane's friend Peter . . . them. "Sorry Mike, but Jane's cake is so fantastic!"

11 A day in Dover

Complete this dialogue with a partner and practise it. – Be careful with the tenses.

Sandra: Where (be) you yesterday, Kevin? I (want) to play table-tennis with you.

Kevin: – Well, I (be) in Dover. First I (try) to find a birthday present for my mother and then I (visit) a friend.

Sandra: Oh, . . . you (stay) at his house all afternoon?

Kevin: – No, I . . . . But it (be) nice. We (listen) to records and (talk) about our hobbies. But we (not talk) about school!

Sandra: . . . you (visit) other people, too?

Kevin: – No, I . . . . I (want) to visit another friend, but he (not be) at home.

Sandra: That (be) a pity. It (be) so nice to see old friends again.

Kevin: – That (be) right. But can we play together this afternoon?

Sandra: Of course. Look, here (be) Liz. Let's ask her, too.

12 Say it in English: *etwas zugeben oder abstreiten*

Wenn Du zugibst, etwas getan zu haben, und Dich auch gleich dafür entschuldigen willst, antwortest Du auf die Frage:

Did you do that?

Yes, I did. I'm sorry.

Wenn Du aber abstreitest, etwas getan zu haben, antwortest Du:

No, I didn't.
No, it wasn't me.

Role-play

Du vermutest, Dein(e) Partner(in) habe Deinen Taschenrechner weggenommen. Dein(e) Partner(in) streitet es ab.

You: Did you take my calculator?
Your partner: No, I didn't. It wasn't me.

Du vermutest, Dein(e) Partner(in) habe . . .	Dein(e) Partner(in) . . .
1. Deine Limo getrunken.	– gibt es zu und entschuldigt sich.
2. Deinen Vogelkäfig aufgemacht.	– gibt es zu und entschuldigt sich.
3. in Dein Englischbuch geschrieben.	– streitet es ab.
4. Deinen Brief gelesen.	– streitet es ab.
5. Deine Süßigkeiten gegessen.	– gibt es zu und entschuldigt sich.

Teacher: Did your dad help you with your homework?
Pupil: No, he did it all.

13 WORDS WORDS WORDS

✓ a **First letter: a**

Complete the sentences with the right prepositions.

1. Sarah is waiting . . . the station.
2. Let's walk . . . the beach.
3. 2F is playing . . . 2B.
4. Where can we get . . . the river?
5. It's dangerous to run . . . a bus.
6. What do you know . . . Loch Ness?

b **When you ride a bike . . .**

1. . . . do not overtake →	in your tyres.
2. . . . it is always a good idea	too fast.
3. . . . check the air	→ on dangerous bends.
4. . . . wait at the traffic lights	to take a repair kit.
5. . . . never go	till they are green.

14 Revision: plurals

girl – girls	child – ?	family – ?	homework – ?	hobby – ?	class – ?
woman – ?	mouse – ?	match – ?	man – ?	furniture – ?	way – ?

15 Revision: your his its their

1. Do you know John's brother and sister? – Yes, his brother is quiet, but his sister is very lively.
2. My sister is small. – Yes, that's right. . . . sister is very small, but you're tall.
3. Where are Dave and Sally? – They're on . . . uncle's farm in Little Missenden.
4. Do you know Peter? – No, I don't. But I know . . . friend John.
5. Look at this BMX bike. It's Jane's birthday present from her parents. – Oh! . . . colours are great.
6. My aunt and uncle from Germany are visiting us at the moment. – What are they like? – Oh, they're OK. But we don't understand . . . English. That's the only problem.
7. What's Hatfield House? – You don't know it? It's a big old house. . . . history is very interesting and it's very popular with tourists.

16 Revision: A mixed bag

1. There's a rabbit in the garden.	– No, . . . two rabbits.
2. This is my English book and this here is my German book.	– No, . . . are my books. . . . are your books.
3. Why isn't Tom at work?	– He's ill. He (sleep).
4. . . . 's Susan?	– In London.
5. . . . is driving Arthur's car?	– Arthur's father.
6. I can't see Sandra.	– She (sit) near that tree.
7. What's Kevin's hobby?	– Oh, he (take) photos.
8. When . . . Kevin (play) football?	– Every Saturday.
9. . . . you (watch) TV?	– Yes, sometimes.
10. And yesterday?	– I (watch) an exciting programme.

17 Listening comprehension: "Animal Hour"

Look at Britain

1

2

3

7

4
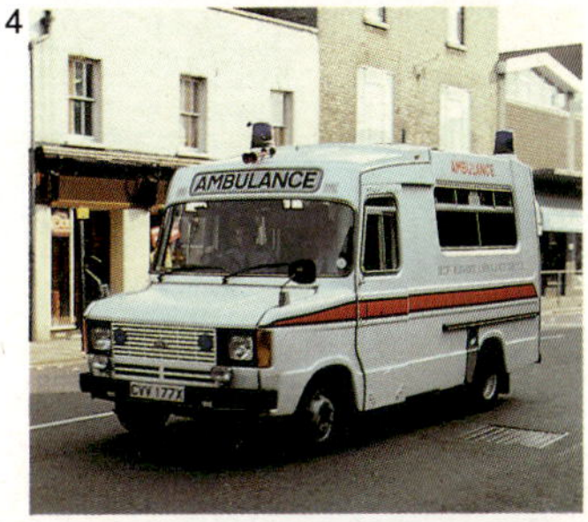

6

5

Work with a partner. Ask her or him questions about the pictures.

Example: Look at the signs in picture 2, Karen. Is Cambridge about 50 or 80 kilometres from London?

Just for fun

Lucy arrived home after her first day at school.
"What did you learn at school today?" her mother asked.
"Not enough," Lucy said. "We must go again tomorrow."

My friend Rory

This is the story
of my friend Rory.
He fell off the wall –
and that's all.

Die einfache Form der Vergangenheit (The simple form of the past tense = The simple past)

1 Gebrauch

My mother **was** in Frankfurt yesterday.
Meine Mutter war gestern in Frankfurt./... ist gestern in Frankfurt gewesen.

Dave and Sally **played** football last Saturday.
Dave und Sally haben am letzten Samstag Fußball gespielt./... spielten am letzten Samstag Fußball.

Man verwendet das *past tense*, wenn man sagt, wann jemand etwas getan hat oder wann etwas geschehen ist. Wenn man über vergangene Ereignisse oder Erlebnisse berichtet oder wenn man eine Geschichte erzählt, benutzt man durchgehend das *past tense*.

2 be (sein)

Positive sentences	
I **was** You **were** He/She **was** We **were** You **were** They **were**	in London yesterday.

Negative sentences	
I **wasn't** You **weren't** He/She **wasn't** We **weren't** You **weren't** They **weren't**	in Hatfield.

Langformen: I/He/She **was not** in Hatfield.
We/You/They **were not** in Hatfield.

Questions	Short answers
Were you in London? **Was** he in Hatfield? **Were** they in London?	Yes, I **was**. No, he **wasn't**. Yes, they **were**.
Where **were** you yesterday?	In London.

3 Regelmäßige Verben (Regular verbs)

a Bildung

Infinitive	Simple past
listen	listen**ed** [-d]
help	help**ed** [-t]

Die Bildung des *simple past* der regelmäßigen Verben ist ganz einfach, weil man nur *-ed* an den Infinitiv anzuhängen braucht.
Alle Personen haben die gleiche Form.

b Besonderheiten der **Aussprache** bei Verben, die auf [-d] oder [-t] enden:

Infinitive	Simple past
nee**d** [-d]	needed [-d**ɪd**]
wan**t** [-t]	wanted [-t**ɪd**]
ha**t**e [-t]	hated [-t**ɪd**]

c **Besonderheiten der Schreibung**

Infinitive	Simple past
arrive stop try	arrived stopped tried

Aber: helped, jumped, ...
Aber: played, stayed, ...

d **Frage**

Positive sentence: Jill **played** tennis yesterday.

Questions: **Did** Anne **play** tennis, too? — **Short answers:** Yes, she **did**.
Did Liz **play** tennis? — No, she **didn't**.
What **did** Liz **play**? — Hockey.

Die Frage im *simple past* wird für alle Personen mit vorangestelltem *did* gebildet.
Das Verb *(play)* steht im Infinitiv (hat also kein angehängtes *-ed*!).

⚠ Auch in Fragen mit dem Vollverb *do* (deutsch: *machen, tun*) muß *did* verwendet werden:
What **did** Sandra **do** before the race? – She checked her brakes.

e **Verneinung**

Positive sentence: Jill **played** tennis yesterday.

Negative sentence: Liz **didn't play** tennis yesterday.

Die Verneinung im *simple past* wird für alle Personen mit *didn't* (Langform: *did not*) gebildet.
Nach *didn't* steht das Verb im Infinitiv (also ohne *-ed*!).

4 Unregelmäßige Verben (Irregular verbs)

a **Bildung**

Infinitive	Simple past
fall overtake ride say	**fell** **overtook** **rode** **said** [sed]

Jedes unregelmäßige Verb hat eine eigene Form für das *simple past*. (So etwas kennst Du auch aus dem Deutschen, z.B. fallen – *fiel*.) Auch die unregelmäßigen *simple past*-Formen sind für alle Personen gleich. Du findest sie sowohl im Vokabular als auch in der Liste am Ende des Buches.
Jede dieser Formen mußt Du gesondert lernen.

b **Frage und Verneinung**

Positive sentence: Kevin **overtook** Andy in the race on Saturday.

Questions: **Did** Tim **overtake** Andy, too? — **Short answers:** No, he **didn't**.
When **did** Kevin **overtake** Andy? — After the bend.

Negative sentence: Liz **didn't overtake** Andy.

Genau wie bei den regelmäßigen Verben wird auch bei den unregelmäßigen Verben die Frage mit *did* und die Verneinung mit *didn't* gebildet.

⚠ In der Frage mit *did* und in der Verneinung mit *didn't* wird also auch bei den unregelmäßigen Verben der Infinitiv *(overtake)* und nicht die *simple past*-Form *(overtook)* verwendet.

1 Some people are not happy when they get up in the morning. ▷

◁ Some people *are* happy.

◁ And some even sing when they are in the bathroom.

And you?

Here is a song. You can sing it when you get up in the morning.

2. wash your hands/Sunday
3. brush your teeth/Monday
4. brush your hair/Tuesday
5. clean your shoes/Wednesday
6. eat your food/Thursday
7. drink your tea/Friday

2 When Merlin the magician gets up, he is usually very happy. He sings in the bathroom and then again in the kitchen.

Merlin always does magic when he makes the breakfast. He stands near the cupboard, opens the doors and says, "OK, plates. Go to the table!" And the plates, the cups and saucers all fly out of the cupboard and land on the table. Then he does the same with the knives, forks and spoons.

3 This morning Merlin wants to show his Aunt Agatha what he can do. But Merlin has got a cold. So his magic is not very good. And when Merlin's magic is bad, some funny things can happen . . .

Dr K. Nickel has got five plates.
He has got a spoon and two forks but no . . . .
He has got . . . .

Merlin's Aunt Agatha has got three . . .
and two . . . but no . . . .
She has got . . . .

Merlin . . .

4 When Merlin goes into the kitchen, he always makes a big breakfast. He has toast or bread with lots of butter and jam. That is a good breakfast for a hungry magician. And he always has five cups of tea with his breakfast because he is very thirsty in the morning. When Aunt Agatha visits Merlin, she finds cornflakes and a boiled egg on the table. And she always drinks coffee. But today she can see some rolls on her plate. They are fresh from Germany. Dr K. Nickel has breakfast at the same time. He eats a carrot, of course. And he sometimes eats a yoghurt, too. He does not like tea or coffee, so he drinks milk or cocoa.

5

Who has toast or bread for breakfast every morning?	– Merlin.	**What does** Merlin **have** with his breakfast?	– (He has) five cups of tea.
Who drinks . . . ?	– Aunt Agatha.	What does . . . drink?	– (He drinks) milk or cocoa.
Who eats . . . ?	– Dr K. Nickel.	What does . . . eat, too?	– (He sometimes eats) a yoghurt. → S 1 · Ex 2, 3

6 It was a lovely day last Sunday. Merlin and Aunt Agatha stayed at home in the garden. The Connors **took** food for a picnic and **went** to the coast. A lot of other people **had** the same idea. The roads were full of cars.
At twelve o'clock the Connors **found** a field for their picnic. Carol **made** some sandwiches. Tina and Mrs Connor **drank** some orange juice. Mr Connor **stood** near the road and watched the other cars. "Why don't they all stay at home and sit in the garden?" he said.

Suddenly Mrs Connor **saw** the huge animal in the field. Of course, Mr Connor is not a farmer, but a bull is a bull. Everybody knows that.
"Back to the car!" Mr Connor shouted.
That day the bull **had** a nice lunch. It **ate** all the sandwiches and drank all the orange juice.

7

Who stayed at home in the garden last Sunday?	– Merlin and Aunt Agatha.	**Why did** Merlin and Aunt Agatha **sit** in the garden?	– Because it was a lovely day.
Who went . . . ?	– The Connors.	Where did . . . have a picnic?	– (They had a picnic) in a field.
Who made the . . . ?	– Carol.	What did . . . see?	– (She saw) . . . .
Who . . . ?	– Mr Connor.	What . . . ?	– (It ate) . . . . → Ex 4, 6

8 People in different countries eat different things, of course. The British like chips. Some people say the British eat chips with everything. And they drink lots of tea with milk. Here are some British meals:

ham salad

sausage, egg and chips

beans on toast

omelette

cheese on toast

roast beef and potatoes

fish and chips

9 This year Carol, Kevin and Tina have lunch at school. But the Connors always have tea together in the evening. They usually have tea at six o'clock when Mr Connor comes home. What did they have last week?

On Monday they had . . . .
On Tuesday . . . .
They had . . . on Wednesday.
. . .

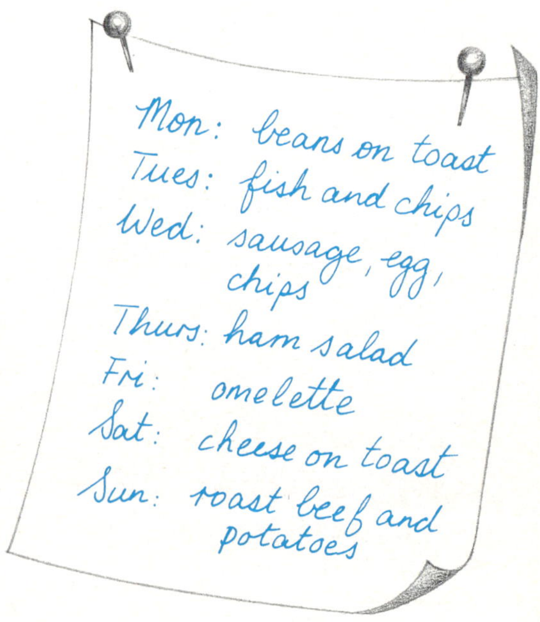

And you?

When do you usually have your evening meal?
Do you have a hot meal or a cold meal in the evening?
When did you have your evening meal last night?
What did you have?

→ Ex 7

10 The Connors usually go to the supermarket every week. Before they leave the house, Mrs Connor always makes a list and writes down what they need. Here is the **Connors'** list for this week. → S 2 · Ex 5

11 This week they need **some** eggs.
They need some . . . .
They . . .

12 They do**n't** need **any** bread.
They don't need any salt.
They . . .

Do they need **any** cheese**?** – Yes. They have**n't** got **any**.
Do they need **any** coffee**?** – No. They've still got **some**.
And oranges?
Do they need any? – No. They've still got some.
Do they . . .? – Yes. . . ./No. . . .

They've still got some bread, but they haven't got any butter.
They've still got some . . . , but they haven't got any . . . .
They . . . → S 3a · Ex 8

13 When the Connors went to the supermarket, they took everything with them: enough money, three bags and a basket, the car and all the children. But **something** was at home on the kitchen table – the list! → S 3b · Ex 9

3 T

Spaghetti trees

Last week class 2F went to a food factory near Hatfield with Miss Green. A man from the factory, Mr Evans, showed them how they fill tins with spaghetti and tomato sauce. It was very noisy.

"You must be careful that nothing falls in the tins," Mr Evans shouted. "A few weeks ago a family found chewing gum in a tin of beans after a school class visited us."

The children laughed, and Dave shouted, "Hey, I've got a new meal: beans and chewing gum on toast." But Miss Green only said, "Oh Dave, please."

When they were near the tins, Dave stood next to Liz. The pupils all watched the tins and listened to Mr Evans. But Dave did not listen. He saw that Liz had a pen in her pocket. He took the pen from Liz. A minute later he said, "Hey, Liz. Where's your pen?"

"Oh no, Miss Green. Help! My pen is in the spaghetti."

Dave laughed.

"Stop the machines," Mr Evans shouted.

Dave said, "It's OK. It's here. It was on the floor."

Miss Green was angry. "Did it fall on the floor, Dave, or did you take it from Liz?"

"Who? Me, miss?" "Yes, you."

"It's OK," Mr Evans said. "Well, have you got any questions?"

"Yes." It was Sandra. "How do you make spaghetti?"

"We don't make it," Mr Evans said. "We buy it in Italy. They've got spaghetti trees there."

"Spaghetti trees?"

"Yes, it comes every week in special boxes, so it's always fresh."

"Is that right?" Sandra asked.

"Yes," Dave said. "And elephants can fly."

"OK, Dave," Miss Green said. "You're so clever. Tomorrow at school you can tell us what spaghetti is and how they make it. OK, everybody, let's go."

→ Ex 1

1 *Look at "Spaghetti trees" on page 34 again.*

a *Right or wrong?*

Examples:
Class 3F went to a food factory last week.
– That's wrong. Class 2F went there.
It was noisy in the factory. – That's right.

1. Mr Evans showed the children how they fill tins with beans.
2. A few weeks ago a family found chewing gum on its toast.
3. Liz had a pencil in her pocket.
4. Dave took Liz's pen.
5. The pen fell in the spaghetti.
6. Miss Green was angry with Dave.
7. The factory buys spaghetti in Italy.

b *Write these sentences in the right order:*

1. Dave played a silly trick with Liz's pen.
2. Dave saw that the story was not true.
3. Mr Evans stopped the machines.
4. Mr Evans decided to tell Sandra a funny story about spaghetti trees.
5. Mr Evans showed the class how they fill spaghetti into tins.
6. Miss Green was angry with Dave.
7. Miss Green was angry with Dave again.
8. Miss Green took class 2F to a food factory near Hatfield.
9. Sandra was not sure if the story was true.

2 Who can remember? *Ask your friends.*

Who
- sells pets?
- thinks farms are boring?
- lives in Woodside?
- sings in the bathroom and the kitchen?
- plays football?
- goes to the park every morning?
- has got 90 cows?
- sleeps in a small blue bedroom?
- paints houses?

I think it's . . . .
That must be . . . .
That's . . . .
. . . , of course.

Kevin and Sally
Dave
Sandra and her mother
Merlin
Aunt Mary and Uncle Ernie
Mr Singh
Mr Hill and Sebastian
Dr K. Nickel
Mr King

3 Who? What? When? Where?

Make two groups, then ask and answer these questions about these children from Park School.

Who?	Susan	Bob	Richard	Julia
What?	the piano	the guitar	football	table-tennis
When?	every afternoon	in the evenings	on Saturdays	after school
Where?	at home	in his room	at the youth club	at a friend's house

Examples: Who plays the piano? – Susan.
What does Bob play? – The guitar.
Where does Richard play football? – At the youth club.
When does Julia play table-tennis? – After school. *Go on.*

4a “Woggle.” – “What did you say?”

Find the correct simple past forms of the verbs and practise the dialogue with a partner. You play Jill’s part.

Example: Yesterday I found (find) an interesting *woggle.*
– What did you find (you/find) yesterday? – An interesting coin.

You (= Jill):	*Your partner:*	*You (= Jill):*
1. I (see) Susan in the precinct *woggle.*	– When (you/see) her?	– Yesterday.
2. We (go) to a *woggle.*	– Where (you/go)?	– To a café.
3. We (drink) some *woggle.*	– What (you/drink)?	– Some tea.
4. *Woggle* (eat) some cake, too.	– Who (eat) cake?	– Susan.
5. We (have) a very nice *woggle.*	– What (you/have)?	– A very nice time.
6. Later I (go) *woggle.*	– Where (you/go)?	– Home.
7. Susan (go) to the cinema with her *woggle.*	– Who (go) with Susan?	– Her sister.
8. My bus was very *woggle.* I (stand) all the way home.	– Why (you/stand) in the bus?	– Because it was so full.

• b *Now complete this text. Remember: use long forms when you write it.*

Jill (be) in Hatfield yesterday, in the precinct. She (want) to go to the bookshop. On her way there she (see) Susan. But Susan (not see) her. Jill (say) “Hallo” to her. They (talk) for a few minutes and then they (go) to a café for a cup of tea. Soon they (find) a nice place. Susan (have) a cup of tea, and she (eat) some cake. Jill (not have) cake, she just (drink) some tea. They (have) a very nice time together. Later Jill (go) home by bus. She (not go) to the bookshop. It (be) too late. Her bus (be) very full. She (stand) all the way home.

5 Friend(s), friend('s) or friend(s')?

Write this short text again with (s), ('s) *or* (s') *in the right places.*

The Connor● flat is not very big, so they cannot have big pet●. They have got a white rabbit. The rabbit● name is Blacky. Blacky● favourite meal is carrot●. Kevin● favourite meal is sausage● with chip●. Carol and Tina are Kevin● sister●. His sister● favourite meal is ham salad, and his parent● favourite is roast beef and potatoe●.

○ Jenny took her dog to the cinema. They saw ‘Animal Farm’. After the film the woman next to Jenny said, “Did your dog like the film?” “Oh yes, he did,” answered Jenny. “I’m very surprised[1],” the woman said. “I’m surprised, too,” said Jenny, “because he didn’t like the book.”

[1] surprised [sə'praɪzd] *überrascht*

6 Stone men

Complete this dialogue, but be careful with the tenses. Some verbs are in the simple past, some are in the simple present.

– Hallo, Liz. You (not come) to the cinema with us yesterday afternoon. Why not?

– Oh, . . . you (go) to the ABC? Peter (see) a super film there last week.

– Well, we (go) to the ABC, but we (not see) that film. There (be) a new film yesterday. – But where (be) you? What (you/do) yesterday afternoon?

– Peter and I (make) a cake with my mother. When it (be) cold, we (eat) some. And we (have) a cup of tea with it. It (be) lovely.

– . . . you (stay) at home all afternoon?

– No, we (not stay) at home all afternoon. At about half past three Peter and I (take) our bikes and (ride) through the woods.

– Who (go) with you?

– My mother and my father. We (find) lots of nice stones in the woods.

– But who (want) stones?

– Well, Peter (collect) them. He (paint) them and then he (make) little stone men from them.

– What (he/do) with these men?

– He (give) them to his friends on their birthdays.

– I (not think) that's a bad idea.

7 Breakfast and lunch

Example:
It is 7.15. The Deans are having breakfast. They usually have breakfast at 7.15. But not at the weekend. They do not have breakfast before nine o'clock then.

Now look at the words and pictures and write three short texts. Use "have breakfast/lunch", but be careful: simple or progressive form?

7.30 – the Kings – breakfast – usually breakfast 7.30 – not at the weekend – not before nine then

one o'clock – Sandra – lunch at school – every day – not at the weekend – lunch at home then

1.30 – the Connors – a cold lunch – usually a cold lunch – not on Sundays – a hot lunch then

8 "some" or "any"?

Make sentences. Be careful and use the right form of the verbs.

a *Example:*

photos of animals	+
pets	–

Tim/have got/in his room

Tim has got some photos of animals in his room, but he has not got any pets.

1. farms	+
factories	–

There/be/in Little Missenden

2. toast	+
cornflakes	–

Merlin/have/for breakfast yesterday morning

3. cake	+
biscuits	–

Carol/eat/yesterday

b *Now work with a partner.*

Example:

sandwiches?
usually for his lunch

Mr Hill/eat/yesterday?

Did Mr Hill eat any sandwiches yesterday?

– Yes, he did, I think. He usually eats some (sandwiches) for his lunch.

1. rabbits?
often in the fields

Aunt Mary/see/ last week?

2. cocoa?
always with their breakfast

The children/drink/yesterday?

3. carrots?
usually on Mondays

Dr K. Nickel/ buy/yesterday?

9 "something" or "anything"?

Complete these short dialogues.

1. I can hear ... outside.
   – I can't hear .... Oh, be quiet.
2. Look at that bird on the tree.
   – Sorry, I can't see ....
3. Where's Tom?
   – He's at the supermarket. He needs ... for his tea.
4. Try Dave's chocolate cake.
   – Sorry, I can't eat .... I ate too much for lunch.
5. What's Tina doing?
   – I don't know. I think she's preparing ... for her guests tonight.
6. Nick doesn't get much pocket-money.
   – Why? Do you know?
   Well, he doesn't do ... at home.
7. Now, Martin, don't tell me that you can't remember ... about our last English lesson.
   – Sorry, Herr Wenzelmann, I can't.
   But you must remember ...!
8. Merlin, tell me ... about your magic.
   – Sorry, Agatha, I can't say ... about it.
9. Here's £5, Janet.
   – Thanks, Mum. Do you want ... from the shops?
10. Did Mary give you ... for your birthday?
    – No, she didn't. I never get ... from her.

10 Revision: British money

1. How many . . . are there in a . . . ? – 100, of course.
2. What are these? – The first is a . . . note, I think. The second is . . . . *Go on.*

3. *Ask your partner how much these things are.*

How much is/are the . . . ? – Oh, it's/they're . . . .
Go on.

4. *Now ask your partner how much the things are in marks. But first ask your teacher how many marks there are in a pound.*
   How much is/are the . . . in marks?
   – Oh, it's/they're about . . . . *Go on.*

11 Revision: on the phone

Julia Buxton is phoning about the furniture.

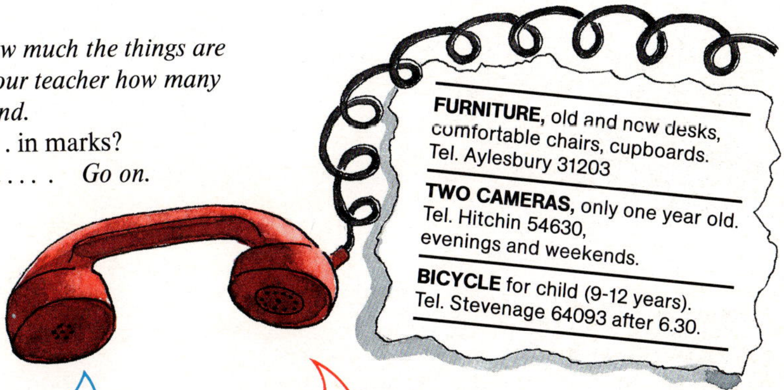

Woman:

Aylesbury three-one-two-o-three, Susan Hill here.

We've got some for £15 and some for £25.

Yes, of course. When can you come?

All right. And your name, please?

7 Market Street. – See you tomorrow afternoon then. Goodbye.

Julia:

– Hallo, I'm phoning about the furniture. How much are the old desks, please?

– I'd like to look at them, please.

– Tomorrow afternoon?

– Buxton. B-U-X-T-O-N. Julia Buxton. What's your address?

– Thank you. Goodbye.

Work with a partner and make dialogues about the other two adverts.

12 WORDS WORDS WORDS

a **German: vor**
English: ago before in front of to

Complete the following sentences with the right words.

1. The next bus leaves at ten . . . six.
2. Jane arrived . . . us.
3. Wait for us . . . the cinema.
4. The accident happened two days . . . his 15th birthday.
5. The boy next to Peter is Jim and the girl . . . him is his sister Mary.
6. I tried to phone Kevin . . . lunch.
7. Meet me at the club at quarter . . . four.
8. Have you got a garden . . . your house?
9. Jeff fell off a ladder two weeks . . . .

b **"Big brothers"**

All the words in list A have got "big brothers" in list B. *Find them and write the combinations down.*

3 S

1 Wortstellung in Fragen mit Fragewörtern (Word order in questions with question words)

	Subject	Verb	Object
Positive sentences:	Dave The Kings Sandra	likes need overtook	toast. a new car. Kevin.
Questions:	**Who** **Who** **Who**	**likes** **needs** **overtook**	toast? a new car? Kevin?

Who? (= Wer?) ist Subjekt der Fragesätze. Wenn das Fragewort gleichzeitig das Subjekt der Frage ist, wird *do/does/did* nicht verwendet.
Das gilt auch, wenn statt *Who?* ein anderes Fragewort Subjekt ist, z.B. *What?* in:

What **happened** yesterday?

Aber vergiß nicht: Fragesätze, in denen das Fragewort nicht Subjekt ist, mußt Du mit Hilfsverben bilden. Du verwendest *do/does* im *simple present*, *did* im *simple past* oder ein anderes Hilfsverb:

Question word	Auxiliary	Subject	Main Verb	Object
What **Where** **When** **Why**	**do** **does** **did** **can't**	the Kings Kevin the Deans Sandra	**need**? **play** **watch** **come**?	 football? the tennis match?

2 Der Genitiv im Plural (The possessive form in the plural)

Singular	Plural
Dave likes his sister's records. ... die Platten seiner Schwester. Are these men Mr Dean's brothers?	Kevin hates his sisters' records. ... die Platten seiner Schwestern. No, they must be the Deans' friends.

's zeigt bei einem Nomen im Singular an, daß etwas oder jemand (zu) einer einzelnen Person gehört (= Genitiv Singular).

Wenn etwas oder jemand aber (zu) mehreren Personen gehört (= Genitiv Plural), dann steht der Apostroph nach dem Plural-s, also s'.

3a some – any

Positive sentences

The Kings need **some** [səm] eggs. – And bread? – No. They've still got **some**. [sʌm]
Die Kings brauchen **(einige/ein paar)** Eier. – Und Brot? – Nein. Sie haben noch **etwas/welches**.

Negative sentences

They do**n't** need **any** oranges. – And butter? – No. They do**n't** need **any**.
Sie brauchen **keine** Apfelsinen. – Und Butter? – Nein. Sie brauchen **keine**.

Questions

Do the Kings need **any** potatoes? Do they want **any** of these? Have they got **any** fruit?
Brauchen die Kings Kartoffeln? Wollen sie **welche** von diesen hier? Haben sie (noch) Obst?

Some wird vor allem in Aussagesätzen, *any* in verneinten Sätzen und in Fragen verwendet.

b somebody, something, somewhere – anybody, anything, anywhere

Positive sentences

There's **somebody** in the garden.
... jemand ...

The dog must be **somewhere** in the garden.
... irgendwo ...

John can see **something** behind the tree.
... etwas ...

Let's go **somewhere** nice.
... irgendwohin, wo es schön ist.

Negative sentences

I ca**n't** see **anybody** in the car.
... niemanden ...

I ca**n't** find my cassettes **anywhere**.
... nirgends ...

There is**n't** **anything** on the table.
... nichts ...

Sandra did**n't** go **anywhere** yesterday.
... nirgendwohin ...

Questions

Can you see **anybody** in the shop?
... (irgend) jemanden ... ?

Is there a bank **anywhere** near here?
... irgendwo ... ?

Can you hear **anything**?
... (irgend) etwas ... ?

Would you like **anything** else?
... sonst noch etwas ... ?

Did you go **anywhere** last night?
... irgendwohin ... ?

Entsprechend dem Gebrauch von *some* und *any* werden die Zusammensetzungen mit *some (somebody, something, somewhere)* in Aussagesätzen, die Zusammensetzungen mit *any (anybody, anything, anywhere)* in verneinten Sätzen und in Fragen verwendet.

EXTRA READING

The film star

It was Monday morning and Kate Price was not at school.

"Where is she?" asked Mr Hill. "Has she got a cold again?"

"She's in London," said Sandra.

"In London? What's she doing there? We've got lessons today."

"She has got an interview for a part in a TV film," said Dave.

"How did that happen?" asked Mr Hill.

"Well, we were in the precinct on Saturday morning," said Sandra. "And two men were there with cameras. Then one of them saw Kate and said 'That girl there'. He's a famous film director. He makes lots of films. Well, he wanted to interview her, so she went to London this morning with her mother."

On Wednesday Kate was back at school, and she had the part.

"What's the film about?" her friends asked.

"Oh," said Kate, "it's about a girl – her name is Angela – and she's crazy about horses. She wants to be a champion. But she has an accident in a competition and that's the end of her career."

"Is that all?" said Dave. "It's not very interesting."

"There are lots of stars in it," said Kate.

"Well, you're very lucky," said Mr Hill.

*

They made the film during the autumn holidays in the television studios in London. Then towards the end of October, the film director wanted to make the last scene in Hatfield. He needed a nice big crowd for the competition when the girl in the story has the accident. Dave and his friends wanted to go, of course. "We can be the crowd," they said.

When the pupils arrived at the sports field, they found hundreds of other people there. The director was in the field. He had a microphone in his hand.

"Listen," he shouted. "Angela is sitting on her horse. This is a very important competition for her. She wants to jump over these fences here. Now, when she jumps over the fences, please shout and cheer. At the fourth fence – and this is very important – the horse stops and Angela falls off her horse. When she falls off, please say 'Oooohhh!'. OK, can we practise now, please? – One, two, three: NOW!" The crowd cheered.

"Good," said the director. "Let's try it."

(line 14) director [dɪ'rektə] *Regisseur/in*
(l. 20) What's the film about? *Wovon handelt der Film?*
(l. 24) competition [kɒmpə'tɪʃn] *Wettbewerb*
career [kə'rɪə] *Karriere, Laufbahn*
(l. 29) during ['djʊərɪŋ] *während*
holidays ['hɒlədɪz, 'hɒlədeɪz] *Ferien*
(l. 31) towards *gegen*
(l. 33) crowd [kraʊd] *Menschenmenge*
(l. 43) fence [fens] *Hindernis*
(l. 45) (to) cheer [tʃɪə] *jubeln, hurra rufen*

Kate rode towards the first fence and jumped over it. The crowd cheered. She jumped over the second fence and the third fence and the crowd cheered again. Then she arrived at the fourth fence and the crowd said "Oooohhh!" – but the horse did not stop. It jumped over it and rode towards the next fence.

"Stop," shouted the director. "Let's try again."

They practised the scene seven times. The crowd always said "Oooohhh!", but the horse did not stop.

"Hurry up, Kate," the pupils shouted. "Stop and fall off."

Then at one o'clock when the crowd was hungry and wanted to have lunch, the horse stopped in front of the fourth fence and Kate fell off. The crowd was so happy that they all shouted and cheered.

"No," shouted the director. "It's 'Oooohhh! Oooohhh!'. Let's do it again."

"That was great," said Dave in the evening. "I liked it. We're all film stars now."

"It was easy for you," said Kate, "but I sat on that horse for six hours."

*

The film was on TV in December. That evening everybody in Hatfield stayed at home and watched it. They waited for the famous fourth fence in the competition. Then they saw the scene. Kate rode towards the fence, the horse stopped, Kate fell off and the crowd said "Oooohhh!". And all the people in front of their TVs in Hatfield cheered and shouted.

Some questions about the text:

(Lines 1-28): 1. Kate Price was not at school on Monday morning. Where was she? Why was she there? 2. How did Kate get the part in the film? 3. What was the film about?
(Lines 29-70): 4. Where did the film director make the last scene of the film? 5. Why did so many people go to the sports field? 6. Why did the crowd cheer when Kate fell off the horse?
(Lines 71-82): 7. For Dave and his friends the day on the sports field was great. Kate did not find it so funny. Why not?

(line 59) time *Mal* (l. 73) easy ['iːzɪ] *leicht, einfach* sat [sæt] *simple past of 'sit'*

Unit 4 A

1 Song: One finger, one thumb

2. One finger, one thumb, one arm, one leg, keep moving, . . .
3. One finger, one thumb, one arm, one leg, one nod of the head, keep moving, . . .
4. One finger, one thumb, one arm, one leg, one nod of the head, stand up, sit down, keep moving, . . .

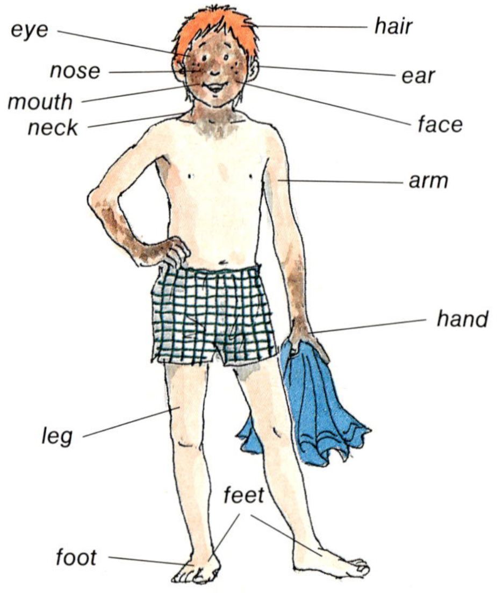

2 Do you know who this is?
It's Kevin after his last BMX race.
He fell into the mud two or three times.
His face is dirty.
But his hair is clean because he wears a helmet.
His . . . are dirty, too.
And . . .

3

When Kevin comes home from a race, he must go to the bathroom and have a bath or a shower. Kevin is usually in a hurry because he is hungry after a race. But his mother always says to him, "And don't come out till you're clean."

4 Dave and his friends often have bike races in the afternoon after school.
Sometimes Dave is **faster than** Kevin.
And sometimes Kevin is faster than Dave.
But Sandra is often the **fastest**.

5

There was a race yesterday.
Kevin won it. Sandra was second.
She was **not as fast as** Kevin. Dave and Liz were third. Liz was **as fast as** Dave.

6 Kevin thinks he has got a good bike.
Dave thinks his bike is **better than** Kevin's.
But Kevin and Dave think Sandra's bike is the **best**.

Kevin's bike is not bad.
It is not **worse than** Dave's.
It is not the **worst** bike.

You and your friends

I'm Peter is ...	taller smaller older younger	than	Anne. ... me.

I'm (not) Katrin is (not) ...	as	tall small old young	as	Dirk. ... me.

→ S 1a, c, 2 · Ex 3, 4

7 A lot of sports are exciting.
For Dave BMX is **more exciting** than football.
But he thinks volleyball is the **most exciting** sport.
For Sally ...
And Kevin thinks ...
...

→ S 1b · Ex 5-7, 12

	football	tennis	BMX	hockey	volleyball
Dave	+		++		+++
Sally	+	+++		++	
Kevin	+++		++		+
Liz		++	+++	+	

8

Whose bike is this? / **Whose** is this bike? – (It's) Tom's.

Whose bikes are these? / **Whose** are these bikes? – (They're) Sally's and Dave's.

→ S 3 · Ex 8

9 **Which bike** is Sandra's? / **Which** is Sandra's bike? – The red bike.

Which helmets are the boys'? / **Which** are the boys' helmets? – The yellow helmets.

Which of the boys is Dave? – The boy in the blue pullover.

→ S 4 · Ex 9

10 Which bike is Dave's? – The blue **one**.

Which are the boys' helmets? – The yellow **ones**.

→ S 5 · Ex 10

11 Some pupils are not at school today.
Miss Green wants to know who they are.

Dave: Kevin is ill, miss.
Kate: And Sandra is ill, too.
Miss Green: Hmm, funny. **Both of them** are ill. Are they really ill, or is there a bike race today?

→ S 6

12

Kevin is at home today. He's ill.
He has got a headache.
He has got a temperature.
His arms and legs are aching.
What's wrong with him?
He has got a bad cold.

And what's wrong with Sandra?
She has got a stomach ache. She has got a temperature, too – and she has got a sore throat. Mrs Bell wants to phone the doctor.

And in your class?

Who is not at school today?
What's wrong with him/her?

13 It is a few days later.

Sandra is still ill.
She must stay in bed.
She **mustn't** get up.

Kevin is feeling better already.
He **needn't** stay in bed.
But he must stay at home. And he must take his medicine.

And you? How are you feeling today?

Terrible.	Oh, I'm all right.
Not very well.	Not bad.
I've got a ...	Fine, thanks.
My ... is/are aching.	Very well, thank you.

→ S 7 · Ex 11

Last Thursday Sandra had a temperature, a stomach ache and a sore throat. So Mrs Bell phoned Dr McPherson.

Dr McPherson is a very nice Scottish woman. She visited Sandra in the morning.

"Well," she said, "How are you feeling, Sandra?"

"Not very well, doctor. I've got a sore throat, a headache, and my arms and legs are aching. And my stomach is aching, too."

"That's terrible."

"What has she got, doctor?"

"Let's see. What's your class doing at school today, Sandra?"

"An English test, doctor."

"An English test? I see. Do you like English, Sandra?"

"No . . ."

Mrs Bell said, "Wait a minute, doctor. Sandra, are you really ill?"

"Let's see what's wrong with you," said Dr McPherson. 'Open your mouth, please." She looked in Sandra's mouth. "Say 'Aah', please." Then she checked Sandra's eyes and her temperature.

"Is she ill, doctor, or is it a trick?" asked Mrs Bell.

"You mean, has she got McPherson's virus?" said the doctor.

"What's that?" asked Mrs Bell.

"Children usually get it on Monday morning – or when they've got a test at school."

"Sandra!"

But Dr McPherson laughed. "No, no. She has really got a very bad cold, Mrs Bell."

"So I can't go to school? And I can't do the English test?"

"No," said Dr McPherson, "You can't go to school." She started to write. "Please fetch this medicine for Sandra, Mrs Bell." Then she looked at Sandra. "And you must stay in bed for the next three days."

"The next three days? But there's a BMX race on Saturday, and I'm in the Park School team."

"Sorry, Sandra," said Dr McPherson. "You must stay in bed."

"Can't I go to school tomorrow, Mum? I'm feeling better already."

"You heard Dr McPherson, Sandra."

"Well, goodbye, Sandra."

"Goodbye, doctor . . ."

"And I hope the Park School team wins."

"Yes, but without me." → Ex 1, 2

4 Ex

1 *Look at "McPherson's virus?" on page 47 again.*

a *Find the mistakes and correct them.*

Last Tuesday Sandra had a temperature, a stomach ache and a sore foot. Dr McPherson phoned Mrs Bell. She visited Sandra in the evening. Sandra's class had a German test at school. Mr Bell asked, "Is it a trick?" Dr McPherson checked Sandra's ears and hair. She said Sandra must go to school and needn't stay in bed. She said, "I hope the Park School team doesn't win."

b *Try to tell the story in your words. Here is some help:*

1. On Thursday – Sandra – not feel very well. 2. Mrs Bell – phone – Dr McPherson.
3. The doctor – visit – morning. 4. Sandra – sore throat – headache – stomach – arms – legs – ache.
5. Dr McPherson – check – eyes – temperature. 6. Sandra – have – bad cold.
7. The doctor – say – "You – must stay – bed – three days." 8. Sandra – happy – English test.
9. There – be – BMX race – Saturday – but Sandra – not be – team. 10. Sandra – not happy.

2 Dave's headache

Look at the pictures and write a short text about Dave.
You can begin: Last Monday morning Dave had a bad . . .

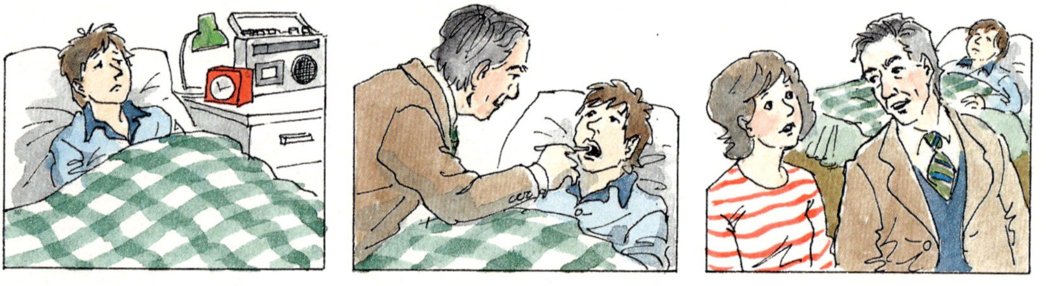

Last – Dave – headache / Mrs King – phone – doctor / "not well – headache" / "Let's see – wrong / open – mouth" – doctor / check – eyes – temperature / "trick – ill?" – Mrs King / "No - high temperature / stay – bed / get up – when – headache – better" / "Thank you" / "Goodbye"

3 A little green man from Mars *Can you answer his questions?*

1. Excuse me, is Hatfield <u>as big as</u> London?

2. Hatfield/small/Woodside?
3. Germany/big/India?
4. bikes/fast/cars?
5. a big house/cheap/a small flat?
6. summers in Scotland/warm/summers in India?
7. winters in Italy/cold/winters in Germany?
8. sweets/good for you/apples?

You:

What a silly question! Of course Hatfield <u>isn't as big as</u> London. *Go on.*

Question: Is the letter "e" ill?
Answer: No, but it's always in bed.

4 "older than" or "not as old as"?

Look at the pictures and make comparisons.

1. The radio is <u>older than</u> the TV. But it is <u>not as old as</u> . . . .

2. Our English lessons . . . German lessons. But they . . . history lessons. *Go on.*

5 I am better.

Why is Miss I. M. Better not very popular with people? What she has got is always more, better, funnier, more exciting, . . . *Complete the following short dialogues.*

1. *Susie:* I know <u>500 French words</u> altogether. I think that's great.
   Miss Better: That's nothing. I know <u>more</u> than that. I know 2000.
2. *Bob:* My friend Jane has always got very <u>good</u> ideas.
   Miss Better: That's nothing. I've got . . . than all your friends.
3. *Sheena:* You must read this comic. It's very <u>funny</u>.
   Miss Better: That's nothing. All my books . . . your silly old comic.
4. *Kelly:* I collect stamps. It's an <u>exciting</u> hobby.
   Miss Better: That's nothing. I collect old English coins. So my hobby . . . your hobby.
5. *Janet:* We've got a very <u>old</u> church. And it's <u>beautiful</u>.
   Miss Better: That's nothing. We've got an old church, too. It's much . . . and . . . your church.
6. *Martin:* I've got a new watch. It's very <u>expensive</u>.
   Miss Better: That's nothing. I've got an old Japanese pocket watch. It must be . . . .
7. *Jerry:* I've got a very <u>clever</u> dog. He can fetch the newspaper.
   Miss Better: That's nothing. My dog can read . . . . So he must . . . .
   Susie: Yes, Miss Better. And you've got a pink elephant. And this elephant is bigger, faster, stronger, cleverer, more dangerous and more fantastic than all other elephants – and of course it can fly, too!

6 The "fourth man"

1. old – oldest small – ?	4. silly – sillier dirty – ?	7. hungry – hungrier happy – ?
2. good – better bad – ?	5. busy – busiest careful – ?	8. young – youngest terrible – ?
3. better – best worse – ?	6. popular – more popular nice – ?	9. clever – cleverer interesting – ?

7 Peanut Superdog – in his dreams . . .

a
1. In his dreams Peanut is always very big. He is often bigger than other dogs. Sometimes he is even the biggest.
2. He is always very strong. He is often . . . the other animals. Sometimes he is even the . . . .
3. Sometimes he is in a race in his dreams. And he is very fast. He is often . . . . Sometimes he is even . . . .
4. Sometimes in a dream he has got a nice new basket. And his basket is . . . all the other dogs' baskets. Sometimes he thinks he has got . . . in the town.
5. When he gets up, he is always very happy. He thinks he is . . . . And he often thinks he is the . . . dog in Britain.

b

popular	clever animal	good singer	angry	beautiful

Write some more sentences about Peanut Superdog.

8 How much do you remember?

Ask questions with "Whose . . . ?". Your partner must then find the right answers.

Whose . . .

. . . favourite food is chips?

. . . pets are Sebastian and Mozart?

. . . Aunt Agatha likes a boiled egg for breakfast?

. . . head is on British coins and notes?

. . . aunt and uncle have got a farm?

. . . clothes are often blue, red and yellow?

. . . pet shop is in Sandfield Street?

. . . lessons finish at four o'clock?

Merlin's
Mr Singh's
British children's
British people's (favourite food)
Sally and Dave King's
Mr Hill's (pets)
The Queen's
BMX riders'

. . . , I think.
. . . , of course.

9 What do you think?

Ask the other pupils in your class questions.

Which
- pet is
- is
- British pop group is
- game is
- English town is
- houses are
- classes are

more interesting, dirtier, more exciting, nicer, cleaner, the noisiest, the cleverest, the craziest, bigger than, more boring, the most popular

- , a dog or a cat?
- to read: a newspaper or a magazine?
- of them all?
- , hockey or tennis?
- Hamburg, West Berlin and Munich?
- to live in: old houses or new houses?
- at our school?

○10 In English, please.

1. Welches von deinen Büchern ist dein Lieblingsbuch? – Das von *(by)* Sally Rider. 2. Welcher Sänger war der beste? – Der große aus York. 3. Welches war das schnellste Auto im Rennen? – Das französische. 4. Wer von deinen Freunden ist Jim Doyle? – Der mit den roten Haaren. 5. Welches ist deine teuerste Briefmarke? – Die alte schwarze aus Deutschland. 6. Welche Übungen sind für morgen [auf]? – Nur die erste auf Seite 55. 7. Wer von euch hat einen Taschenrechner? – Wir alle. 8. Wer von euch kann mir die Antwort geben? – Ich.

Question: What time is it when an elephant sits on your bike?
Answer: Time to buy a new one.

Question: Which month has got twenty-eight days?
Answer: They all have.

11 *Put the two parts of the sentences together with "mustn't" or "needn't".*

When doctors are ill, they ...
Everybody knows that you ...
In a BMX race, riders ...
People in a train ...
Fast trains ...
Without a bell or lights you ...
In a car race, the best driver ...
In Britain, you ...
In most winters, drivers in England ...
When the traffic lights are red for pedestrians, you ...

... **mustn't** ...
... **needn't** ...

... drive your car through a pedestrian precinct.
... always win.
... drive on the right.
... go to another doctor.
... go across the road.
... open the doors before the train stops.
... use special winter tyres.
... ride a BMX bike in the streets.
... ride without a helmet.
... stop at every station.

12 Say it in English: *nach einer Meinung fragen; eine Meinung äußern*

So kannst Du jemanden auf englisch nach seiner Meinung fragen:

> **What do you think about** Mr Smith?
> **What's your opinion about** pop music?
> **How do you like** my idea?

Und so kannst Du Deine Meinung äußern:

> **I think/I don't think** . . . .
> **In my opinion,** . . . .

Eine Meinung kannst Du aber auch so erfragen:

> **Do you think** Mr Smith is a good teacher?

Mögliche Antworten hierauf sind:

> **Yes, I think so./No, I don't think so.**
> **I think/I don't think** . . . .
> **In my opinion,** . . . .

Bist Du Dir nicht ganz sicher, so kannst Du auf alle vier Fragen antworten:

> **Well, I'm not sure.**
> **I can't really say.**

a Imagine some pupils from England are asking your opinion about schools in England and in Germany.

Wendy: We wear uniforms at our school. What do you think about that?
You: . . .
Tony: Do you think your friends would like to wear a uniform?
You: . . .

Anne: We only go to school from Monday to Friday. Do you think that's better than lessons on Saturday?
You: . . .
David: We've got five lessons in the morning and three in the afternoon. What's your opinion about that?
You: . . .

b *Ask your partner what she/he thinks about pop music/Eintracht Frankfurt (or Hamburg or . . .)/ short hair/pets/computers/. . .*
In your answers you can use these words: good, interesting, boring, terrible, great, fantastic, silly, noisy, nice, crazy, expensive, . . .

Just for fun

1. 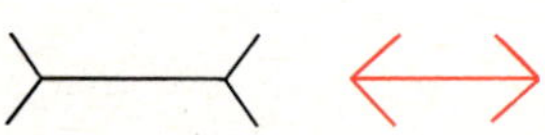

Which line is longer?
The red one or the black one?

2. 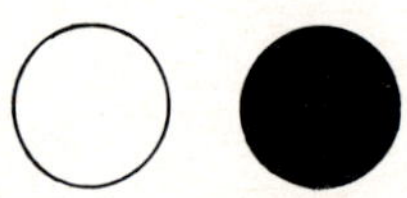

Is the white ball bigger or smaller than the black ball?

Some funny questions:

3. Can you jump as high as a house?
4. Which has got more ears, one cat or no cat?
5. Which word can you make longer, but then it is shorter?

(You can find the answers on page 183.)

13 WORDS WORDS WORDS

a *Which words from A go together with which words from B?* *Example:* brother and sister

A

1. brother 2. right 3. summer
4. pen 5. father 6. man 7. aunt
8. town 9. hands 10. cup 11. knife
12. tea 13. bread 14. fish 15. day

B

coffee uncle feet saucer
sister chips country wrong
night butter winter fork
woman pencil mother

b *Take three or four combinations of words and try to make sentences with them.*

Examples: Sandra has not got any brothers or sisters./Put some cups and saucers on the table.

c **Hidden words** *Find 16 hidden words. Or can you find more than 16?*

1. Good, better, best.
2. Simple past of "eat".
3. Please . . . the window.
4. She gets £2.50 . . . hour for her work.
5. Why don't you . . . your orange?
6. I can run very . . . .
7. A ten pound . . . .
8. "went" is the simple . . . of "go".
9. My . . . writes in red.

B	F	M
H	E	A
P	S	T
A	P	O
E	N	C

10. A hamster is a . . . .
11. Take the letter to the . . . office, please.
12. When the traffic lights are red, you must . . . .
13. The colours are not different, they are the . . . .
14. It is much bigger than a lake.
15. It is a drink and a meal.
16. 11 footballers.

14 Revision: simple present or present progressive? What are these children's hobbies?

1. Brian often makes model cars, but today he is making a model plane.
2. Helen often reads cowboy books, but today she is . . . . *Go on.*

15 Listening comprehension: Jeremy's accident

1 Die Steigerung der Adjektive (The comparison of adjectives)

Im Englischen gibt es zwei Arten der Steigerung: eine mit *-er/-est* und eine mit *more/most*.

a Durch Anhängen der Endungen *-er/-est* werden gesteigert:

		comparative:	superlative:
1. alle einsilbigen Adjektive:	cheap billig	cheap**er** billiger	cheap**est** (der/die/das) billigste . . . , am billigsten
	old	old**er**	old**est**
2. zweisilbige Adjektive, die auf *-y* enden:	funny happy	funni**er** happi**er**	funni**est** happi**est**
Beachte folgende Besonderheiten bei der Schreibung und Aussprache:	nic**e** bi**g** laz**y** lo**ng** [-ŋ]	nic**er** bi**gg**er laz**i**er lo**ng**er [-ŋgə]	nic**est** bi**gg**est laz**i**est lo**ng**est [-ŋgɪst]

b Durch Voranstellen von *more/most* werden gesteigert:

1. die meisten zweisilbigen Adjektive, die nicht auf *-y* enden:	careful vorsichtig	**more** careful vorsichtiger	**most** careful (der/die/das) vorsichtigste . . . , am vorsichtigsten
	boring	**more** boring	**most** boring
2. alle Adjektive mit mehr als zwei Silben:	exciting expensive	**more** exciting **more** expensive	**most** exciting **most** expensive

c Die Adjektive *good* und *bad* sowie *much/many* haben besondere Steigerungsformen:

	good	**better**	**best**
	bad	**worse** [wɜ:s]	**worst** [wɜ:st]
	much/many viel/viele	**more** mehr	**most** (der/die/das) meiste . . . , am meisten

2 Sätze mit Vergleichen (Sentences with comparisons)

Jane is taller **than** Fred.
. . . größer **als** . . .

She's **as** tall **as** Peter.
. . . **so** groß **wie** . . .

But she is**n't as** tall **as** Dave.
. . . **nicht so** groß **wie** . . .

⚠ Peter is younger than **me**.
. . . als **ich**.

3 Das Fragewort „whose" (The question word "whose")

Whose bike is this? – (It's) Tom's.
Wessen Fahrrad ist das? – Toms.

Oder: **Whose is** this bike? – (It's) Tom's.
Wem gehört dieses Fahrrad? – Tom.

Whose sisters argue all the time? – Kevin's.
Wessen Schwestern . . . ?

Mit *Whose . . . ?* [hu:z] fragt man danach, (zu) wem etwas oder jemand gehört.

⚠ **Who is** this girl? – (It's) Sandra.
Whose is this bike? – (It's) Sandra's.

4 Das Fragewort „which“ (The question word “which”)

Which boy is taller, Kevin or Dave?
Welcher Junge ist größer, Kevin oder Dave?

Which are the fastest girls in 2F?
Welche(s) sind die schnellsten Mädchen in Klasse 2F?

We've got seven BMX bikes. **Which** would you like? – **Which of** the bikes is the fastest?
Welches möchtest du? **Welches von** den Rädern ist das schnellste?

Mit *Which ... ?* fragt man nach Personen oder Sachen aus einer begrenzten Anzahl:
Welcher Junge (von den beiden)? Welche Mädchen (aus Klasse 2F)? Welches Rad (von den sieben)?

⚠ **Who** watched the film last night? – Aber: **Which of you** watched the film last night?
What colour are your eyes? – Aber: **Which** colour would you like, blue or yellow?

5 Das Stützwort „one“ (The prop-word “one”)

The Millers have got three dogs – a big **one** and two small **ones**
... einen großen und zwei kleine.

These tomatoes aren't as good as the **ones** from our garden.
... wie die aus unserem Garten.

Das Stützwort *one* muß verwendet werden, wenn man ein schon genanntes Nomen *(dogs, tomatoes)* nicht wiederholen will. Anstelle eines Nomens im Singular steht *one (a big dog – a big one)*, anstelle eines Nomens im Plural steht *ones (two small dogs – two small ones)*.
Im Deutschen bleibt das Stützwort *one* meist unübersetzt.

6 both

Both boys play the piano.
Beide Jungen ...

Oder: **Both the boys** play the piano.
Beide Jungen .../Die beiden Jungen ...

Both these girls play the piano, too.
Diese beiden Mädchen ...

Both her children play the piano, too.
Ihre beiden Kinder ...

Both bedeutet „alle beide“ (= der eine wie der andere). *Both* steht immer vor dem bestimmten Artikel *the* oder einem anderen Bestimmungswort (z.B. *these, her*).

⚠ **Both of them** are very good.
Sie beide ...

Both of us like music.
Wir beide ...

Ebenso: **All of us** like music.
Wir alle ...

7 mustn't, needn't

Peter is ill. He must stay in bed. He **mustn't** get up.
Er **darf nicht** aufstehen.

Must Carol stay in bed, too? – No, she **needn't** stay in bed. She can get up.
Nein, sie **braucht nicht** im Bett zu bleiben.
Nein, sie **muß nicht** im Bett bleiben.

Mustn't ['mʌsnt] (Langform: *must not*) und *needn't* (Langform: *need not*) haben für alle Personen die gleiche Form.

Also: I **mustn't** play, you **mustn't** play, he **mustn't** play, she **mustn't** play, ...

⚠ I **mustn't** come = ich **darf nicht** kommen
I **needn't** come = ich **brauche nicht** zu kommen, ich **muß nicht** kommen

Unit 5 A

Über Sport sprechen; sagen, ob man Sport mag oder nicht mag

1

I like sport very much. I'm a member of a sports club in town. My favourite sport is tennis. I'm in the tennis club at school, too. We practise every Wednesday and Friday.

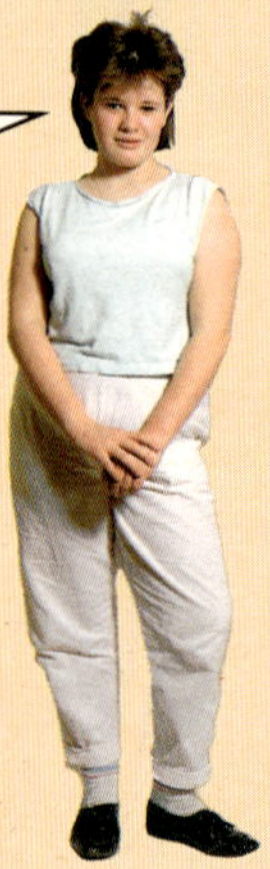

I like basketball. But I'm not in a school team. I'm not good enough. I sometimes practise with friends. I always watch basketball matches on TV.

What's your opinion about sport?

Do you like sport?
Do you think sport is boring?
Are you a member of a sports club?
Or do you only watch sport on TV?

I'm crazy about sport. My favourite sport is football. I'd like to play for one of the London clubs when I leave school – West Ham or Crystal Palace. My favourite player is Jeff Beckham.

I think sport is boring. I'm not a member of a club. But I sometimes watch international matches on TV. I like music better and other things like that.

→ Ex 10

2 What are your favourite sports? What sports do you do? Are you interested in any of these?

weightlifting

riding

gymnastics

ice-skating

skiing

cycling

running

swimming

My favourite sport is . . . I like/love . . . I'm crazy about . . . I'm interested in . . . I'm not interested in . . . I don't like . . . I hate . . .	swimming. ice-skating. skiing. riding. table-tennis. tennis. volleyball. judo. handball.	cycling. running. weightlifting. basketball. hockey. gymnastics. football. squash.

And your friends?

3 You must be strong for weightlifting.
You must be . . . .

I'm good at . . . because I'm . . . .
I'm not very good at . . . because I'm too . . . .
I'm interested in . . . , but I'm not . . . enough.

I play/do . . . , but I'm not very . . . .

4 Sally King is good at tennis. She almost never loses a match. She is quick, strong and fit. When Sally plays against her friends, she always beats them. She is in the Park School team, and there are often matches against other schools. There was a match against Grove School last Saturday. Sally played against Martina Jackson. Martina is very good, too. She is a confident player. A tennis match against her is never easy. So Sally was nervous before the match started.

5 In the first ten minutes Sally played **nervously**, and she lost the first set 2-6. Martina played confidently as always, but then Sally started to play confidently, too.

6 Sally did not win. She played **well**, but Martina was better. The ball sometimes came over the net so **fast** that Sally did not see it. Martina beat Sally 6-2, 4-6, 7-5. It was a hard match and Martina did not win easily.

Ask a partner.

Are you good or bad at . . . ?
What other sports are you good at/bad at?

Do you play . . . well or badly?
What other sports do you play well/badly?

→ S 1a, b, c · Ex 2

7 Sally is often nervous before a match, but yesterday she did not play nervously.

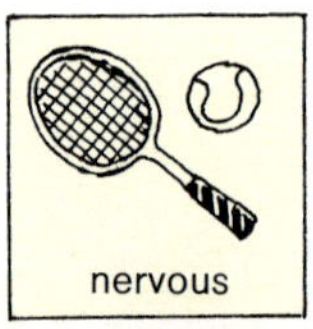

Park School has got a . . . football team. But they did not play very . . . last Saturday.

Tim is a . . . table-tennis player. He always plays . . . .

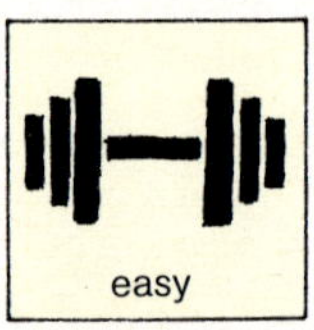

Weightlifting is not . . . . But Tom can lift 100 kilos . . . .

Hockey is not a . . . game, but some people play . . . .

You must be . . . when you play tennis. Martina can run very . . . .

→ Ex 3-5

8 Sandra's cousin Michael is disabled. He cannot walk, so he must use a wheelchair. But, like lots of other disabled children, he enjoys sport. Every week he goes to a special centre where disabled children meet. There they play basketball and take part in other games. They do weightlifting or train for other sports. Sometimes there are competitions with disabled children from other towns or centres. Last month Michael was very successful. He won a prize when he beat all the others in a wheelchair race.

9 It is not easy to do sports when you are in a wheelchair. But many disabled children learn to do sports quite successfully. They can do some sports **more successfully** than other sports, of course. Michael, for example, can play basketball more easily than tennis. → S 1d · Ex 6

10

There is a notice in the Centre about new sports. Everybody can choose one sport. Michael likes volleyball, but he cannot play it.
"**I'm going to write** my name under Group A. What **are** you **going to do**, Alan?"
"I'm going to learn basketball."
Susie **is not going to choose** volleyball or basketball. She is going to play tennis. → S 2

11 The pupils at Park School are going to learn some new things this year, too.

Dave is going to learn chess.
Liz and Sally . . . learn judo.
. . .

And you?

Are you going to learn a new sport/instrument this year?
What are you going to do tonight/at the weekend/next . . . ?

→ Ex 7-9

JUNIOR WORLD MAGAZINE

Sport for everybody

Alison, Andrew, Tom, Paul and Carol from St. Albans are all members of a sports club for disabled people. Last month they all took part in a sports competition.

Alison Brown won a prize for swimming. She did 50 metres in 61 seconds. It is her favourite sport and she practises every day. She was in a basketball match in the competition, too. Her other hobby is riding. She started it in the summer holidays. But Alison cannot do a lot of other things because she is disabled. She had a bad car accident when she was ten years old.

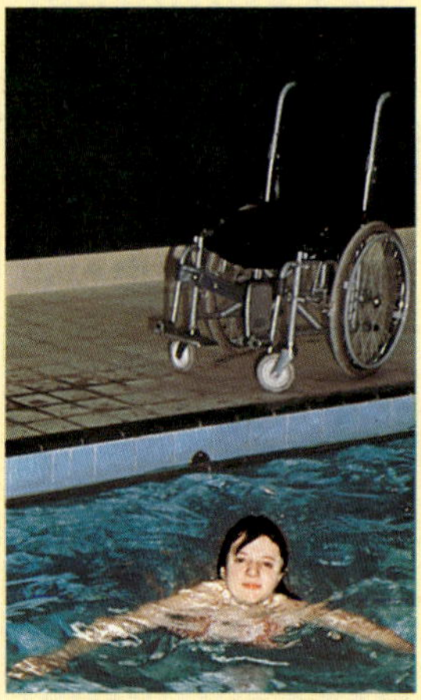

"I often come to the swimming-pool with my friends. They aren't disabled but we all like swimming. And when I'm in the water, I can swim as well as my friends."

Tom Davis had polio when he was young, and he must use a wheelchair now. He was in the sports competition, too. He won a prize for weightlifting. He lifted 102 kilos.

"I can't walk but I can lift 102 kilos easily. I must practise very often, of course. My other sport is volleyball."

Andrew Lee won a wheelchair race. Races in a wheelchair are difficult, and you must practise regularly. Andrew did 60 metres in 16 seconds in the competition.

"I play basketball and I'm going to learn volleyball. I'd like to do sports every day, but I must do lots of homework for school, too."

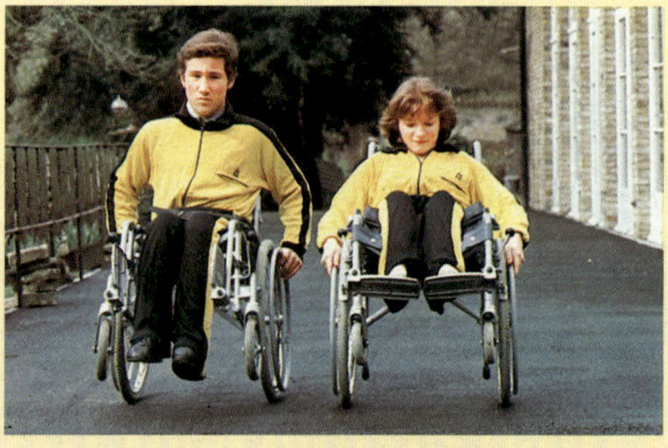

Paul Fox and **Carol Hunt:** "We're training for the London Marathon. We hope to do it in under three hours."

→ Ex 1

1a *Look at "Sport for everybody" on page 60 again and answer these questions.*

1. What did Alison win?
2. How fast did she swim?
3. What other sports does she do?
4. Why is Alison disabled?
5. What did Andrew win?
6. What does the text say about wheelchair races?
7. Why doesn't Andrew do sports every day?
8. What did Tom win?
9. How much did he lift?
10. What is his other sport?
11. What are Paul and Carol training for?
12. How fast do they hope to be?

b *Write 3 short texts.*

1. Alison Brown swam . . . . Swimming . . . , but she likes . . . , too. She is disabled because . . . .

2. Andrew Lee . . . a prize in a . . . . In this competition he did . . . . He plays . . . and he is going to . . . . He would like to do sports . . . , but . . . .

3. Tom Davis is . . . because he had . . . when he . . . . He . . . walk, but . . . good at . . . . 102 kilos. Of course he must . . . very often. Tom plays . . . , too.

2 Sandfield v. Woodside *Make adverbs from the adjectives in ( ) and complete the sentences.*

Last week Kevin's football team, Sandfield Youth Club, won their match (easy). They usually play very (confident) and win most of their matches. But yesterday things did not go so (good). They did not play (careful) enough, and so they lost against Woodside Sports Club. The Woodside team played very (clever), sometimes (fast) and sometimes (slow). After a short time the boys in Kevin's team ran round the field (nervous) and started to play (bad). Kevin had a very bad day – he played (terrible). Soon it was 3-1 for Woodside. The Sandfield boys tried very (hard), but the Woodside team played too (strong) for them. Woodside won the match 5-1.

Question: Why is Sunday the strongest day?
Answer: Because the others are weekdays – 'weak days'.

3 Sport

Adjective or adverb? – Practise with a partner.

1. The school volleyball team played (good) on Saturday.
   – Oh, did they win? Their last match was (terrible).

2. West Ham were so (bad) last week that they lost against Luton. But yesterday they beat Everton (easy).
   – Everton often play (bad) against weaker teams.

3. Did you hear about the cycling race on TV? Jim Kelly was (fantastic).
   – We only watched the first part. But that was very (exciting).

4. Basketball is very (popular) at this school. Do you think I can play in your team?
   – Can you run (fast)? Can you jump (good)? And can you move (quick)? Then you're all right.

4 They aren't feeling very well.

Adjective or adverb?

bad careful clever dangerous good happy hard high lucky quick terrible (2×) wrong

1. What's your temperature? Is it . . . ?
   – I don't know. I think I must check it . . . .

2. Yesterday Tom rode his new bike very . . . . He fell and broke his right arm . . . .
   – Oh, that's . . . . He usually rides quite . . . .

3. My throat is aching . . . .
   – Take this medicine here. It's very . . . for sore throats.

4. There's not much . . . with Sandra. I think she's . . . . She has got McPherson's virus.
   – She's . . . . She's sitting . . . in front of the TV and we're working . . . here at school.

○5 The answers in English, too, please.

1. What did John say? – Ich weiß nicht. Er spricht so schnell, daß es nicht leicht ist, ihn zu verstehen.
2. Does Bettina play tennis? – O ja! Sehr gut. Sie ist eine sehr starke Spielerin. Aber letzten Sonntag hat sie schlecht gespielt. Sie war zu nervös.
3. Who is Karen White? – Ein neues Mitglied in unserem Tennisclub. Sie spielt sehr gut, sehr selbstbewußt.
4. Is Jenny Johnson a good pupil? – Oh ja. Sehr gut. Sie arbeitet sehr hart, aber nicht immer sorgfältig.

6 Who talks most slowly? *Find the answer as fast as you can. Work with a partner.*

Janet talks more slowly than Kate. Kate talks faster than Tim. John talks more slowly than Janet, but not as slowly as Carol. Carol talks more slowly than Tim. Who talks most slowly?

7 What are they going to do?

Find the right answers to the questions and complete them.

Example: Why's your mother taking the car out of the garage? – Because she's going to wash it.

1. Why are you painting your bike so carefully?
2. Why isn't Tom going home with us?
3. Why are you wearing your oldest clothes?
4. Why are you two making so many cakes?
5. Why's your sister learning French?
6. Why are you interested in the prices of guitars?
7. Why can't you play cards with us on Saturday?
8. Why isn't Jane doing her homework?
9. Why is everybody going to the dining-room?
10. Why didn't Sally buy a ticket for the match?

. . . sell it soon.
. . . have lunch in a minute.
. . . father . . . fetch him.
. . . work in the garden.
. . . watch it on TV. . . . have a party.
. . . work in France next year.
. . . paint my room at the weekend.
. . . she and Dave . . . do it together later.
. . . buy one next year.

8 What are their plans?

Write short dialogues.

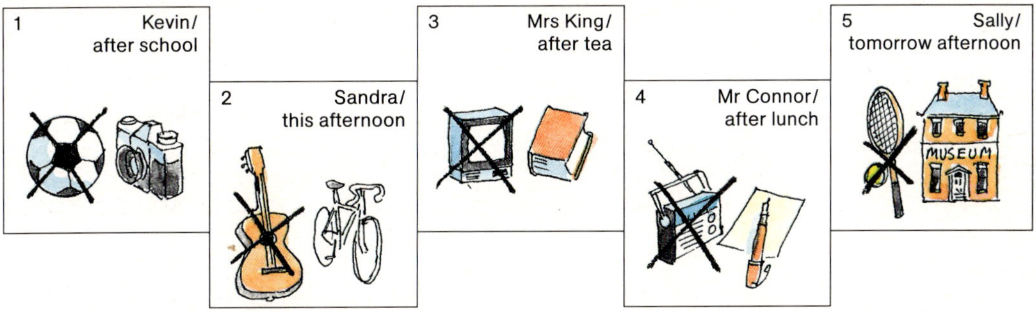

1. What are you going to do after school, Kevin? Are you going to play football?
– No, I'm going to take some photos with the photo club. *Go on.*

9a Plans for the weekend

Liz Dean is staying with her German pen-friend Anja in Kiedrich.

Put in the correct "going to" forms.

What are your parents' plans for the weekend? . . . (we/visit) the Gutenberg Museum in Mainz?

– No, my parents (take) us to Burg Eltz on Saturday.

How . . . (we/get) there?

– Well, first we (drive) to Moselkern. That's a little village on the River Mosel. We (park) the car there and then we (walk) through the woods for about an hour.

Oh, lovely. – . . . (we/take) Rex, too?

– No, we (not take) him. He always barks when it's hot in the car. We (give) him to the Kuhns for the day.

That's very nice of them.

– It is. But next week we (feed) their cat, too. We usually help them and they help us.

b *Tell your partner about your plans for next Saturday/Sunday/weekend. What are you going to do? Your partner can tell you about her/his plans. Write a short text about your partner's plans; she/he can write about your plans. Read your texts to the class.*

"How did you find your steak, sir?"
– "Quite easily. I looked under a potato – and there it was."

10 Say it in English: *sagen, was man mag, was man nicht mag und was man lieber mag*

Wenn Du auf englisch sagen willst, was Du magst oder nicht magst, kannst Du folgende Ausdrücke benutzen:

		Ich mag/esse Cornflakes
+	I **love** cornflakes.	▷ . . . sehr, sehr gern.
↑	I **like** cornflakes **very much**.	▷ . . . sehr gern.
	I **like** cornflakes.	▷ . . . gern.
	I **quite like** cornflakes.	▷ . . . ziemlich/ganz gern.
↓	I **don't like** cornflakes.	▷ Ich mag Cornflakes nicht.
–	I **hate** cornflakes.	▷ Ich kann Cornflakes nicht ausstehen.

Wenn Du etwas lieber magst als anderes, kannst Du sagen:

I **like** coffee **better than** tea.	▷ Ich mag/trinke Kaffee lieber als Tee.
I **like** cocoa **best**.	▷ Ich mag/trinke Kakao am liebsten.

a *Work with a partner.*
Ask him/her what he/she likes for breakfast.

You: What do you like for breakfast?
Partner: Oh, I like/love . . . and I quite like . . . .
You: Which do you like better, toast or rolls?
Partner: I like . . . better than . . . .
You: And yoghurt? Do you like yoghurt?
Partner: Oh, I love/quite like/hate . . . .
You: And what do you drink for breakfast?
Partner: Well, I like . . . best.

b *Now it is your partner's turn to ask you questions about lunch or tea. Your partner can ask you*

– what you like for lunch/tea.
– which you like better: chips or sandwiches, pizza or spaghetti, cheese or sausages, . . .
– if you like chicken, fish, beans, . . .

c *Now work with a different partner.*
Ask him/her what he/she doesn't like for breakfast or lunch and what he/she hates for tea.

11 WORDS WORDS WORDS

a New words – new friends

Which words often go together? Some words have got more than one friend.

run
take part in
train for
lose
play
be good at
win
beat
be a member of
enjoy

a prize
a competition
sport
football
the 200 metres
basketball
the first set
somebody at chess
a race
a sports club

b Why? *Find the right adjectives.*

1. Sandra ate two pizzas. She was very . . . .
2. You can never hear Peter when he's in his room. He's a really . . . boy.
3. Her record-player was only £20. It was very . . . .
4. I washed our car on Sunday. It was . . . .
5. Kevin was last in the race. He was too . . . .
6. I don't want to watch TV. I want to finish my book. It's so . . . .
7. Sorry, I can't carry the box for you. I'm too . . . .
8. Mr Hill was angry when Liz came into the classroom at five past nine. She was . . . again.
9. Dave drank three cups of tea. He was very . . . after the race.
10. I made the tea an hour ago, so you can't drink it. It's . . . now.
11. Caroline never takes Rex for walks. She's a very . . . girl.
12. Simon makes too many silly mistakes in his work. He's very . . . in tests.

c What is wrong with them?

The letters **a**, **e**, **i**, **o** and **u** are missing in the underlined words.

Read the sentences, then write them.

1. I can't speak very well today. I've got a sr thrt, you know.
2. My foot is chng. I hope it isn't brkn.
3. I can't do the test. I've got a terrible hdch.
4. Mr Connor is in bd. He's ll. He has got a bad cld.
5. You must stay in bed and tk yr mdcn.
6. Tom had an ccdnt yesterday. He's in hsptl.
7. Kevin can't come with us. He has got a tmprtr.
8. Sarah ate a green apple yesterday. Now her stmch is chng.

9. There was a terrible accident last night. An mblnc took five people to hsptl.
10. I'm sorry I can't help you. Let's phone a dctr.
11. There's no mdcn for this vrs.
12. Mrs Bell flt very bd yesterday. But she's flng better today.

○12 In English, please: Katrin's letter

Your English friend Penny wants to know what is in this letter. Can you translate it for her?

> Lieber Thomas,
> was hast Du am Samstag vor? Hoffentlich hast Du [noch] keine Pläne. Möchtest Du nicht mit uns auf Onkel Georgs Bauernhof fahren? Wir werden dort reiten und vielleicht Onkel Georg helfen, die Tiere zu füttern.
> Peter und Michael haben auch vor mitzukommen. Kannst Du Dich an sie erinnern? Die beiden spielen sehr gut Fußball. Wie Du Dir vorstellen kannst, werden sie am Samstag auch Fußball spielen. Aber ich habe nicht vor zuzuschauen. Ich finde Fußball langweilig und spiele schlecht. Ich werde im Wald spazieren gehen. Kommst Du mit?
>
> Viele Grüße
> Deine Katrin

13 Revision: simple past

Yesterday was a terrible day for Mr Brown.

Say what happened. – Put in the simple past forms of the verbs.

arrive, take, sleep, get, want, crash, break, try, argue, fall

In the morning Mr Brown slept too long. Then, of course, he . . . at the office too late. His boss was angry and Mr Brown . . . with him. After work Mr Brown . . . into a tree in his nice new car. Then he . . . to go home by bus. But he . . . the wrong bus. When he . . . home, there was not anybody there. He . . . to climb through the window, but he . . . off the ladder and he . . . his arm. It was not Mr Brown's lucky day!

14 Revision: simple past Friday 13th or 14th?

Complete the following story. But be careful: In some sentences you must use negative verb forms.

Yesterday Mrs Goodman (get up) and (feel) happy. Why? She (know). She (look) at her calendar and (see) 'Friday 14th'. "Ah, good," she (think), "not Friday 13th!" When she (listen) to the radio, she (hear) her favourite song. She (sit down) at the kitchen table and (have) a nice breakfast.
She (be) in a hurry, so she (go) by bus. She (walk) to the office. At the office everybody (be) quiet. Mrs Goodman (look) at the office calendar: 'Friday 13th'. Now she (understand). And her calendar at home – (be) it wrong? "Well, let's do some magic," she (think). At lunch time she (buy) some very nice cakes and back at the office she (make) some tea. Then she (ask) everybody to have a cup of tea and some cakes with her. "What a nice idea," they all (say). Soon everybody (be) as happy as Mrs Goodman. Was it really Friday 13th?
When Mrs Goodman (arrive) home, she (go) into the kitchen – and (see) that the window (be) broken. There (be) a football on the floor. "I think I must go and check my calendar," Mrs Goodman (say) quietly.

15 Revision: A mixed bag

Be careful: sometimes you must use more than one word.

1. I'd like . . . butter and some eggs, please.
   – How . . . eggs would you like?
   Oh, only six.
   – Here you are. Would you like . . . else?
2. Dad, get up! There's . . . in the garden. He's standing behind a tree.
   – Oh, go back to bed and . . . silly, David. I can't see . . . .
3. Where's Dave?
   – I don't know. Perhaps he . . . to records in his room.
4. . . . pullover is this? I like the colours. It's much nicer . . . my new pullover.
5. Is John . . . old as you?
   – No, he's a year younger than . . . .
6. It's all right, Kevin. You . . . wash the car. I did it this morning.
7. You . . . get up, Sandra. You've still got a temperature.
8. Look, what nice pictures! . . . do you like best?
9. Both of us like music. And both our children . . . the piano.
10. . . . you in London yesterday?
    – Yes, I . . . . But I . . . buy any new clothes.

Look at Britain

A 1. Two brothers have got tickets for the sports centre. What sport are they going to do?
2. What sport is their father going to do?

B 3. When does the junior judo club meet?
4. Can adults learn judo on Wednesday?

C 5. Can you play squash at the sports centre?
6. Can you buy food there?

1 **Die Adverbien der Art und Weise** (The adverbs of manner)

a **Gebrauch**

Adjektiv: Mrs Connor is always **careful**.
. . . ist immer vorsichtig.

She is a **careful** driver.
. . . eine vorsichtige Fahrerin.

Adverb: Mrs Connor drives **carefully**.
. . . fährt vorsichtig.

Adjektive beschreiben ein Nomen näher. Wir benutzen sie oft nach *be* (z.B. *is careful*) oder vor einem Nomen (z.B. *a careful driver*). Sie sagen etwas über die Eigenschaften einer Person oder Sache aus: Mrs Connor ist ein vorsichtiger Mensch/eine vorsichtige Fahrerin.

Adverbien der Art und Weise beschreiben ein Verb näher. Sie sagen aus, wie oder auf welche Art und Weise jemand etwas tut: Mrs Connor fährt vorsichtig.

Im Deutschen haben Adjektive und Adverbien die gleiche Form. Im Englischen dagegen haben Adverbien zumeist eine andere Form als Adjektive.

b **Bildung**

Adjective	Adverb
a strong player She is quick. a dangerous driver	She plays strong**ly**. She can run quick**ly**. He drives dangerous**ly**.

Ein Adverb wird durch Anfügen von *-ly* an das Adjektiv gebildet.

an eas**y** job What a terrib**le** headache!	We can do it eas**i**ly. It is aching terrib**ly**.

⚠ Bei der Schreibung sind einige Besonderheiten zu beachten.

He is **good** at tennis.	He plays it **well**.
I am as **fast** as you are. We had a **hard** test yesterday.	Don't run too **fast**. We worked **hard** for it.

Das Adjektiv *good* hat die besondere Adverbform *well*.

Fast und *hard* haben als Adjektiv und Adverb die gleiche Form.

c **Wortstellung**

	Verb	Adverb
Kevin often	works	**quickly**.

In Sätzen ohne Objekt stehen die Adverbien der Art und Weise gleich nach dem Verb.

	Verb	Object	Adverb
Our teacher	**speaks**	English	**well**.

. . . **spricht gut** Englisch.

⚠ Adverbien dürfen nie zwischen Verb und Objekt stehen.

d **Steigerung**

Adverbien mit der Endung *-ly* werden mit *more/most* gesteigert:	Bill works slowly.	Susie works **more** slowly.	But Jack works **most** slowly.
⚠ Einsilbige Adverbien wie *fast* und *hard* werden mit *-er/-est* gesteigert:	fast hard	fast**er** hard**er**	fast**est** hard**est**
Die Adverbien *well* und *badly* haben besondere Steigerungsformen:	well badly	**better** **worse**	**best** **worst**

2 Das Futur mit „going to" (The going to-future)

a **Bildung**

Positive sentences	
I**'m going to** You**'re going to** He**'s**/She**'s going to** We**'re going to** You**'re going to** They**'re going to**	**read**.

Negative sentences	
I**'m not going to** You **aren't going to** He/She **isn't going to** We **aren't going to** You **aren't going to** They **aren't going to**	**watch** TV.

Questions	Short answers
Are you **going to read**? **Is** he **going to watch** TV? **Are** they **going to read**?	Yes, I **am**. No, he **isn't**. Yes, they **are**.
What **are** they **going to read**?	The newspaper.

Das *going to-future* wird mit *am/are/is going to* + Infinitiv gebildet.

b **Gebrauch**

Sandra: What **are** you **going to do** at the weekend, Dave?
Was hast du am Wochenende vor, Dave?
Was wirst/willst du am Wochenende machen, Dave?

Are you **going to watch** the football match?
Hast du die Absicht, dir das Fußballspiel anzuschauen?

Dave: No, I**'m not**. We**'re going to visit** Aunt Mary and Uncle Ernie.
Nein. Wir haben vor, Tante Mary und Onkel Ernie zu besuchen.

Das *going to-future* wird verwendet, wenn man sagt oder fragt, was jemand vorhat.

EXTRA READING

Every year at Park School there is a sports day. In the afternoon there is a pupil-teacher football match. This is very popular because the pupils usually win. But this year, things were a bit different.

When the teachers came on the field, everybody started to laugh. Some were old, some had white legs, others had big stomachs, and some had no hair. But there was one player – he was small, but he was strong and very fit. He was the new German teacher, Herr Meier.

Mr Hill was the captain, but he was not very good. He fell in the mud during the first five minutes. Herr Meier was very good. Soon it was 1-0 (one-nil) for the teachers. Then Frank Whittle scored for the pupils, and it was 1-1 (one-all). But Herr Meier soon scored his second goal, and it was 2-1.

After the first half, one of the pupils said, "What can we do? Can't we stop him?"

"I can stop him," said Alex Murphy. Alex was big and strong, a weightlifter. "Give him the ball when I'm near him."

They started the second half, and Alex ran towards Herr Meier. Dave Bennett kicked the ball across the field. Herr Meier stopped it and ran with it.

Alex ran towards him - and crashed into him. The pupils shut their eyes. When they opened them, Alex was on the grass. Two teachers carried him off the field.

Towards the end of the match it was 3-2 for the teachers, and Tim Walsh had the ball. The teachers all ran towards him, but he ran between them easily. And then he was there. The goal was in front of him. It was easy. But Herr Meier was behind him. Tim remembered Alex; he remembered Herr Meier's goals. The pupils started to shout. Tim kicked the ball – and missed. It flew past the goal, and Herr Meier flew past Tim like an express train.

"Always watch the ball and not the other players," Herr Meier shouted.

After the match there were the questions. "Who is Herr Meier?" "Why can he play so well?"

And Dave Bennett soon had the answer: "He played for a German club before he was a teacher. They've got a strange name – Eintracht Frankfurt."

"Are they good?" asked Alex.

Talk about the text:

1. *Why is the pupil-teacher match so popular?*
2. *What can you say about the teachers on the sports field?*
3. *What happened in the first half of the match?*
4. *What did Alex do in the second half of the match?*
5. *Why did Tim miss the goal?*
6. *Why did Herr Meier play so well?*

(line 5) a bit *ein bißchen, etwas* (l. 12) captain [ˈkæptɪn] *Mannschaftskapitän*
(l. 13) during [ˈdjʊərɪŋ] *während* (l. 16/18) (to) score (a goal) [skɔː, gəʊl] *(ein Tor) schießen*
(l. 19) half *Spielhälfte, Halbzeit* (l. 25) (to) kick *treten, stoßen*
(l. 31) off the field *vom Spielfeld (herunter)* (l. 40) (to) miss *verfehlen; hier: danebenschießen*
(l. 40) past the goal *am Tor vorbei* (l. 41) express train [ɪkˈspres] *Schnellzug*
(l. 49) strange [streɪndʒ] *seltsam, sonderbar*

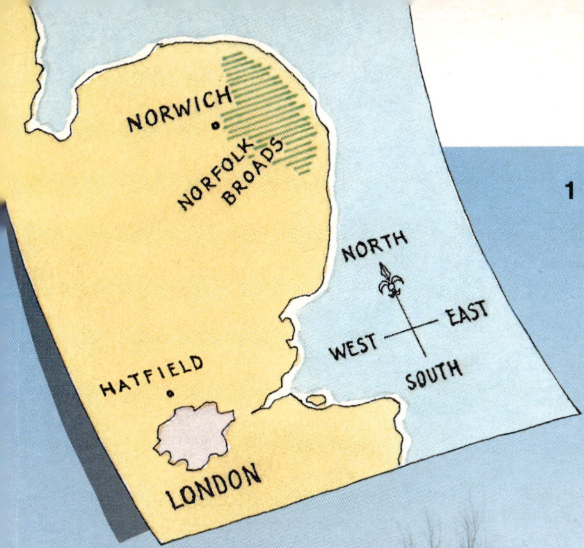

Unit 6 A

1 The Norfolk Broads are a very popular part of Britain. They are about 120 miles north of London. There are no hills or mountains, so it is very flat. But there are lots of rivers, lakes and canals.

In the summer many families hire a boat for their holidays. Some boats are quite big with several beds, a shower, a toilet and a kitchen. But you can also hire smaller boats, or take your own canoe, of course.

2 Every year Mr Hill takes one of his classes on a trip to the Norfolk Broads. He usually goes during the Easter holidays. This year he is going to take a group of pupils from class 2F to Potter Heigham. They are going to camp there for three days. So they need tents, warm clothes and lots of food.

The pupils are loading everything into the coach. Two other teachers, Mr Duncan and Miss Green, are helping them. They are also going on the trip.

... And at last they are all on their way.

3 They **have arrived** in Potter Heigham.
The coach **has stopped** at a farm.
They are going to camp in the farmer's field.
The children are unloading all the things.

4 Now the children **have unloaded** everything.
They have unloaded the food.
They have unloaded . . . .
They have . . .

→ S 1, 2a, 3a, 4a · Ex 2

5 The teachers **have given** the pupils different jobs.
Dave and Kevin must put up the tents.
Brian must fetch the water.
Paul and Kate must collect wood for a fire.
And Liz, Sandra and Tim must cook the evening meal.
But, as you know, pupils do not always do what their teachers tell them.

→ S 3b · List of irregular verbs p. 154

6 Dave and Kevin have put up the tents for the boys, but they **have not put up** any tents for the girls.
Brian **has not fetched** the water **yet** because he cannot find a canister.

→ S 2b · Ex 3, 4

7 *Miss Green:* Kate, Paul, **have** you **collected** the wood for the fire yet?
Kate: No, not yet, miss.
Miss Green: Well, hurry up before Mr Duncan returns from the village.
Brian, have you . . . ?
Brian: No, miss, I haven't. I can't . . . .
Mr Hill: Dave, Kevin, have . . . ?
Dave: Well, we've . . . , but . . . .

*

Mr Duncan: Hallo, Tim and Liz. What **have** you **cooked**?
Tim: Potatoes, sausages and beans.
Mr Duncan: Well, I hope we can eat it.
Liz: It's OK. Miss Green has helped us.

→ S 2 c · Ex 5-7

8 *Sandra:* Mr Duncan, we've just made some tea. Would you like a cup?
Mr Duncan: Yes, please. That's very nice of you.
Derek: Is it true that you're going to visit Norwich tomorrow?
Mr Duncan: Mm. Do you want to come?
Derek: Yes, please. → Ex 11

9 *Mr Duncan:* Have you ever been to Norwich before?
Liz: I've been to the Norfolk Broads, but I've never visited Norwich.
Sandra: I've often been to Norwich. I've got relatives there.

And you? And your partner?

Have you been to an interesting or beautiful town? – Yes, of course. I've been to . . . .
Have you ever been to Heidelberg/Hamburg/Düsseldorf/. . . ? – Yes, I have./No, I haven't but I've been to . . . .

→ S 4 b · Ex 8-10

10

Now the children have finished everything at last.
They have . . . all the tents.
They have . . . the evening meal.
And . . . a big fire.

Miss Green and Mr Duncan have brought their guitars. After the meal they are all going to sing some folk songs. Later, after they have sung the songs, Mr Hill is going to tell them a ghost story. Lots of people do not believe in ghosts, of course. But when the night is dark, and there is no moon and there are no stars, some strange things can happen . . .

The Old Woman

The evening is dark and warm. The pupils from Park School have made a nice big fire and they have sung some songs with Miss Green and Mr Duncan. Now everybody is quiet. It is late, but nobody wants to go to bed. They want to hear a ghost story from Mr Hill.

Mr Hill: All right then. Listen. Many years ago there was a house on this field. It was a very nice house with a big garden. An old woman lived in it with her son. One day he went out to sea in his boat and he never came back. The old woman went to the coast and asked all the people, "Have you seen my son?" But the answer was always "No." The days and weeks went by and he didn't come home. And then one day people found his boat on the beach and everybody knew that he was dead. But the old woman didn't believe it. Every day she sat on the beach and waited.

Without her son, the old woman had no money. Now, there was a man in the village, Mr Fenwick, and he wanted the old woman's house. He offered her five hundred pounds. The old woman wanted more, but Mr Fenwick knew she was very poor and needed the money. At last the old woman took the five hundred pounds and Mr Fenwick was the new owner of the beautiful old house with its nice big garden. A few days later the old woman left the village. For a long time nobody saw her.

*

But a year and a day later somebody knocked on Mr Fenwick's door. It was evening, after nine o'clock. Mr Fenwick opened the door and saw the old woman.

"I've been to the coast," she said, "I've waited a year and a day. I've told my son about the house and the five hundred pounds. He's going to return tonight. He wants the house back."

Mr Fenwick was very angry. "Go away," he said. "This is my house now." And he shut the door loudly. But the old woman stayed outside in the garden. "He's going to return tonight," she said. "He's going to come back from the sea."

Mrs Fenwick was in the living-room. "Can it be true?" she asked.

"Of course not," said Mr Fenwick angrily. "Dead people don't come back from the sea."

But then Mrs Fenwick said, "I've just remembered. Old people say that you can sit next to a grave for a year and a day and the dead person comes back. But the ghost must return before the morning. We must shut all the windows and doors, and we mustn't leave the house before the morning."

"That's a silly story," said Mr Fenwick.

Two hours later they heard the old woman outside in the garden again.

"He's coming," she said. "I know it. It's ten miles from here to the coast. But he's on his way."

Mr Fenwick opened a window and shouted "Go away!" But the garden was empty. And it was very dark. There was no moon and there were no stars. Then in the next village the dogs started to bark.

"Shut the window," said Mrs Fenwick. "I'm frightened."

"What time is it?" said Mr Fenwick.

"Half past eleven," said his wife.

They sat in the living-room and waited. The minutes went by slowly.

"Why are those dogs barking?" asked Mrs Fenwick.

"I don't know," Mr Fenwick said. More dogs started to bark. Then, suddenly, somebody knocked on the door.

"Don't go," said Mrs Fenwick. "Please . . ."

But Mr Fenwick walked into the hall. He went to the door and opened it – and there was a terrible scream.

Mrs Fenwick ran into the hall. Her husband was on the floor, his mouth and eyes open. Outside, the night was very dark, but there was somebody, or something, there. It came towards her, slowly . . .

Of course everybody thought the old woman was the ghost, but they never found her. And when new people bought the house, the same strange things always happened. On the first night when there was no moon and there were no stars and it was very dark, the dogs started to bark and somebody knocked on the door. So for many years the house was empty, because nobody wanted to live in it. Then a farmer bought the land and pulled down the house.

*

Mr Hill stopped. "And I've just remembered something. Tonight it's very dark. There's no moon and there are no stars, and we've got our tents on the old woman's field. And listen."

In the next village the dogs started to bark . . .

"I hope you all sleep well," Mr Hill said.

→ Ex 1

Some British folk songs

Old MacDonald had a farm

2. . . . some ducks (quack-quack)
3. . . . some geese (gabble-gabble)
4. . . . some pigs (oink-oink)
5. . . . some dogs (bow-wow)
6. . . . some chickens (cluck-cluck)

One man went to mow

2. Two men went to mow, went to mow a meadow.
   Two men, one man and his dog went to mow a meadow.

3. Three men went . . . Three men, two men, one man and his dog . . .
4.-10.

Good night, ladies

2. Farewell, ladies, farewell, ladies, farewell, ladies,
   we're going to leave you now.

1 *Look at "The old woman" on pages 74-75 again.*

a *Do you think these sentences are right? Try to explain your answers.*

Examples: The old woman and her son did not have a nice house. – I don't think that's right. They had a very nice house with a big garden.
The son had an accident in his boat. – I think that's right. One day he went out to sea and he never came back again.

1. Mr Fenwick, a man in the village, wanted to help the old woman.
2. The old woman was happy when Mr Fenwick gave her the money.
3. She believed that her son was dead.
4. Later she wanted to have the house back.
5. Mr Fenwick was nice to her when she came back.
6. The old woman spoke to Mr Fenwick about her son.
7. Mr Fenwick did not believe the old woman's story, but Mrs Fenwick believed it.
8. Mrs Fenwick was not frightened when the dogs started to bark.
9. Perhaps the dogs saw the ghost.
10. After many years a farmer wanted to live in the house.

b *Let's talk about the text.*

1. Say something about the night when the old woman came back to Mr Fenwick's house.
2. Why was Mr Fenwick so angry with the old woman?
3. Why did Mrs Fenwick want to shut all the windows and doors?
4. What happened to Mr Fenwick when he opened the door on that dark night?
5. And what happened to his wife?
6. What happened when people bought the old woman's house?
7. Do you like ghost stories like "The old woman"?
   Do you think they are exciting/boring/silly/. . . ?
   Can ghosts come back from their graves? What do you think?

2 **Jobs at home** *Use the correct present perfect forms of these verbs:*

ask clean cook dry finish help repair tidy up unload wash

1. You must wash your car today.
   – Can't you see that I . . . it?
2. Oh, I must cook the lunch now.
   – No, it's OK. Kevin . . . it today.
3. I must clean the windows, but I've really got no time for it.
   – It's okay. Look, I . . . them for you.
4. Can I watch television, Dad?
   – Not before you . . . your room.
5. Why must I help Mum with the housework, Dad? Can't Tina do it?
   – No, it's your turn, Carol. Tina . . . me in the garden.
6. You can't go on Mum's old bike. It's broken.
   – No, it isn't. Dad . . . it.
7. Oh, no! It's raining and I must unload the car.
   – Don't worry, Mum. I . . . it for you.
8. Let's go to the cinema this evening, John.
   – Yes, OK. But not before we . . . the housework.
9. I'm going to dry the dishes now, Dad.
   – You're too late. I . . . them for you.
10. I hope Mr King can paint the house next week.
    – Yes, he can. Mum . . . him.

3 Angry teachers, worried teachers
Complete the sentences.

1. Mr Hill is angry because Dave and Kevin have not put up (not put up) any tents.
2. Miss Green is angry because the boys (not unload) all the things.
3. Mr Hill is angry because the girls (not help) the boys.
4. Mr Duncan is angry because Brian (not fetch) the water from the farmhouse.
5. Miss Green is angry because Paul and Kate (not collect) any wood for the fire.
6. Mr Hill is worried because some girls (not arrive).
7. Mr Duncan is angry because Kevin (not help) the other boys with the dishes.
8. Miss Green is worried because some pupils (not phone) their parents.
9. Mr Hill is angry because John and Helen (not clean) the tables.
10. They are all angry because Liz and Tim (not cook) the evening meal.

4 *Complete the following short dialogues with the right forms of the verbs. With some of the verbs you must use "not".*

arrive cook finish have lose phone say wash

1. I can't give you my four-colour pen.
   – Why not?
   I've lost it.
2. You can't wear your jeans tonight.
   – Why not?
   I . . . them yet.
3. You needn't answer Susan's letter.
   – Why not?
   Mother . . . Susan.
4. Liz can't take part in the BMX race.
   – Why not?
   She . . . an accident with her bike.
5. I hope nothing has happened to the girls.
   – Why?
   They . . . yet. And it's already four o'clock.
6. We can't have lunch today.
   – Why not?
   I . . . anything.
7. Sorry, I can't go with you.
   – Why not?
   I . . . my homework yet.
8. I'm not going to ask Tim for help.
   – Why not? I think he's very nice.
   Well, Tim . . . some silly things about me.

Jack: I've lost my dog.
Jill: Why don't you put an advert in the paper?
Jack: Don't be silly, my dog can't read.

5 *Make questions with the present perfect.*

1. who/put up/for the younger children/the tents/has?
2. why/she/hasn't/her bedroom/tidied up?
3. you/tried/our new jam/have?
4. the Kings/hired/have/a caravan/why?
5. how much/Derek/has/money/saved?
6. completed/have/you/the exercises on page 22?
7. you/used/Peter's bike/again/have/why?
8. have/for lunch/what/you/Mum/cooked?
9. phoned/your sister/haven't/you/why?
10. they/haven't/a drink/given/why/you?
11. the men/unloaded/how much/have/furniture
12. yet/the dishes/you/dried/haven't/why/Sandra?

6 *Complete the questions. Use one of these verbs in the present perfect.*

arrive buy cook feed finish find give have make read repair
save sell shut wash

1. Have you finished that letter to Uncle Bob? – No, I haven't. I'm still writing.
2. ... Helen ... a present for Tom? – Not yet. She's still looking for something.
3. ... Mr Hill ... back the English tests? – No. He hasn't looked at them yet.
4. ... the London train ... yet? – Yes. It's at platform nine.
5. ... Kate ... the paper? – Yes, she has. You can have it now.
6. ... Mary ... lunch? – No, she isn't hungry.
7. ... Andy ... your record-player? – No, it's still broken.
8. ... you ... the cakes for the party yet? – No. I'm going to make some tonight.
9. ... you ... your old bike? – Yes, but I still haven't got enough money for a new one.
10. ... Mum ... my white pullover yet? – I don't know. Why don't you ask her?
11. ... the children ... enough for a new radio? – Almost. But they still need £5.
12. ... you ... all the windows? – I think so. But I'm not sure about the bathroom.
13. ... Sally ... her bag? – No. I think it's still in the bus.
14. What ... you ... for lunch? – Roast beef, beans and chips.
15. Why haven't you ... the dog? – Because Jill is taking it for a walk in the park.

7 *Ask your partner questions about the pictures. Use the present perfect.*

1 Kevin

2 Carol and Tina

3 Nick and Paul

4 Susie

5 Mr Singh

6 Janet

7 Liz and Sandra

8 Dr K. Nickel

1. *You:* Has Kevin cleaned his bike?
Partner: Yes, he has. Now he can play with us.

2. *Partner:* Have Carol and Tina ... their rooms?
You: No, they haven't. I must tell them again.

Now go on.

8 *Ask your friends.*

Have	you		cooked a meal? made a cake? repaired a lamp? argued with a friend? wanted to be big and strong? lived in a big town?	– Yes, / – Of course: I have. I . . . / he has. He . . . / she has. She . . . – I think he has/she has. He/She . . .
Has	Merlin Christoph Bärbel . . .	ever	lived in a village? milked a cow? had an accident? found any money in the street? been to Britain? read an Enid Blyton book? tried weightlifting? slept in a tent?	– No, I haven't/he hasn't/she hasn't. – No, never. – Of course I haven't/he hasn't/she hasn't. – I don't think I have/he has/she has. – I don't know. Why don't you ask him/her?

9 Camping in Potter Heigham *Complete the answers with the correct present perfect forms.*

1. *Mr Hill:* Isn't it your turn to make the tea, Angela?
   Miss Green: I (just make) some, Roger. Do you want a cup?
2. *Mary:* Can you give me 50p for sweets?
   Nina: Sorry, I can't. I (already spend) my pocket-money for this week.
3. *Peter:* Isn't our tent great?
   Andy: I'm not too sure about it. I (never sleep) in a tent before.
4. *Miss Green:* Did you know that Dave and Kevin are cooking the lunch, George?
   Mr Duncan: Oh, yes. The two (often cook) meals before, you know.
5. *Tom:* Look at Mr Hill, Derek. His face is green.
   Derek: You're right. I don't think he (ever be) on a boat before.
6. *Paul:* Do you want to play football with us?
   Sandra: I can't. I must phone my mum. I (not phone) her yet.
7. *Dave:* Let's tell Mr Hill that we can't dry the dishes this evening.
   Kevin: Too late. I (already tell) him.
8. *Liz:* Have you heard? We're going to visit Norwich on Saturday.
   Sandra: Oh! I wanted to go to Great Yarmouth. I (never be) there before.

○ **10 In English, please: Rita in England**

Rita kennt England nicht sehr gut. Und sie ist [noch] nie in Norwich gewesen, wo ihre neue Brieffreundin Jane wohnt. Jane hat Rita schon viele interessante Briefe geschrieben. Und nun hat sie Rita nach Norwich eingeladen. Sie hat ihr auch ein Buch mit Bildern der Norfolk Broads geschenkt. Rita hat schon viel über diese Gegend *(part)* Englands gehört. Und ihre Englischlehrerin hat ihr viel darüber erzählt. Rita hat [schon] immer dorthin fahren wollen, aber sie hat nie genug Geld gehabt. Aber diesmal hat sie Glück. Ihre Großeltern haben ihr gerade DM 200,– geschenkt. Und sie hat schon fast DM 300,– gespart. Am Samstag hat sie Geburtstag, und ihre Mutter wird ihr auch etwas Geld geben.

Two teachers came into the room. One was the father of the other one's son.
Can you explain that?

11 Say it in English: *jemanden einladen*

So kannst Du jemanden auf englisch einladen:

I'm going to have a party on . . . .
I want to go to . . . with my parents.
Would you like to come?/**Do you want to** come?

So kannst Du die Einladung annehmen:

Yes, please. That's very nice of you.
Yes, **I'd like to** (come).
Yes, **I'd love to** (come).
Thank you. I'd like to come very much.

Und so kannst Du sie ablehnen:

I'm afraid I can't. I must . . . .
I'm sorry, but I can't.
I'd like to come, but . . . .
That's very nice of you, but . . . .

Role-play

a Your class wants to have a party on Friday afternoon. You want to invite your English teacher, Mr Williams. But he cannot come because he must go to the doctor.

You: Excuse me, Mr Williams. We're going to have . . . on . . . .
Would you . . . ?
Partner: That's very . . . , but I'm afraid . . .
You: That's all right. Perhaps another time.

b Imagine it is your birthday next week and you want to have a party. *Invite your partner. Ask him/her if he/she knows where you live and if he/she can come at three o'clock.*

You: It's my . . . next . . . . I . . . a party. Do you . . . ?
Partner: Yes, I'd . . . .
You: Do you know . . . ?
Partner: . . .
You: Can you come . . . ?
Partner: . . .

c – You want to go with your parents to a lake next weekend. *Invite your partner to come with you.*
– You are going to visit your uncle's farm next Saturday. *Invite your partner to come with you.*

12 WORDS WORDS WORDS

a *Find the right words for the "woggle" words in these sentences. All the words are new in this unit.*

1. I don't want to fly to England. Can't we go by *woggle* this time? 2. I'm thirsty. – All the bottles are *woggle*, so I can't *woggle* you a drink. 3. Liz likes pop music, but she *woggle* likes folk songs. 4. A group of children are collecting wood for a *woggle*. *Woggles* are nice on cold evenings. 5. London isn't in the *woggle* of England, but York is. London is in the *woggle*. 6. Derek can tell fantastic *woggles*. 7. He told us that he saw a ghost with his *woggle* eyes. 8. My friend Tim didn't think this story was true, but I *woggled* him. 9. Come here, Dave. Help me to *unwoggle* the bus. And you, Kevin. Take this *woggle* and fetch some water. 10. We all want to go on a *woggle* to England over *woggle*. *Woggle* is at the end of March this year.

○b Wie war das? – In English, please.

1. *Wie* ist der Unfall passiert?
   How did . . . ?
2. *Wie* viele andere behinderte Kinder treibt Mike gern Sport *(enjoy).*
3. *Wie* heißt „Rollstuhl" auf englisch?
4. Sally läuft so schnell *wie* Dave.
5. Mein Vater kann schwimmen *wie* ein Fisch.
6. *Wie* ist Ihr Name?
7. Hatfield, *wie* ihr alle wißt, ist nördlich von London.
8. Wir brauchen jemanden *wie* deine Schwester in unserer Hockey-Mannschaft.

13 Revision: A mixed bag

Write a short text about the picture. Use verbs in the present progressive, "there is . . . /there are . . . " and prepositions like "across, in front of, behind".
You can start like this: There are . . . in the picture. On the left a man is . . .

14 Revision: mixed tenses

Liz and Sandra are talking about last weekend. – *Write a dialogue and be careful with the tenses.*

Hallo – Liz / not see you – precinct – Saturday

– be – at home

Why – stay at home? / usually – go there – Saturday morning

– aunt – uncle – from Scotland visit us – at the moment

What – do with them – last weekend?

– Hatfield House – Saturday afternoon / Sunday – coast

Where – go there?

– go – Southwold – near Norwich / know it?

Yes – lovely little town / But – beach – not so nice now

– right – lots of oil – on beach / But they – clean it – for the tourists – next month

always – clean it – before the summer / We – go – last summer – and it – be – beautiful

15 Listening comprehension: Blake House

The cathedral

NORWICH

△ The Tourist Information Centre

△ Elm Hill, the oldest street in Norwich

◁ Swan Lane pedestrian precinct

△ The market

Das Perfekt (The present perfect)

1 Gebrauch

I've collected a lot of photos of my favourite animals.
Ich habe viele Fotos meiner Lieblingstiere gesammelt.

Liz **has phoned** Dave. The Connors **have arrived** in London.
Liz hat Dave angerufen. Die Connors sind in London angekommen.

Man verwendet das *present perfect*, wenn man mitteilen will, daß (nicht: wann!) jemand etwas getan hat oder daß (nicht: wann!) etwas geschehen ist.

2 Bildung

a

Positive sentences	
have/has + Past participle	
I**'ve cleaned**	the bikes.
You**'ve cleaned**	
He/She **has cleaned**	
We**'ve cleaned**	
You**'ve cleaned**	
They**'ve cleaned**	

b

Negative sentences	
haven't/hasn't + Past participle	
I **haven't cleaned**	the car.
You **haven't cleaned**	
He/She **hasn't cleaned**	
We **haven't cleaned**	
You **haven't cleaned**	
They **haven't cleaned**	

Langformen:

I/You/We/They **have** cleaned the bikes.

In Aussagesätzen mit der 3. Person Singular verwenden wir in diesem Buch nur die Langform:

He/She **has** cleaned the bikes.

Langformen:

I/You/We/They **have not** cleaned the car.
He/She **has not** cleaned the car.

Das *present perfect* wird immer mit *have/has* + Partizip Perfekt *(past participle)* gebildet.

⚠ Zur Bildung des *present perfect* wird also auch dann *have* verwendet, wenn die entsprechenden Verben im Deutschen mit „sein" gebraucht werden.

Vergleiche: Dave **has finished** his homework. Sandra **has arrived**.
Dave **hat** seine Hausaufgaben **erledigt**. Sandra **ist angekommen**.

c

Questions	Short answers
Have you **cleaned** the bikes?	Yes, I **have**.
Has he **cleaned** the car?	No, he **hasn't**.
Have they **cleaned** the bikes?	Yes, they **have**.
What **have** you **cooked**?	Potatoes and sausages.

3 Das Partizip Perfekt (The past participle)

a Das Partizip Perfekt der regelmäßigen Verben (The past participle of regular verbs)

Infinitive	Past participle
clean fetch	clean**ed** [-d] = geputzt fetch**ed** [-t] = geholt

Die Bildung des Partizip Perfekt der regelmäßigen Verben ist sehr einfach, weil man nur *-ed* an den Infinitiv anzuhängen braucht.

⚠ Für die Aussprache und Schreibung des Partizip Perfekt bestimmter regelmäßiger Verben gelten dieselben Besonderheiten, die Du schon beim *simple past* (Summary Unit 2, 3b und 3c) kennengelernt hast. Beachte also die Formen *painted* [-tɪd], *phoned, stopped, tried* usw.

b Das Partizip Perfekt der unregelmäßigen Verben (The past participle of irregular verbs)

Infinitive	Past participle
give make be	**given** = gegeben **made** = gemacht **been** = gewesen

Die unregelmäßigen Verben haben eigene Formen für das Partizip Perfekt. Du findest sie sowohl im Vokabular als auch in der Liste am Ende des Buches.
Jede dieser Formen mußt Du wie die unregelmäßigen *simple past*-Formen gesondert lernen.

4 Wortstellung (Word order with the present perfect)

a

	Past participle	Object
Sandra **has**	**painted**	her room.
Sandra **hat** ihr Zimmer **gestrichen**.		

	Past participle	Adverbial of place
Have the children	**arrived**	in Potter Heigham?
Sind die Kinder in Potter Heigham **angekommen**?		

⚠ Anders als im Deutschen müssen ein Objekt oder eine Adverbialbestimmung immer nach dem Partizip Perfekt stehen.

b already, always, ever, just, never, often, sometimes

	Adverb	Past participle	
I've	**just**	made	some tea.
She has	**often**	been	to Italy.
He hasn't	**ever**	played	football.
Have you	**ever**	worked	on a farm?

Die Adverbien *already, always, ever, just, never, often, sometimes* stehen unmittelbar vor dem Partizip Perfekt.

⚠ Beachte, daß *before, yet, (not) yet* am Satzende stehen:

Have you been to Norwich **before**? = Bist du **schon mal** in Norwich gewesen?
Has Sandra arrived **yet**? = Ist Sandra **schon** angekommen?
Kevin has**n't** phoned me **yet**. = Kevin hat mich **noch nicht** angerufen.

1 What's in Sally's wardrobe?
– There's a skirt. There are some trousers.*
There's/There are . . .

2 Sally does not like some of the clothes in her wardrobe. Some are very old. And some are too small for her because she has grown. Her red dress still fits her. But her green blouse and her black skirt are very tight.

Sally: I think I've grown, Liz.
Dave: You haven't grown. You're fatter.

And you?

What are you wearing today?
What's your partner wearing?
Do your clothes still fit?
Do you need any new clothes because you've grown?

*

You can say:	some my the these those	trousers jeans shorts	⚠ But never:	~~a~~ ~~one~~ ~~this~~ ~~that~~	trousers jeans shorts

3 Sally's grandparents have given her a cheque for £25 for her birthday. She has decided to buy some new clothes with the money. She and Liz have gone to London Girl, a clothes shop in the precinct. Liz wants to buy a pullover there.

Sally: I like this white blouse. And it's my size.
Liz: What size do you take?
Sally: Ten usually. Sometimes twelve. What do you think? Does the blouse suit me?
Liz: Yes, it suits you very well.

4 Sally and Liz have tried on a lot of different clothes, and now they have decided what they want. Sally has chosen the white blouse, and she has found a yellow T-shirt and some nice socks. Liz has bought a red pullover.

And you?

Are there any good clothes shops in your town/village?
What would you like to buy there?
Does your friend/mother/father go with you when you buy clothes?
Do you pay for your own clothes?

5 It is Wednesday evening now. Sally is at the youth club. She has put on her new blouse.

Sandra: Hey, you've bought a new blouse.
Sally: Yes. Do you like it?
Sandra: It's super. What have you done with your green blouse?
Sally: Mum has given it to people from the church. They're collecting things.
Sandra: Oh, we also want to collect things. We want to give them to the Oxfam shop.

→ Ex 2, 3

INFO BOX

Oxfam shops

There are Oxfam shops in many British towns. People often take old clothes, books, toys and even furniture to the shops. The shops then sell these things. With the money they buy food and medicine for poor and hungry people in the Third World. Young people often help in the Oxfam shops because these shops cannot pay many assistants.

6 Sandra and her friends went from house to house during the next week and collected things. People gave them toys, old clothes, records and books.

→ Ex 4-6

7 Now it is Saturday morning and the children are at the Oxfam shop. They have collected a lot of things.

Kevin **has collected** some trousers.
He **collected** them from Mr Warren on Monday.
Liz has collected . . . .

→ Ex 7

8 Sally has now arrived at the shop, too. She has got so many coats and hats that she almost fell when she came into the shop.

Sally: **I've collected** five coats and seven old hats. What **have** you **collected**?
Dave: Look here. Everything is on the table.
Liz: I hope it's all worth lots of money.
Sally: Just imagine. I **went** to Mr Warren's house on Thursday and he said, "Not another! You're the fourth." **Did** you **go** there, too?
Kevin: Yes, I went on Monday.
Sandra: And I went on Tuesday.
Liz: I went there on Wednesday.
Tom: I went last night, but he didn't open the door. He looked out of the window and said, "Go away. The house is empty. I'm not here."

And you?

Have you and your friends ever collected clothes or other things for the church/school/youth club/. . . ?

Have you ever done anything to help poor people in Third World countries?

– No, I/we haven't.
– Yes, we have. We collected . . . last month/last year/. . . .
And we . . .

→ S · Ex 8-12

The red stamp

It was Friday evening. The youth club members had a lot of things for the Oxfam shop. Liz looked at the dirty old book in her hand.

"The shop can't sell this book, Sandra. It's too dirty. Let's throw it away."

Something fell out of the book. It was an old envelope.

"No, some people collect old books. But you can throw that old envelope away," said Sandra. "Or is there a letter in it?"

"No, there isn't. But look at this." There was a red stamp on the envelope.

"I haven't seen this stamp before. It must be very old. Do you think it's worth lots of money?" Liz asked.

"I don't know," said Sandra. "But there are stamp catalogues at the library. Perhaps the stamp is in one of the catalogues. Let's meet at the library at nine o'clock tomorrow."

The next morning Sandra and Liz went to the library and looked at the stamp catalogues.

"Here. I've found it," said Sandra. "*D* on the left and *I* on the right. It's a Penny Red – 1854. And it's worth £150!"

"We must find the owner," said Liz. "What's the address on the envelope?"

"Mrs Ellen Sharp, 22 Hanover Street, Hatfield. I haven't heard of that street before." Sandra fetched a map of Hatfield, but there was no Hanover Street. Then she had an idea.

"Let's look at the old maps. Perhaps the street has got a new name."

Liz fetched an old map.

"Look. Here it is. Hanover Street. That's where Albert Road is now. Let's go!"

An old woman opened the door at 22 Albert Road.

"Our youth club collected some books from you last week," said Liz. "And we found this envelope in one of the books. The stamp is very old. We found out that it's worth £150."

"Oh!" said the old woman. "Ellen Sharp was my grandmother. And the stamp is worth £150? Well!"

Three days later a letter arrived at the youth club.

→ Ex 1

1a *Look at "The red stamp" on page 89 again. Now find the mistakes in these sentences and correct them.*

It was Thursday evening. Liz was at the library. She had a new book in her hand. She found an envelope with a blue stamp on it. The stamp was worth £100. It was from 1954. Liz and Sandra went to 22 Hanover Street. Ellen Sharp was happy to have the stamp back. She did not sell it to a stamp shop. Miss Sharp gave the children a cheque – £25 for the Oxfam shop.

b **An interview with Mary Sharp, Liz and Sandra** *Work in groups and ask and answer the questions.*

1. Miss Sharp, why did the children come to your house last Saturday?
2. Liz, you wanted to throw the book away. Why?
3. And why did you want to go to the library, Sandra?
4. You found out something interesting about the stamp, Sandra and Liz. What was that?
5. And was it difficult to find the owner's address? How did you find it out, Liz?
6. Why did you two go to Albert Road?
7. Miss Sharp, why did you write a letter to the youth club members?
8. Liz and Sandra, what did your youth club spend the money on?

2 Simon was ill for two weeks, but now he is back at school and wants to know what has happened. *Complete his questions with the right present perfect form, find the right answers and complete them, too.*

1. . . . you (do) the English test yet?
2. And our French test? . . . Miss Green (give) it back?
3. . . . you (practise) for the pupil-teacher football match?
4. . . . anybody (watch) the teachers' team?
5. . . . you (talk) about our school trip to London?
6. Mr Hill's old car isn't standing in front of the school. . . . he (buy) a new one?

a) Of course, we . . . . Our team is in top form.

b) No, we . . . . But Mr Hill is going to give us some information about the trip very soon.

c) You're lucky. We . . . . So you needn't do it.

d) Yes, Kevin . . . . He thinks Herr Meier is their best player.

e) No, he . . . . He came by bike today.

f) No, she . . . . We're still waiting for it.

Doctor, doctor, I've eaten a pencil. What can I do?
– Use a pen.

3 *Look at the pictures and ask your partner questions with "Why . . . ?". Your partner must use the present perfect in her/his answers.*

1. Mrs Dean – angry?

2. Mr Hill – tired?

3. Kevin – feeling terrible?

4. Aunt Mary – frightened?

5. Karen – dirty?

6. Mrs White – happy?

7. Mr Dean – unhappy?

8. Sandra's room – so untidy?

1. Why's Mrs Dean so angry?
   – Well, Peanut has just eaten the newspaper.
   Oh, that's terrible.

2. Why's Mr Hill . . . ?
   – Well, he . . . the housework.
   I can understand him. I hate housework, too.

Go on.

4 Revision: simple past

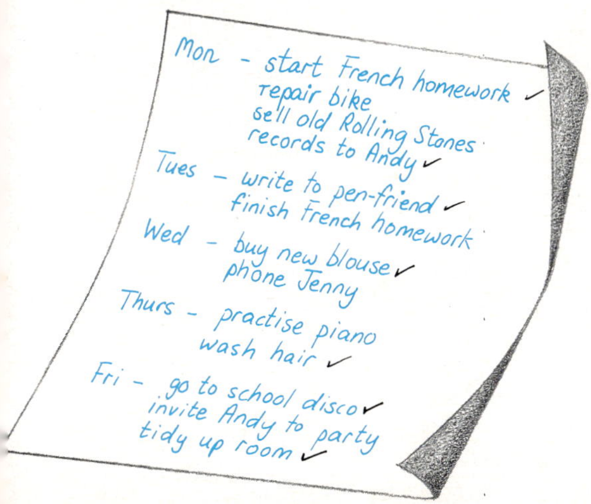

Look at Liz's list. It tells you what she did and what she did not do last week.

a What things did she do last week?

On Monday Liz started her French homework.
And she sold her old . . .
Go on.

b What things did she not do last week?

On Monday she did not repair her bike.
On Tuesday . . .
Go on.

5 Revision: simple past **The new shirt** *Complete the sentences.*

Andrew went (go) into town last Friday and (buy) a new shirt. Then he (take) it home and (show) it to his mother. His mother (like) the style, but she (not like) the colour. "It's terrible, Andrew," she (say). "Why . . . you (take) it? . . . they (not have) any nicer colours?" Andrew (look) at the shirt, (think) for a long time and (agree). "Yes," he (decide), "it (look) OK in the shop, but not in this light."
There (be) no problem at the shop the next day. " . . . it (not fit)?" the assistant (ask) and (offer) Andrew his money back. But Andrew (not want) his money back. He (choose) a different shirt this time. It (be) the same style but a nicer colour.

6 Revision: simple past

Franz and Gudrun Schmidt from Wolfsburg are talking to some American friends, Gary and Jo-Ann Mayer, about holidays. – *Complete their questions and answers.*

1. *Gary:* Where . . . you (go) last year, Gudrun?
   Gudrun: We (go) to . . . , Gary. It (be) a lovely holiday.
2. *Jo-Ann:* . . . you (go) by . . . ?
   Franz: No, we (fly) there, Jo-Ann. They drive on the . . . in England, you know, and we (not want) to try that.
3. *Jo-Ann:* Where . . . you (fly) to? London?
   Gudrun: Yes, that's right. We (land) at Heathrow Airport.
4. *Gary:* How . . . you (get) from Heathrow to the city centre?
   Gudrun: We (go) by Underground, Gary. That's the quickest . . . .
5. *Gary:* . . . you (sleep) at a friend's . . . ?
   Franz: No, we (stay) at a . . . .
6. *Jo-Ann:* . . . you (walk) from the . . . station to your . . . ?
   Franz: No, we (take) a taxi.
7. *Gary:* When . . . you (arrive) at your . . . ? Morning or evening?
   Gudrun: We (arrive) there at . . . , I think. Yes, about then.
8. *Jo-Ann:* . . . you (have) lunch at the hotel?
   Franz: No, we (eat) some . . . in a . . . near Buckingham Palace.

7 The children in the pictures have bought new clothes. They bought them last week. – *Make one sentence with the present perfect, then one with the simple past.*

Saturday Tuesday Friday Wednesday Thursday

1. Look, Liz has bought a new blouse.
   – Yes, I know. She bought it last Saturday.
2. Kevin . . . tie.
   – Yes, . . . last Tuesday. It's terrible. *Go on.*

8 *Which adverb or adverbial phrase goes with which sentence?*

Dave King has ● been on TV.
The first men walked on the moon ●.
Men have ● walked on Mars ●.
Have you ● been to Scotland or Wales?
Miss Green went to church ●.
Sally is tired because she went to bed ●.
Open the door. Aunt Mary has ● arrived.
The Connors went to Germany on holiday ●.
It is not Herr Schneider's first trip to London. He has been there ●.

● in August
● on Sunday
● at 11 o'clock
● in 1969
● never
● before
● just
● not ● yet
● ever

9 *Make negative sentences with the present perfect and the simple past.*

Sandra Dave Kevin	has not did not	(go) to school (do) her/his homework (see) the film (spend) all her/his pocket-money (read) "Robinson Crusoe"	last night. before. on Tuesday. at the weekend. yet

Examples: Sandra has not done her homework yet.
Dave did not read "Robinson Crusoe" last night.

10 Have you ever . . . ? *Complete these short dialogues with the present perfect or the simple past.*

Example: *Liz:* Have you ever seen a fire? (you/ever/see)
Sandra: Yes, I have.
Liz: When did you see one?
Sandra: I saw one in York some years ago.

1. *Kate:* . . . any money? (you/ever/lose)
Paul: Yes, ...
Kate: How much . . . ?
Paul: I . . . £10, I think.

2. *Brian:* . . . anything in the street? (you/ever/find)
Dave: In the street? . . .
Brian: What . . . ?
Dave: Well, I . . . a knife.

3. *Tim:* . . . you? (Kate/ever/visit)
Paul: Kate? . . .
Tim: Oh! When . . . ?
Paul: She . . . me last July, I think.

4. *Anne:* . . . to Germany? (you/ever/be)
Clare: Me? Of course . . .
Anne: And where . . . ?
Clare: Oh, I . . . in Bonn.

5. *Peter:* . . . a white budgie? (you/ever/see)
Pam: A white budgie? . . .
Peter: Where . . . ?
Pam: I . . . one at Mr Singh's pet shop.

6. *Kevin:* . . . too much? (you/ever/eat)
Dave: Of course . . .
Kevin: When . . . ?
Dave: I . . . at my father's birthday party.

○

Doctor, I've lost my memory[1].
– When did this happen?
When did what happen?

You need glasses[2], Mrs Biggs.
– That's right. But how do you know, doctor?
You've just walked through the window.

[1] memory ['meməri] *Gedächtnis*   [2] glasses ['glɑːsɪz] *eine Brille*

11 Where are Sandra and Liz? *Present perfect or simple past?*

Mr Hill: Ah Dave, ... Sandra (show) you her photos of the Norfolk Broads yet?
Dave: Yes, sir. She (show) them to me yesterday. They're great.
Mr Hill: Yes, I agree. But where's Sandra today? ... you (see) her yet?
Dave: Well, I (see) her at about half past eight, Mr Hill. She (be) on her way to school.
Mr Hill: Well, nobody at school (see) her yet.
Dave: Nobody? ... you (ask) Liz, too?
Mr Hill: No, I haven't. I don't think Liz (arrive) yet. – Ah, there is Sandra!
Sandra: I'm late, I know, Mr Hill. I'm sorry. I (get) to school at nine o'clock. But then I suddenly (remember) my homework and I (decide) to go home and fetch it.
Mr Hill: That's okay. And Liz? ... you (see) her on your way to school?
Sandra: Oh, Liz. She (phone) me last night. She has got a temperature and must stay in bed.

○ **12 In English, please:** *Frage Deinen Partner/Deine Partnerin, ...*

1. ob er/sie schon mal in England gewesen ist.
2. wo er/sie gestern abend war.
3. ob er/sie letzte Nacht einen interessanten Traum *(dream)* gehabt hat.
4. ob er/sie je „Oliver Twist" gelesen hat.
5. was er/sie gestern zum Frühstück gegessen hat.
6. ob er/sie schon mal geflogen ist.
7. ob er/sie je im Krankenhaus war.
8. ob er/sie am Wochenende Spaghetti gegessen hat.
9. wann er/sie den neuen Plattenspieler gekauft hat.
10. ob er/sie letzte Woche auf einer Party war.
11. warum er/sie Dich gestern nachmittag nicht angerufen hat.
12. ob er/sie je einen Unfall mit seinem/ihrem Fahrrad gehabt hat.

13 Revision: A mixed bag

At school *Complete the sentences.*

1. We haven't got ... French books, Miss Green.
   – Well, go to the school library and fetch ... books.
2. Sorry, sir, I ... my homework.
   – Not again. ... it for tomorrow, then.
3. Can you see Mr Duncan?
   – Yes, he ... to Miss Green over there.
4. Are ... your pencils, Dave?
   – No, miss. ... Tim's, I think.
5. When ... Anne (arrive) at school this morning?
   – Her bus ... (usually/arrive) at 8.30.
6. ... Jenny (win) the tennis match yesterday?
   – No, she ... (lose). She played very ... (nervous).
7. Yesterday's English lesson ... really bad.
   – You're lucky you weren't there the day before yesterday. It was even ... .
8. Mr Hill is ... a funny tie today.
   – Oh, he always ... funny clothes.
9. Can I sit ... Mary today, miss?
   – No, you ... . And ... ask me again.
10. My mum ... my maths homework for me yesterday. ... you like to see it?

○14 Revision: her his their she's he's they're – In English, please.

Some children are talking about their friends:
Can you translate what they are saying into English?

1. Martina ist ganz nett, aber ich mag ihren kleinen Bruder nicht.
   – Ach, ich weiß nicht. Der ist in Ordnung.
2. Ich mag Peter ganz gern, aber seine große Schwester ist furchtbar.
   – Das stimmt. Sie ist furchtbar.
3. Weißt du, warum Sarah und Susie so unglücklich sind?
   – Ja. Ihre Eltern wollen von hier weggehen und in London wohnen.
4. Ich mag David und Ruth, aber ich mag ihre Hunde nicht.
   – Du magst sie nicht? Sie sind aber schön.
5. Ich muß Michael und Iris zu meiner Party einladen. Sie sind so lustig.
   – Lustig? Ich finde ihre Geschichten langweilig.
6. Hast du Karen gesehen?
   – Ja. Sie ist ganz glücklich. Ihre Eltern wollen ihr mehr Taschengeld geben.

7. Martin hat einen Hund zum Geburtstag bekommen.
   – Der hat Glück. Seine Eltern schenken ihm immer ganz tolle Sachen.
8. Anja und ihr Bruder wollen morgen eine Party geben.
   – Na, ja. Ich mag ihre Partys nicht. Sie spielen nie gute Platten.

15 Revision: comparisons

What is your opinion? *Choose an adjective from the left.*

Example: French is easier than German, I think. – Well, I don't know. French can be difficult, too.

or – You're right. French is easier.

boring, difficult, nice, fast, exciting, interesting, noisy, quiet, good, bad, easy, cold, funny, warm

1. Bonn/Mainz
2. July/August
3. cars/trains
4. lessons/weekends
5. cowboy films/animal films
6. comics/history books
7. housework/homework
8. chess/card games
9. green/blue
10. carrots/tomatoes

16 Revision: mixed tenses *Find the right combinations.*

1. Last Saturday Sandra ...
2. Look, Sally is ...
3. When Liz is in a clothes shop, she often ...
4. It's much too cold, so I haven't ...
5. Next Saturday Kevin is going ...
6. Dave's coat is too small for him, so he ...

... has bought a new coat.
... tries on lots of different clothes.
... bought a new pullover.
... wearing some new summer shoes.
... to buy some new trousers.
... taken any summer clothes with me.

17 WORDS WORDS WORDS

a *Look at the pictures and make six lists from these words. Several words can be in more than one list.*

answer	finger	leg	(to) read	(to) sing	(to) touch
(to) argue	folk song	(to) listen	record	sock	(to) walk
arm	football	(to) look	(to) repair	sound	(to) watch
book	hair	loud	(to) run	spoon	word
brake	handlebars	music	(to) say	(to) stand	(to) write
cycling	hat	neck	scream	story	
(to) draw	headache	nod	(to) see	(to) talk	
drink	(to) hear	noisy	shoe	(to) tell	
(to) eat	helmet	nose	(to) shout	(to) think	
film	(to) jump	(to) pronounce	sign	thumb	

arm	hair	brake	answer	book	answer
brake	hat	cycling	(to) argue	film	folk song
...	...	...	...	...	...

b **How well can you spell?**

Read the following sentences, then write them down.

1. Everybody <u>knows</u> [nəʊz] that Bill has got a <u>nose</u> [nəʊz] like a potato.
2. When I [sɔ:] him last night, he had a [sɔ:] throat.
3. Last [wi:k] Sandra was ill and too [wi:k] to get up.
4. [aɪ] can't see very well with my left [aɪ].
5. Do you [nəʊ] Mary Sharp? – [nəʊ], I don't.
6. Have you [red] the little [red] book?
7. Kevin [rəʊd] along the [rəʊd] on his bike.
8. You can [si:] the [si:] from here.
9. But you can't [hɪə] the traffic in [hɪə].
10. The old woman's [sʌn] loved the [sʌn].
11. The children [θru:] a ball [θru:] the window.
12. [waɪ] can't I spell "tries" with a "[waɪ]"?
13. Sally [wʌn] only [wʌn] set of the tennis match against Martina yesterday.
14. Did you [breɪk] my bike? – Well, I only wanted to check the [breɪk].
15. Of course Anne isn't my [nju:] friend. I [nju:] her when I was six.
16. [weə] are my jeans? I want to [weə] them today.
17. Your sentence isn't [raɪt]. Try to [raɪt] it again.
18. You want to eat [tu:] chickens? Isn't that [tu:] much for you?

How often can you say these tongue twisters?
Say them slowly first, then try to say them more quickly.

1. Red ladder, yellow ladder. Red ladder, yellow ladder. ...
2. Mixed biscuits. Mixed biscuits. ...
3. She sells shoes in a special shoe shop.
4. Simon's short shirt and Sandra's school skirt.
5. Phone Phil for fine fresh fish.

The present perfect and the simple past

Sowohl das *present perfect* als auch das *simple past* werden verwendet, um über Ereignisse in der Vergangenheit zu sprechen:

Present perfect

Liz: Look, Sally. I**'ve bought** a new pullover. **(a)** →

Mit dem Satz im *present perfect* will Liz Sally auf ihren neuen Pullover aufmerksam machen. Sie sagt damit nur, daß sie sich irgendwann einen neuen Pullover gekauft hat.

Tim: Dave, **have** you ever **seen** a Charlie Chaplin film? **(c)**
Dave: Yes, I **have**. **(a)** →

Mit der Frage im *present perfect* erkundigt sich Tim, ob Dave überhaupt schon mal einen Charlie-Chaplin-Film gesehen hat.

Simple past

I **bought** it at London Girl last Saturday. **(b)**

Mit dem Satz im *simple past* fügt Liz nun hinzu, wann (und wo) sie sich ihren Pullover gekauft hat (nämlich am letzten Samstag bei London Girl).

Tim: When **did** you **see** your first Charlie Chaplin film? **(d)**
Dave: When I **was** five. **(e)** I really **liked** it. **(f)**

Mit der *When?*-Frage im *simple past* erkundigt sich Tim, wann Dave den ersten Charlie-Chaplin-Film gesehen hat. Dave nennt den Zeitpunkt (als er fünf war) und sagt, daß er den Film sehr mochte. (Dabei wiederholt Dave den Zeitpunkt natürlich nicht, denn es ist ja klar, von welchem Film er spricht.)

Man verwendet das *present perfect:*

- wenn man mitteilen will, daß jemand etwas getan hat **(a)** oder daß etwas geschehen ist,
- wenn man fragen will, ob jemand etwas schon irgendwann mal getan hat **(c)** oder ob etwas irgendwann geschehen ist.

Der genaue Zeitpunkt ist dabei unwichtig und darf nicht genannt werden.

Man verwendet das *simple past:*

- wenn man (in einer Aussage oder Frage) den genauen Zeitpunkt eines vergangenen Ereignisses nennt **(b, e)** sowie immer in *When?*-Fragen **(d)**,
- wenn man über eine bereits erwähnte Sache spricht und dazu etwas fragt **(d)** oder sagt **(f)**,
- wenn man über ein vergangenes Ereignis berichtet (z.B. das BMX-Rennen auf S. 21) oder wenn man eine Geschichte erzählt (z.B. Mr Hills Geistergeschichte auf S. 74/75).

In Sätzen mit dem *present perfect* findet man häufig Adverbien wie:
already, before, ever, just, never, often, (not) yet.

In Sätzen mit dem *simple past* findet man häufig Zeitangaben wie:
two days ago, three years ago; at one o'clock, at the weekend; in 1980; last night, last week; on Monday; yesterday; Fragewort *When . . . ?*

Merke also: *Yesterday, ago* und *last* fordern immer *simple past.*

⚠ Ich **bin** gestern im Kino **gewesen**.
Ich **war** gestern im Kino. } I **was** at the cinema yesterday.

Im Deutschen ist es oft unwichtig, ob man in einem Satz das Perfekt („bin . . . gewesen") oder das Präteritum („war") benutzt. Aber im Englischen sind das *present perfect* ("have been") und das *simple past* ("was") nicht austauschbar. Im deutschen Beispielsatz steht die Zeitangabe „gestern", und deshalb kann man im entsprechenden englischen Satz nur das *simple past* verwenden.

Unit 8 A

1 Noah's ark

Which animals are already on the ark?
Which animals are still coming towards the ark?
Which animals are behind it?
Which are in front of the ark?

2

Song: The animals went in two by two

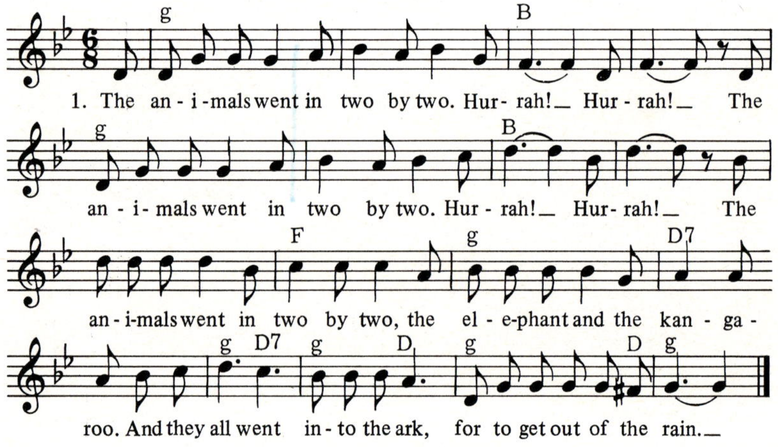

3 Game: Guess my animal.

You: It's black and white and has got four legs.
Your partner: Oh, that's a zebra.

Your partner: My animal has got a long neck.
You: Oh, that's a giraffe.

You: It lives . . . *Go on.*

– black and white, four legs
– long neck
– lives in trees, bananas
– grey, big ears, long nose
– big cat, dangerous
– lots of colours, can fly and talk
– swims in the water, big eyes
– can jump, carries its babies in a pocket
– big, brown, lives in the mountains
– white, dangerous, lives where it is cold
– lives in hot countries, carries things
– black and white, seabird, cannot fly, can swim
– huge animal, big head, big mouth, small ears

And you?

Do you remember the names of other animals?
Write down the names of six or seven.
What are your favourite animals?
What can you say about them?

4 All the animals from Noah's ark live in different countries in the world. But you have probably seen most of them already because they live in zoos, too. In Britain the biggest and most famous zoo is London Zoo.

And you?

Have you ever been to a zoo?
Is there a zoo in or near your town?
When did you go there the last time?
How did you like it?

5

Sally, Dave and their friends went to London Zoo in early spring. Mrs King went with them. There were a lot of baby animals then, and the children wanted to see them.
When they arrived at the zoo, Mrs King bought the tickets and gave them to the children.
"This is your ticket, Liz," she said. "And this is **yours**, Sandra."
"Where are **ours**?" asked Dave and Kevin.
"Wait a minute, please. Here you are. Where's Sally? She needs a ticket, too."
"She's buying an ice-cream," Liz said.
"Well, this is **hers**. Now I haven't got a ticket. Who has got **mine**?"
"I've got two," said Dave. → S 1 · Ex 3-5

6 First Mrs King and the children visited the monkeys and the gorillas. It was very loud and very smelly.
"Remember what's on the sign," said Mrs King. "Don't feed the animals or try to touch them. It's dangerous."
"But can't we touch the ponies and animals like that?" asked Liz.
"Only in the children's zoo. We can go there later."

7 They met a very nice zoo keeper. He took them to a special cage with a baby gorilla.
"This is Susie," he said. "She's five days old. Her mother didn't want her. So we must look after her."
"Why didn't her mother want her?" asked Sally.
"A lot of animals in zoos are frightened when they see their baby for the first time," said the zoo keeper.
"They don't know what it is. And they don't know what they must do with it."

Some animals in zoos are so frightened when they see their baby for the first time that they run to their keeper and hide behind him. Then the keeper must take the baby or give it to another 'mother'. But it is not easy. You can sometimes give a baby lion to a tiger, but you cannot put a baby chimp together with a gorilla.

8 "What **will happen** to Susie now? **Will** she **die**?" Dave asked.
"Well, she **won't die**, but we must feed her every two or three hours. And one of us must take her home every night. **It'll be** hard work for us. But after six months she'll be strong enough to go into a cage with other gorillas."
→ S 2a

9 At quarter to two it was feeding-time for the sea lions. There were a lot of children there, so the keeper played some games with the sea lions. He put the fish in his mouth and the sea lions jumped out of the water and took the fish from him.

Feeding times

IN SUMMER (April to Sept.)		IN WINTER (Oct. to Mar.)
3.30 pm	sea lions (not Fridays)	1.45 pm
2.45 pm	penguins	2.45 pm
4.30 pm	gorillas (not Mondays)	2.30 pm
3.30 pm	polar bears	3.00 pm

10

"That was great," said Dave as they walked towards the children's zoo. "I think **I'll work** in a zoo **when** I **leave** school."
Sally started to laugh. "I'm sure the chimps **will think** you're one of their relatives. The zoo **will** probably **make** a special cage: 'The Hatfield Monster'."
"Ha, ha, very funny," said Dave. "And I suppose you**'ll come** and feed me every day."
"You two are so silly," said Liz. "I like animals very much. And you know what? Lots of animals are dying out. Perhaps they**'ll** only **live** in zoos in the future."
"Oh, I don't think it**'ll be** so bad," said Dave.

And you?

Have you read, heard or seen films about animals in danger?

→ S 2b · Ex 6-9

Lions and tigers

Not long ago the Connors visited Longleat House near Bath. That is 120 miles from Hatfield. This beautiful sixteenth-century house is very popular with tourists because it has got a big safari park with lots of wild animals. But these animals are not in cages as in a zoo. They walk through the fields freely. Tourists can drive through the park and look at the animals. But they must not leave their cars.

It was a quiet day and there were not many tourists in the park. Mr Connor was not too happy when he saw the monkeys and the elephants. The Connors had a new car. It was only one week old.

"I hope these animals won't run after us or jump on the car," he said.

Soon they drove through a large gate and they saw the famous Longleat lions. There are over thirty lions in Longleat Park. Some of them sat on the grass; some walked across the fields; and some looked at the Connors in their car. Kevin took lots of photos.

"Are they dangerous?" asked Carol.

"They're very dangerous when they're hungry," said Mrs Connor.

And then Tina said, "Dad, what's that red light?"

Mr Connor looked behind the steering wheel where all the lights were. One light was red. "I don't know," he said.

There were lights for everything: for water, petrol, oil, the lights, even for the door.

"Perhaps we need some petrol," said Mrs Connor.

"Or some oil," said Carol.

"No," said Mr Connor, "I think we need some water."

"I've got some lemonade," said Kevin.

"You can't put lemonade in a car," said Carol.

"Be quiet," said Mr Connor. He stopped and opened the door. "I think I must check the water and the oil," he said. But the lions saw him. And they walked towards him.

"John," said Mrs Connor, "Quick. You mustn't leave the car. It's dangerous."

Mr Connor climbed back into the car. And soon there were twenty lions in front of them.

"Dad," said Tina, "Will they eat us?"

"I don't know. But let's leave before they try."

He drove slowly through the lions. And still the light was red. Then a few minutes later they came to another gate and there were no more lions – only tigers.

"Dad," said Tina, "Why's your shirt wet?"

Mr Connor was angry now. "Tina, I don't want to hear more of your silly questions."

"Throw her to the tigers," said Kevin.

They drove through the tigers and everybody in the car watched the light. It was still red.

"Carol," said Mr Connor, "Look in the handbook and tell me what this light is."

"I can't find the handbook," said Carol.

After the tigers there were the wolves – angry grey wolves.

"How big is the park?" said Mr Connor. "Will it never finish?"

A few minutes later they arrived at the end of the park. Mr Connor jumped out of the car – it did not need any oil and it did not need any water. And it still had lots of petrol.

"What was the red light then?" asked Mrs Connor.

Carol now had the handbook and she soon had the answer, too. "It was the handbrake, Dad. You didn't release the handbrake properly."

Mr Connor looked where the red light was. "The handbrake?" he said. "Well, I'm sure in the future I'll remember what that light means."

→ Ex 1, 2

1a *Look at "Lions and tigers" on pages 102-103 again. Are these sentences right? – Try to explain your answers.*

Examples: Longleat House is popular with tourists because it has got a good restaurant.
– That's not right. It's popular with tourists because it has got a big safari park.
Tourists must stay in their cars in the safari park.
– That's right. There are dangerous animals in the park.

1. Mr Connor was happy when he saw the monkeys and elephants and zebras round his car.
2. He was not sure what the red light in his car was.
3. All this was funny for the children.
4. Mr Connor was not frightened when there were lions - and later tigers - round his car.
5. Mr Connor made a silly mistake.

Have you/your parents ever made a silly mistake? Tell the class about it.

b **Tina's story** The day after they visited Longleat House Tina told her friend:

Yesterday – Longleat Park / safari park with wild animals / not many tourists / through park in new car / Kevin – photos / Suddenly I – red light behind steering wheel / Dad – out of car – but lions / Dad – back into car – leave / then tigers and wolves / Everybody – nervous / At last – end of park / Carol – handbook – to Dad "You – not release handbrake properly"

2 **Humphrey's holiday** *Look at the pictures and words and tell the story about Humphrey the hippo. You can start like this:* One day the door of Humphrey's cage was open. The zoo keeper . . .

1. One day – the door – open / zoo keeper – not there / Humphrey – leave cage / lucky – nobody see him / walk out of zoo
2. Near zoo – wood – lots of trees / nice hot day / Humphrey – through the trees
3. Soon – see big house – large garden / Humphrey – into garden / nobody – there / see swimming-pool – decide to swim
4. A few minutes later – woman – come into garden / want to swim / before jump into water – see Humphrey / frightened – shout – "Help!"
5. woman – back into house – phone police / "There's a . . .," she said
6. Ten minutes later – zoo keeper and police arrive / Humphrey – still in water / not want to leave / zoo keeper fetch crane / lift Humphrey – out of swimming-pool / Poor Humphrey – holiday short

Question: What is a good name for a camel with three humps[1]? *Answer:* Humphrey ['hʌmfri:], of course!

[1]hump [hʌmp] *Höcker*

3 In the hall after the party *Complete the sentences. Use possessive pronouns.*

1. Is this your bag, Liz?
   – No, mine is black.
2. Carol and Tina say these brown coats aren't . . . .
   – Of course not. . . . are on that chair over there.
3. Is this Dave's watch, Sally?
   – Yes, it's . . . .
4. This isn't my pullover. It must be . . . , Sandra.
5. Peter, here's your jacket.
   – Sorry, but this isn't . . . .
6. Whose shoes are these? Are they Carol's, Tina?
   – No, . . . are blue.
7. Whose tickets are those on the floor? Are they . . . , Sally and Dave?
   – No, we've got . . . .

4 At the bus stop *Put in:*

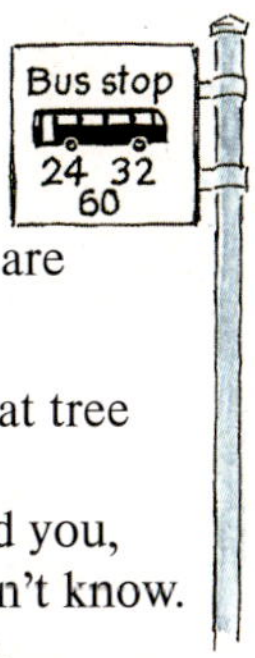

theirs there's they're their there are

1. The bus is late again. – Yes, well, . . . so much traffic.
2. Can you see the brown dog under that tree there? I think it's the Parkers'. – No, it can't be. . . . is a small young dog. And . . . on holiday with it at the moment.
3. Look at the two young people behind you, Mrs Davis. . . . hairstyle is, well, I don't know. – You know what young people are like these days.
4. Listen to those women in front of us, Keith. . . . talking about our hair. – Oh, let them talk. . . . a lot of funny old people.
5. Look, isn't that the Connors' car over there? – No, I don't think it's . . . . car is much bigger.
6. You know, I think I'd like a cup of tea. – Well, . . . a nice café in Victoria Street. Let's go there. We can take a later bus. . . . lots of buses in the early evening.

○ **5 In English, please.**

1. Anne hatte den Pullover ihres Bruders an. Er hatte ihren an.
   Anne wore her brother's pullover. He wore hers.
2. Peter hatte den Pullover seiner Schwester an. Sie hatte seinen an.
3. Kevin hat seine Hausaufgaben gemacht, aber Tina und Carol haben ihre noch nicht gemacht.
4. Wir mögen euren Plan. – Wir mögen euren auch.
5. Ich kann meinen Bleistift nicht finden. – Nimm meinen.
6. Ich habe gerade einen Brief von meinen Eltern bekommen. Hast du von deinen gehört?
7. Gestern besuchten wir die Browns in ihrem neuen Haus. Das Haus ist viel größer als unseres.
8. Ihrs ist vielleicht größer, aber euers ist schöner.
9. Wessen Auto ist das? – Es ist meins. Gefällt es dir?

6 Sandra's party Groups of Sandra's guests are talking noisily.
Complete the sentences with "'ll" or "won't".

1. I like Sandra's new cassette-recorder. I'd like to buy one like it.
   – Well, it . . . be cheap, I can tell you.
2. We're going to see the new film at the Apollo tomorrow. Have you seen it?
   – Oh yes, it's great. You . . . enjoy it.
3. I can't see Terry here. Is he still ill?
   – Yes, he is, I'm afraid. And he . . . be back at school this week or next week.
4. Why aren't you wearing your red dress, Sally?
   – I don't like it. Do you want to have it? It . . . fit you, I'm sure.
   Well, yes. But I don't think it . . . suit me.
5. It's still raining.
   – Yes, I don't think it . . . ever stop.
6. Oh, look at the time. We must leave. It's 11.30 already. What . . . my parents say?
   – Oh, it . . . be okay, I'm sure. They . . . understand.

7 What will I be? Sarah is talking to her brother Mark about what she will be when she is older.
Complete the sentences with "'ll", "will" or "won't".

I've decided I want to be a racing driver.

– Oh, that's very dangerous.

It is, yes. But you . . . see, I . . . be famous.

– And I'm sure that one day you . . . crash and that . . . be the end of you.

No, I . . . .

– Do you really think you . . . find a job? Remember you're a girl.

Of course I . . . . I . . . show them that I can drive as well as a man.

– They . . . listen to you.

Perhaps they . . . , perhaps they . . . . But I still want to be a racing driver.

– Well, we . . . see.

8 Dave's week in Scotland
Complete the sentences with the correct verb form: simple present or will-future.

1. Dave is going to visit his cousin John in Glasgow for a week. He hopes John and his aunt and uncle (be) at the station when he (arrive).
2. Dave (be) very happy when he (see) John again. The two are really good friends.
3. When they (get) to his cousin's house, Dave (phone) his parents in Hatfield.
4. Of course, Dave and John (not sleep) very much when they (be) together. They (tell) ghost stories and (talk) all night.
5. When John's parents (come) home from work in the evening, they (go) out with the boys – perhaps to the cinema. Later, they (play) games together.
6. And, when the weather (be) nice, they (take) Dave and John to the coast or into the mountains.
7. Dave (not think) about Hatfield much when he (be) in Scotland. But he (write) postcards to all his friends, of course.

9 Say it in English: *Vermutungen über die Zukunft äußern*

So kannst Du auf englisch Vermutungen über die Zukunft äußern:

I imagine it'll	▷ Ich stelle mir vor, .../Ich denke mir, ...
I suppose you'll	▷ Ich nehme an, ...
I'm sure she'll	▷ Ich bin sicher/überzeugt, ...
I (don't) think we'll	▷ Ich meine (nicht)/glaube (nicht), ...
Perhaps they'll	▷ Vielleicht . . . .
I'll **probably**	▷ Wahrscheinlich . . . .

a What presents do you think your family and friends will give you on your next birthday?
Use I imagine, I suppose, I'm sure, I (don't) think, perhaps, probably *in your answer.*

Example: I imagine my sister will give me a book. Perhaps one of my friends will give me a poster for my room. I don't think anybody will give me a TV. But I think I'll get some cassettes from my father.

Now it is your turn.

b A reporter is asking some school children how they see their futures.
What are they saying (in English, of course)?

1. *Susie:* Ich glaube, daß ich in einem Krankenhaus arbeiten werde.

2. *Iris:* Ich werde vielleicht irgendwo Zoowärterin sein.

3. *Anne:* Ich nehme an, daß ich für meinen Vater arbeiten werde.

4. *Thomas:* Wahrscheinlich werde ich mit Kindern arbeiten.

5. *Alex:* Oh, ich bin sicher, daß ich ein berühmter Sänger sein werde.

1. *Susie:* I think I'll work . . . . 2. *Iris:* Perhaps I'll be a . . . . *Go on.*

c Sandra and her friends are talking about what clothes people will wear in fifty years from now.
What do they think?

1. Sandra meint, daß Frauen wieder mehr Röcke tragen werden.
2. Sally ist sicher, daß Männer keine Röcke tragen werden.
3. Kevin sagt, daß Jeans wahrscheinlich immer noch beliebt sein werden.
4. Dave stellt sich vor, daß die Kleidung ganz anders als heute sein wird.
5. Carol meint, Pink wird vielleicht die beliebteste Farbe sein.
6. Kevin glaubt nicht, daß Männer noch Schlipse tragen werden.

10 WORDS WORDS WORDS

a *What is missing from these adjectives?* -al -ar -ed -ing -ous *or* -y*?*

1. angr-	6. danger-	11. happ-	16. laz-	21. regul-
2. boil-	7. disabl-	12. hungr-	17. miss-	22. speci-
3. bor-	8. eas-	13. interest-	18. nerv-	23. thirst-
4. bus-	9. excit-	14. interest-	19. nois-	24. tir-
5. craz-	10. fam-	15. internation-	20. popul-	25. worri-

1. angry 2. boiled 3. . . . *Go on.*

b *Find nouns for the adjectives in 10a and make phrases.*

Examples: 1. an angry tiger 2. a boiled egg *Go on.*

c *Now make sentences with the phrases from 10b.*

Examples: 1. An angry tiger can be dangerous. 2. Would you like a boiled egg for breakfast? *Go on.*

d **How quick are you with words?**

Try to find the opposites of all the following words and write them down.
The first letter of every word is 's'. Look at your watch and see how long you need.
Three minutes is very good. One minute is super!

1. big	small	6. land	s__?	11. (to) open	s__?
2. (to) buy	sell	7. (to) listen	s__?	12. (to) sit	s__?
3. clever	s__?	8. long	s__?	13. (to) spend	s__?
4. fast	s__?	9. nobody	s__?	14. weak	s__?
5. (to) finish	s__?	10. north	s__?	15. winter	s__?

e **Jane Longfingers' hidden message**

When Johnny Pinch came home last night, he found this message on the floor.

To find the hidden message put the words in three groups:

1. clothes	2. furniture	3. hidden message
jeans	chair	wait
. . .	. . .	. . .

11 Revision: do – does

Make questions with "do" or "does". Your partner must try to answer the question, then it is his/her turn to ask the next question.

What / When / Where / What animals / How / How much pocket-money + do / does + apples grow? / school start in Britain? / the winter start? / you like best? / you get? / cows live? / a rabbit eat? / "competition" mean? / your best friend get? / a cat drink? / you buy stamps? / you spell the plural of "mouse"?

Examples:

You: Where do apples grow? – *Your partner:* On apple trees, of course.

Your partner: When does school start in Britain? – *You:* At 9 o'clock, I think.

12 Revision: adjective or adverb?

Some pupils at Park School are talking about their teachers:

1. I saw Miss Green at the tennis club last night. She won against Miss Black. She's a very confident (confident) player.
   – Well, yes. She usually plays confidently (confident). But Miss Black often wins, too.

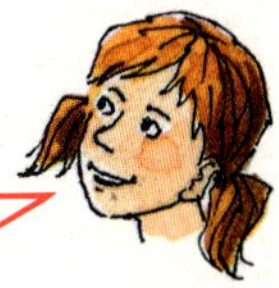

2. Tomorrow is the big match against the teachers. It won't be (easy).
   – Oh, I don't agree. It'll be no problem. We'll win (easy).
3. Is Mr Hill (good) at football?
   – No, he doesn't play very (good).
4. The new music teacher plays the piano (beautiful).
   – And she can sing (beautiful), too.
5. I can never understand Mr Duncan. He explains things so (terrible) that I never know what he wants.
   – Yes, he's a (terrible) teacher.

13 Revision: mixed tenses

Complete these dialogues with the correct verb form.

1. *Jane:* Hallo, Kate. ... you (see) Sally? I want to speak to her.
   Kate: She (just go) into town.
   Jane: Oh! When ... she (leave)?
   Kate: About 20 minutes ago. She (take) the three o'clock bus.
2. *Pete:* What ... you (do) next weekend, Andy?
   Andy: I (watch) the football match.
   Pete: I (not watch) it. We always (lose).
3. *Tracy:* Janet and I (go) to the history museum now. ... you (want) to come with us?
   Bill: No, thanks. I (not like) museums.
4. *Sarah:* ... you (ever be) to England, Heike?
   Heike: Yes, I (go) to Manchester last summer with my parents.
   Sarah: How ... you (go) there? By boat?
   Heike: No, we (fly). It (be) great.
5. *Derek:* Hallo, Judy. ... you (just arrive)?
   Judy: Yes. Sorry I'm late. ... the meeting (start) yet?
   Derek: I think so. Mr Cook (go in) a few minutes ago.

14 Listening comprehension: The new jacket

Adverts

You sometimes see adverts in windows of newspaper shops.

1. You would like one of the rabbits. Write a short letter and start your letter like this: Dear Sir or Madam, ...
2. You want to buy the cassette-recorder. Work with a partner and make a phone call. Your partner answers the phone like this: "Hallo, Hatfield 25374."
3. Tony is telling his friend John about the advert for maths lessons. John is very bad at maths. Write a short dialogue between the two.
4. You want to buy or sell something. Write an advert for a shop window.

Just for fun

"Waiter, there's an insect in my tea."
– "Not so loud, or everybody will want one."

"Now we'll see if that expensive German course on cassette was worth the money, Roger."

1 Die Possessivpronomen: nominaler Gebrauch (The possessive pronouns)

This isn't my pen. **Mine** (= my pen) is green.
I can't find my ruler. Can I have **yours** (= your ruler)?
Where are Dave's shoes? Those aren't **his** (= his shoes).
Dave has done his homework, but Sally hasn't done **hers** (= her homework).

I don't think these things are **ours** (= our things).
My birthday is in May. When are **yours** (= your birthdays), Liz and Peter?
This isn't the Deans' house. **Theirs** (= their house) is much bigger.

Mine, yours, his usw. beziehen sich auf ein vorangehendes Nomen, das man nicht wiederholen will.
Sie stehen anstelle von *my, your, his* usw. + Nomen. Singular und Plural haben die gleiche Form.

2 Das Futur mit „will" (The will-future)

a Bildung

Positive sentence
Tomorrow it**'ll be** nice.

Negative sentence
I **won't have** time to tidy up my room.

Langformen: . . . it **will** . . . I **will not** . . .

Questions
Will you **be** at home tomorrow?
What **will** your friends **say**?

Short answers
Yes, we **will**./No, we **won't**.
Nothing.

Das *will-future* wird mit *will* bzw. *won't* + Infinitiv gebildet. Es hat für alle Personen die gleiche Form.
Also: I**'ll**, you**'ll**, she**'ll**, . . . bzw. I **won't**, you **won't**, she **won't**, . . .
(Statt *will* bzw. *won't* sind in der 1. Person auch die Formen *shall* [ʃæl] bzw. *shan't* [ʃɑːnt] gebräuchlich.)

b Gebrauch

Kevin **will be** fourteen next year.
Kevin wird nächstes Jahr vierzehn sein/werden.

You **won't find** a job.
Du wirst keine Stelle finden.

Das *will-future* wird verwendet, wenn man über Dinge in der Zukunft spricht, auf die man keinen Einfluß hat, und um Vorhersagen zu machen.

I'm sure they**'ll come back** soon.
Sie kommen sicher bald zurück.

Perhaps we **won't have** enough to eat in the year 2500.
Vielleicht werden wir im Jahr 2500 nicht genug zu essen haben.

Oft verwendet man Ausdrücke wie *I imagine, I'm sure, I suppose, I think, perhaps, probably* mit dem *will-future*, um Vermutungen über die Zukunft zu äußern.

⚠ I suppose we**'ll arrive** soon.
Vermutlich **kommen** wir bald **an**. Oder: Vermutlich **werden** wir bald **ankommen**.

Im Deutschen ist es meist unwichtig, ob man das Präsens („kommen . . . an") oder das Futur („werden . . . ankommen") benutzt, wenn man über die Zukunft spricht.
Im Englischen muß man in solchen Fällen das *will-future* verwenden (nicht das *simple present*!).
Diese Regel gilt jedoch nicht für Nebensätze mit *when*. In solchen Nebensätzen wird das *simple present* (nicht das *will-future*) verwendet. Z.B.: I think **I'll be** a teacher when I **leave** school.

EXTRA READING

The world after the year 2000

Liz and Dave have written down their ideas about the future.

This is what Dave thinks:

"I think the world after the year 2000 will be fantastic. We won't have any problems because we will have the answers to everything. I do not think we will work like our parents. We will have machines for every job, so people will have much longer holidays. Perhaps they will work only one or two days a week. They will fly to the moon for their holidays or they will spend their holidays in spacehotels a hundred miles over the earth.

There will probably be factories in space, too, and people will travel to them from the earth. Perhaps we will even have factories on other planets.

In the future we won't have cars. Every family will have a helicopter, so there won't be any traffic jams in the streets.

A lot of people will live and work on farms under the sea. They will have fish on their farms instead of pigs and cows. Perhaps there will be big towns under the sea, too, and people will use submarines instead of buses and trains.

Doctors will have medicines for every illness and we won't need any hospitals.

I think the future will be great."

(line 11) (to) spend *(Zeit) verbringen* space [speɪs] *Weltraum* (l. 12) earth [ɜːθ] *Erde*
(l. 16) planet ['plænɪt] (l. 18) helicopter ['helɪkɒptə] *Hubschrauber*
(l. 19) traffic jam ['træfɪk dʒæm] *Verkehrsstau(ung)* (l. 22) instead of [ɪn'sted‿əv] *anstelle von, statt*
(l. 24) submarine [sʌbmə'riːn] *Unterseeboot, U-Boot* (l. 26) illness ['ɪlnɪs] *Krankheit*

Liz's ideas are very different:

"I do not think the world will be a very nice place in the future. The trees will all be dead. There will be no green fields where children can play football or games like that. So they will sit inside all day.

My children won't see horses or cows. Farms will all be like factories and the animals will never leave them. Without green fields and trees we won't see any birds. Perhaps there won't be any wild animals in the world because they have all died out. Or we will only see them in zoos.

In the future every family will have even more cars than they have today. There will be traffic jams on all the roads. It will be very noisy everywhere. I suppose our windows will be shut day and night because the air will be so dirty. Outside we will wear masks over our mouths and noses. Perhaps we won't even see the sun through the dirty air.

Only a few people will live in houses with gardens. There will be so many people that we will all live in small flats like cages.

There will be millions more people in the world. What will they all eat and drink? Perhaps we won't have enough to eat, or perhaps we will all eat pills instead of fresh vegetables, meat and fruit. Our water will come from the sea, but perhaps even the sea will be too dirty to drink.

I do not think people will be very happy in the future."

Talk about the text:

1. *Make a list of Dave's and Liz's ideas.*
   What are the main differences[1]?
2. *Who do you think is right, Liz or Dave? Can you say why?*
3. *Would you like to live in Dave's/Liz's world?*
   Why/Why not?

And you?

Write a short text:
"My ideas about the future."

(line 17) everywhere *überall* (l. 19) mask [mɑːsk] *Maske* (l. 20) not even *nicht einmal*
(l. 28) pill [pɪl] *Tablette, Pille* vegetables [ˈvedʒtəblz] *Gemüse* (l. 29) meat [miːt] *Fleisch*
[1] main difference [ˈmeɪn ˈdɪfrəns] *Hauptunterschied*

Summer holidays

1 Soon the summer holidays will begin.
What are your plans?
What are you going to do?

> We**'re going to visit** . . . .
> We'd like to . . . .
> We've decided to . . . .

Or are you not sure yet?

> I think I'll go to . . . with my parents.
> We probably won't go to . . . this year.
> I hope we**'ll visit** . . . .

→ S 1 · Ex 2, 3

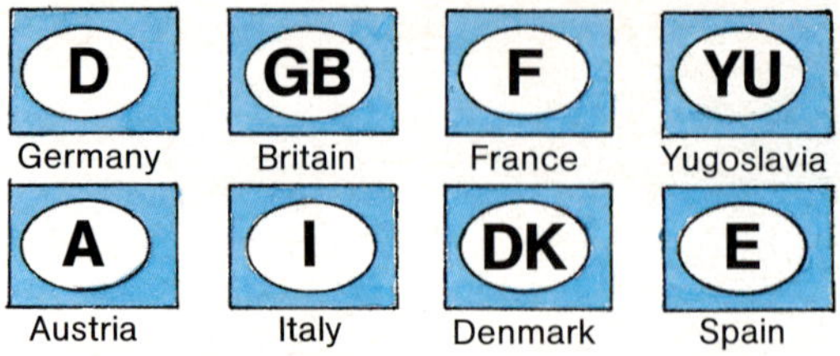

2 Holidays are fun. You can
- play your favourite games.
- swim in the sea.
- lie on the beach and enjoy the sun.
- . . .

But you need not stay on the beach all the time. You can do other interesting things, too. You can
- go into the countryside.
- see how the people live.
- learn about their history.
- . . .

3 Now let us look at Cornwall. This part of Britain is very popular with tourists.

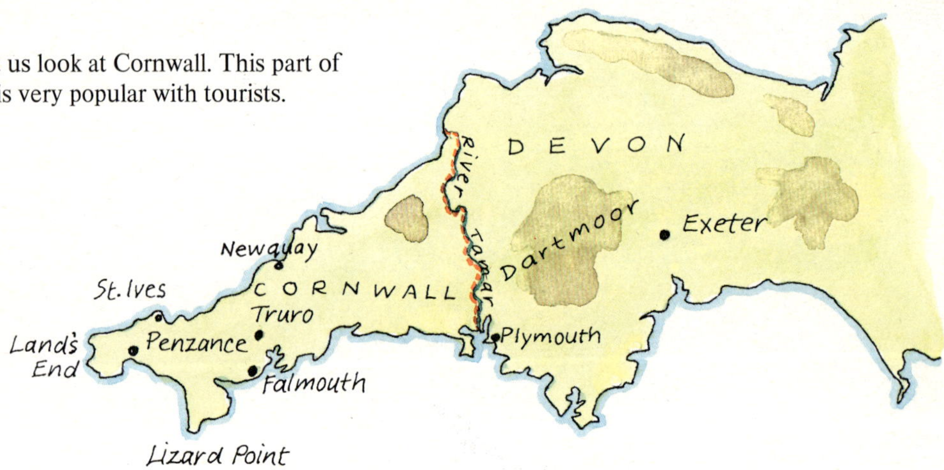

Cornwall

Cornwall is one of the most beautiful parts of Britain. And its coast is one of the most famous in the country. Along the north coast the beaches are flat with beautiful sand. But the south coast is wild and dangerous. Over the centuries hundreds of ships have sunk on the rocks here. In some places one wreck lies on top of the other. Between the rocks there are lots of caves. Some are famous as smugglers' caves.

The ruins of old tin mines are a typical sight in Cornwall. The tunnels in the mines were narrow, dark and very dangerous. Some of the tunnels were over 2000 feet under the ground and went over half a mile under the sea. A few mines are still working and at some mines you can go on a guided tour.

The people along the coast have always lived from the sea. In the small fishing villages with their narrow streets and small houses, life is quiet and slow. But fishing on a wild sea is not an easy job.

And you?

Write to the British Tourist Office and ask them to send you some information about Cornwall.

What beautiful parts of Germany do you know?
Do you know any famous or interesting sights there?
Choose an interesting part of Germany for a handbook for English tourists, and write a few sentences about it.

4 The people of Cornwall often say that they are Cornish and not English. Did you know that there is a Cornish language? It died out a few centuries ago. Some people in Cornwall are now trying to learn the old Cornish language again.

5 During the eighteenth century tea, sugar, tobacco and other things were very expensive in England. As the Cornish coast is near France and things were cheaper there, many Cornishmen became smugglers. They **were not allowed to bring** the things from France into the country, of course. So they hid everything in the caves along the coast. → S 3a

6 There are also many stories about Cornish wreckers. These people knew that in a storm the sailors on the sea **could not see** where the dangerous rocks were. So the wreckers put lamps on these rocks. The sailors often believed the lights were other ships and followed them. Then their ship hit the rocks, and the wreckers climbed onto it and took what they **could find**. → S 3b

7

The captain could not save the ship. It hit the rocks and all the sailors drowned.

8 When the ship hit the rocks, it **was following** the lights of another ship.
a strong wind was blowing.
all the sailors **were working** on deck.

→ S 2 · Ex 4, 5

9 Not everybody, of course, was a smuggler or a wrecker. Many people tried to help the sailors on the ships in danger. The lifeline, for example, was a Cornish invention.
When a ship hit the rocks in those days, the people **had to swim** to the coast. Many drowned in the sea or died on the rocks. With a lifeline the people could leave the ships safely and quickly. They **did not have to swim** through the wild sea. → S 3c · Ex 6, 7

10 Every year ships near the Cornish coast get into trouble during bad weather. Then the men from the villages go out in their lifeboats to help them. It is a very dangerous job. In December 1981, eight men from Mousehole ['maʊzl], a village near Penzance, went out in a terrible storm to help the sailors on a ship, but they never came back. All eight men died. In the village of Mousehole (1500 people) twelve children lost their fathers in that one night.

9T

THE WRECKERS

There were eight men in the King's Head. They were dirty, wild and dangerous. When the nights were dark and there were terrible storms outside, they met in the King's Head.

They waited with Jake, the owner of the King's Head, and his friend, the beggar. Jake was a big man with black hair and black eyes. The beggar was smaller with long hair.

It was four o'clock in the morning and outside they heard the wind and the rain. "It's time to go," said Jake. "It's a good storm. It's time to start work. Beggar, take the waggon and the horses. We can follow you."

It was two miles to the coast, where the wild sea rolled over the black rocks. One of the men climbed onto a huge rock with a lamp. The other men went to the beach and waited. Soon they saw a ship. It started to follow the lamp. It sailed towards the rocks. And then over the noise of the sea and the storm they heard it: the ship was on the rocks.

Boxes and people fell from the ship into the water. Quickly the men ran through the sea and over the rocks.

"Put everything into the waggon," the beggar shouted.

They carried people out of the sea, took everything out of their pockets and left them on the beach. And soon the morning came with big grey clouds.

"Let's go," shouted Jake.

But the waggon did not move. "It has sunk in the sand," the beggar shouted. Suddenly the man with the lamp ran down from the rock. "Quickly! Some riders are coming."

"Take the horses," Jake shouted. "And leave the waggon."

But Harry, one of the men, shouted, "They'll know it's ours. They'll know we've done this."

Jake hit the man hard. Then the beggar took some bags from the waggon and put them on the horses.

"We've only got two horses," another man shouted.

"Well, only two of us can leave," the beggar said, and he and Jake rode away from the coast. They left the other men on the beach, behind them the wild sea, in front of them the riders from the next town.

"Harry was right," the beggar said. "They'll know we did this. We must leave Cornwall."

"But first we must go back to the King's Head," said Jake. "There's still gold there."

"How much?"

"More than you'll ever have."

They rode back to the King's Head. They ran into the empty house and up the stairs.

"This room here," said Jake and gave the beggar a lamp. It was a small dark room with no windows.

"Where is it?"

"Under the floor."

The beggar went into the room and Jake locked the door behind him. "Goodbye, beggar. I need the two horses. One for the gold and one for me."

Quickly Jake went into another room where he fetched some bags with gold coins. And then he left the house.

He rode along the path. Soon he was in the hills. He knew these paths better than all the other people in Cornwall. He wanted to ride east across the hills and into Devon.

He rode slowly. But after some time grey clouds came from the sea and fell on the land. Soon Jake could not see a thing. He stopped. Where was he? And where was the path? Everything was grey: There was no sun, nothing, only the clouds as they came down and touched the ground. And then he saw the people. They were in a group in front of him.

"Who are you?" he shouted, and a man came through the grey clouds towards him. It was a sailor and he was wet from the sea. Behind him there were others: women and children.

"No!" Jake shouted and rode through them. He rode through the fog where there was no path and when he looked back, the people were always behind him.

Jake did not know where he was. He rode wildly across the hills till his horse fell and he fell with it. He was angry and frightened. Slowly the fog went away and then he saw where he was. He was back at the King's Head. The riders from the next town were there. They had the beggar. And now they had him.

→ Ex 1

1 *Look at "The wreckers" on pages 118-119 again.*

a *Complete these sentences.*

There were eight men . . . .
Outside, there was . . . .
At four o'clock in the morning . . . .
When they were on the beach, they saw . . . .
Soon the ship . . . .
The men carried . . . .
The waggon . . . .
The beggar and Jake . . . .
They ran into . . . .
When the beggar was in the room, Jake . . . .
He fetched . . . .
Jake rode away and soon . . . .
Then he saw . . . .
When the fog went away, he saw . . . .
The riders from the next town . . . .

b *Answer these questions.*

1. Who was Jake and what did he look like?
2. Why did the wreckers choose this night to meet?
3. What happened when the ship followed the wreckers' lamp?
4. What did the beggar and Jake do when the waggon sank in the sand?
5. What did Jake want to do at the King's Head?
6. What happened to the beggar?
7. Why did Jake not get to Devon?
8. Who were the people in the fog? What do you think?

c *Write a newspaper story:*
"Jake and the beggar caught."
Begin like this: Early yesterday morning a ship hit some rocks and sank. . . .

Question: What do sea monsters eat?
Answer: Fish and ships.

2a **Holiday plans** Sandra is going to visit Yugoslavia with her mother during the summer holidays. Kevin is asking her questions about their plans. – *Complete the dialogue.*

1. When <u>are you going to</u> leave? – <u>We're going to</u> leave in three weeks.
2. How long . . . stay in Yugoslavia? – . . . for about two weeks.
3. How . . . get there? – . . . fly.
4. Where . . . stay? – . . . in a small hotel in Split, on the coast.
5. What . . . do? – . . . swim and enjoy the sun.
6. How many books . . . take with you? – I . . . not . . . take any books, just magazines.

b **How do you see your friends' futures?** *Say what you think. – Here is some help.*

I think I'm sure I don't think	Jürgen Ute . . .	will won't	remember me in 50 years. find a job easily. have more than one child. stay in this town/village. work in another country. be very successful in his/her job. like his/her work. . . .

3 Plans or no plans? *"going to" or "will"?*

1. It is Janet's birthday on February 2nd. She ... be eleven then.
2. Her parents have decided to give her a pet. They ... buy a hamster.
3. The Whites want to fly to Austria for a skiing holiday. They must take lots of warm clothes because it ... be cold there.
4. The pop singer Mike Walker has given an interview about his plans for the future. He ... write a book about all his pop songs.
5. It rained all day yesterday. It ... probably rain tomorrow, too.
6. Perhaps Helen ... work for her father when she leaves school. He paints houses and she often helps him.
7. Sally has written to Uncle Ernie and Aunt Mary. She ... visit them next weekend.
8. Liz is sure she ... see lots of baby animals at the zoo in the spring.
9. Andy has decided to learn the guitar. He ... practise every day, too.
10. Mr Hill wants to go to Spain in the summer. He is sure the sun ... shine and the sea ... be much warmer than in Britain.

4 *Find the right combinations.*

When	Miss Green came into the classroom, ...	... she was trying on another coat.
	Brian saw Lucy at the party, ...	... they were watching TV.
	we arrived at the cinema, ...	... two boys were arguing.
	Anne and Liz left Sue in the shop, ...	... the sun was shining.
	Sandra found Carol and Tina, ...	... she was sitting next to Philip.
	I got up this morning, ...	... Ben and Jo were buying tickets.

5 What were they doing when the accident happened? *Use the past progressive in your answers.*

1. When the accident happened, Anne was drinking lemonade at a café.
2. Dave was ... *Go on.*

6 *Work with a partner and complete the dialogues. Use the past tense forms of "can", "can't", "must", "mustn't" and "needn't".*

1. My brother can drive a car. He's only 18.
   – My mum could drive a car when she was 17.
2. Dave must repair his bike.
   – Again? He . . . repair it last week, too.
3. Can you have bike races in the park?
   – I don't think so. You . . . have bike races in the park last year.
4. Peter has got a bad cold. He must stay in bed.
   – Oh, Liz had a cold two weeks ago, but she . . . stay in bed.
5. Can you do this puzzle?
   – Well, I can try, but I . . . do it yesterday.
6. Can I go to the cinema tonight, Mum? Sally . . . go last night.

○7 In English, please: Carol's accident

1. Es war fünf Uhr nachmittags. Carol mußte zehn Minuten später im Jugendclub sein.

It was five o'clock in the afternoon. Carol had to be at the youth club ten minutes later.

2. Deshalb mußte sie rennen.
3. Als sie über die Straße lief, konnte sie einen roten Sportwagen sehen.
4. Der Autofahrer konnte nicht schnell genug anhalten und stieß mit Carol zusammen.
5. Carol mußte vier Wochen im Krankenhaus bleiben.
6. Sie mußte im Bett bleiben und durfte nicht aufstehen.
7. Sie konnte ihren rechten Arm nicht bewegen.
8. Ihre Eltern durften sie jeden Tag besuchen.
9. Am Ende des Monats durfte sie nach Hause gehen.

8 Revision: word order

a **Quiz: How much do you remember from units 1-8?** *Find the right word order for the following questions, then try to answer them. There is one question about every unit.*

1. on a farm/like/to live/would/who?
2. the BMX race/who/won?
3. Dave/what/take/did/at the food factory/from Liz?
4. what/check/Dr McPherson/did?
5. do/does/Alison Brown/what sports?
6. usually/during the Easter holidays/a class/takes/who/to the Norfolk Broads?
7. helps/often/in the Oxfam shops/who?
8. about Longleat Park/what/you/do/know?

b *Choose the right verbs. Then make questions and find the right answers in the box. Use the simple present.*

buy do eat go know look after sing write

1. Who – animals in a zoo?
2. What – people – at birthday parties?
3. Who – often – to school by bike?
4. What – people – from Oxfam shops?
5. What – you – in the evening?
6. "You've all heard the question," Mr Hill said. "Who – the answer?"
7. "What – cows – ?" Miss Green asked.
8. What – you – at the end of a letter to a friend?

Old clothes, I think.
"Me."
"Love."
A zoo keeper, of course.
I usually play with my friends.
"Happy birthday."
Liz and Sandra.
"Grass!" everybody shouted.

9 Revision: simple present or present progressive?

1. Mrs Evans works (work) at a bank.
   She (start) work at 9.00 every morning.
   She is leaving (leave) the bank now. She (go) home.
2. Lucy and Mike (do) their homework together today.
   They (go) to the same school.
3. Susan (read) "The Computer" every Friday.
   But she (not read) the magazine at the moment. She (sit) in the garden and (sleep).
4. It is 7.15 and Jimmy (cook) the breakfast.
   Jimmy (have) breakfast at 7.15 every morning.
5. Hilda Hopper is a doctor. When people are ill, she (help) them.
   Dr Hopper (talk) to a man now.
6. Usually, Growler (bark) a lot.
   But he (sleep) now. So he (not bark).

○10 Revision: simple past
In English, please.

Christiane is staying with her pen-friend Jenny in Los Angeles. Here is her letter to her friend in Tübingen.
Can you translate the letter into English?

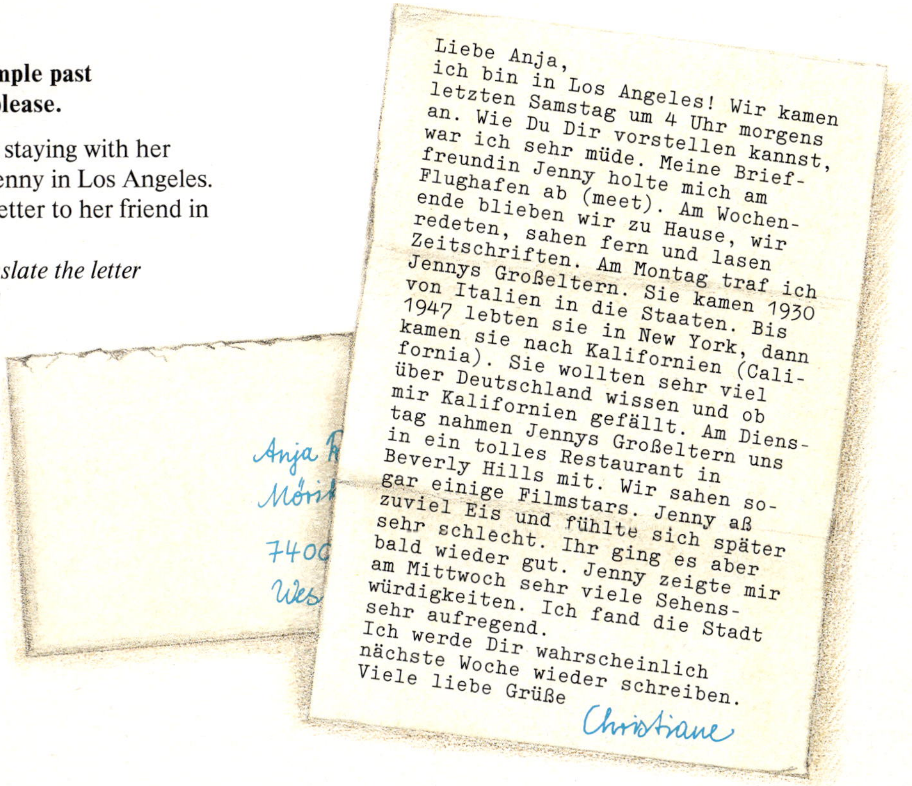

Liebe Anja,
ich bin in Los Angeles! Wir kamen letzten Samstag um 4 Uhr morgens an. Wie Du Dir vorstellen kannst, war ich sehr müde. Meine Brieffreundin Jenny holte mich am Flughafen ab (meet). Am Wochenende blieben wir zu Hause, wir redeten, sahen fern und lasen Zeitschriften. Am Montag traf ich Jennys Großeltern. Sie kamen 1930 von Italien in die Staaten. Bis 1947 lebten sie in New York, dann kamen sie nach Kalifornien (California). Sie wollten sehr viel über Deutschland wissen und ob mir Kalifornien gefällt. Am Dienstag nahmen Jennys Großeltern uns in ein tolles Restaurant in Beverly Hills mit. Wir sahen sogar einige Filmstars. Jenny aß zuviel Eis und fühlte sich später sehr schlecht. Ihr ging es aber bald wieder gut. Jenny zeigte mir am Mittwoch sehr viele Sehenswürdigkeiten. Ich fand die Stadt sehr aufregend.
Ich werde Dir wahrscheinlich nächste Woche wieder schreiben.
Viele liebe Grüße
Christiane

11 Revision: present perfect or simple past? *Choose the right verbs for the questions.*

arrive   be   eat   invite   read   ride   say   sleep   take

1. When ... you ... ?
   – A few minutes ago. The bus was late.
2. ... you ... yet? – No, but I'm not hungry.
3. ... you ever ... to New York?
   – No, but I hope to go there next year.
4. What ... Anita ... to you yesterday?
   – Nothing. Well, nothing much.
5. ... you ... your radio to the shop yet?
   – Oh yes, it's back again already.
6. ... you ... a BMX bike before?
   – No, this is the first time.
7. ... you ... well last night?
   – Yes, I feel great. What's for breakfast?
8. ... you ... the newspaper yet?
   – No, why?
9. How many people ... you ... to your party?
   – Well, there'll be six girls and six boys.
   Do you want to know their names?

1 The going to-future and the will-future

Jill **is going to work** on a farm this summer.
Jill plant, in diesem Sommer auf einem Bauernhof zu arbeiten.

I don't think she**'ll like** it.
Ich glaube nicht, daß es ihr gefallen wird.

We**'re going to fly** to Italy next year.
Wir haben vor, nächstes Jahr nach Italien zu fliegen.

You**'ll have** nice weather in Italy.
In Italien werdet ihr schönes Wetter haben.

Das *going to-future* verwendet man, wenn man sagen will, was jemand plant oder vorhat.
Das *will-future* wird verwendet, wenn man über Dinge in der Zukunft spricht, auf die man keinen Einfluß hat, und um Vorhersagen zu machen. Oft handelt es sich dabei um Vermutungen.

2 Die Verlaufsform der Vergangenheit (The past progressive)

a Bildung

Positive sentences	
I **was reading**	at ten o'clock last night.
You **were reading**	
He/She **was reading**	
We **were reading**	
You **were reading**	
They **were reading**	

Negative sentences	
I **wasn't watching**	TV.
You **weren't watching**	
He/She **wasn't watching**	
We **weren't watching**	
You **weren't watching**	
They **weren't watching**	

Questions		Short answers
Were you **reading**	at ten o'clock last night?	Yes, I **was**.
Was he **watching** TV		No, he **wasn't**.
Were they **reading**		Yes, they **were**.
What **were** they **reading**?		"Animal Farm".

Das *past progressive* wird mit *was/were + -ing form* des Verbs gebildet.

b Gebrauch

Yesterday at five o'clock Dave **was doing** his homework.
Gestern um fünf Uhr hat Dave seine Hausaufgaben gemacht.

He **was doing** his homework when his father came home.
Er machte seine Hausaufgaben, als sein Vater nach Hause kam.

Das *past progressive* wird verwendet, wenn man sagen will, daß eine Handlung oder ein Vorgang zu einem bestimmten Zeitpunkt in der Vergangenheit gerade im Gange war: Dave war um fünf Uhr dabei, seine Hausaufgaben zu machen. Er saß über seinen Hausaufgaben, als sein Vater heimkam.

3 Die Vergangenheit der Hilfsverben „can", „mustn't", „must" und „needn't"
(The past tense forms of the auxiliaries "can", "mustn't", "must" and "needn't")

a **can** (darf) — **was/were allowed to** (durfte),
mustn't (darf nicht) — **was/were not allowed to** (durfte nicht)

I **can go** to the cinema tonight. But I **mustn't come** home late.
Ich darf heute abend ins Kino gehen. Aber ich darf nicht zu spät nach Hause kommen.

Positive sentence: I **was allowed to go** to the cinema last week, too.
Ich durfte letzte Woche auch ins Kino gehen.

Negative sentence: But my friends **weren't allowed to go** to the cinema last week.
Aber meine Freunde durften letzte Woche nicht ins Kino gehen.

Question: **Were** you **allowed to go** to the cinema last week**?** — No, I **wasn't**.
Durftest du letzte Woche ins Kino gehen? — Nein.

Wenn man sagen will, was jemand in der Vergangenheit tun durfte oder nicht tun durfte, verwendet man *was/were allowed to* + Infinitiv bzw. *was/were not allowed to* + Infinitiv.

b **can** (kann) — **could** (konnte), **can't** (kann nicht) — **couldn't** (konnte nicht)

I **can play** the piano.
Ich kann Klavier spielen.

Positive sentence: My grandmother **could play** the piano, too.
Meine Großmutter konnte auch Klavier spielen.

Negative sentence: But my grandfather **couldn't play** the piano.
Aber mein Großvater konnte nicht Klavier spielen.

Question: **Could** your grandparents **play** the piano**?** — Yes, they **could**.
Konnten deine Großeltern Klavier spielen? — Ja.

Wenn man sagen will, was jemand in der Vergangenheit tun konnte oder nicht tun konnte, verwendet man für alle Personen *could* + Infinitiv bzw. *couldn't* (Langform: *could not*) + Infinitiv.

c **must** (muß) — **had to** (mußte), **needn't** (braucht/muß nicht) — **didn't have to** (brauchte/mußte nicht)

Sandra **must repair** her bike. She **needn't ask** anybody for help.
Sandra muß ihr Fahrrad reparieren. Sie braucht niemanden um Hilfe zu bitten.

Positive sentence: She **had to repair** it last month, too.
Sie mußte es auch im letzten Monat reparieren.

Negative sentence: Sandra **didn't have to take** it to a repair shop.
Sandra brauchte es nicht in eine Reparaturwerkstatt zu bringen.

Question: **Did** she **have to ask** her friends for help**?** — No, she **didn't**.
Mußte sie ihre Freunde um Hilfe bitten? — Nein.

Wenn man sagen will, was jemand in der Vergangenheit tun mußte oder nicht zu tun brauchte, verwendet man für alle Personen *had to* + Infinitiv bzw. *didn't have to* + Infinitiv.

⚠ In Fragen muß man *did* und in verneinten Sätzen muß man *didn't* verwenden!

1

Amy Connor is Kevin Connor's American cousin. She lives with her parents and her little brother Jonathan in New Rochelle, a suburb of New York City. Kevin and his family visited them last summer. They had a great time while they were in America. The children cannot wait until they go back again.

The American Connors all love camping. They have got a small motorhome and they go fishing and walking in the mountains as often as they can.

Amy usually cuts the grass at home and for another family in the next street on Saturday mornings. She is saving her money so that she can go to Girl Scout camp in August.

2 The Connors have invited their neighbours, the Minardis, to a backyard picnic. Nick Minardi is in Amy's class at school.

Nick: Only three weeks till summer vacation starts. Three months without school – fantastic!

Amy: Are you going to stay at that camp site in Florida again this year?

Mr Minardi: No, we're going to visit my sister Nancy in Denver. She has got a new baby. And if we've got time, we'll go to other parts of Colorado, too.

Nick: I hate babies, Dad. They're boring. I want to go to Florida again. I love the beaches and Disney World .... Just imagine, four days in the car – just to see a baby! If you like babies so much, you can go without me. Can I have the ketchup, please?

Mr Minardi: Oh, Nick. I know you don't mean that.

Mrs Connor: My dad lives in Miami now. He loves it. He's 81, but he still plays golf every day.

Amy: He has got a girlfriend, too. Her name is Lucy.

Mr Connor: *Girl*friend? She's 75!

Mrs Connor: Let's go to Florida this year and see what Grandpa is doing!

And you?

If I've got time tomorrow, I'll ...
If the weather is fine next weekend, we'll/I'll ...

→ [S 1 · Ex 2-5]

S 1, 2 sowie Ex 2-6, 10 sind fakultativ in Bundesländern, deren Lehrplan die Behandlung von *if-clauses* bzw. *reported speech* nicht für Klasse 6 vorschreibt.

3 The Connors have got a family tradition. Every Sunday evening Mr Connor makes waffles for the family. Last Sunday, while he was cooking, the phone rang. Amy answered it.

→ [S 2 · Ex 6]

4 Here is a postcard from Amy to her cousin Kevin in Hatfield.

Write a postcard to a pen-friend in New York.

→ Ex 7

10 A

FLORIDA

THE SUNSHINE STATE

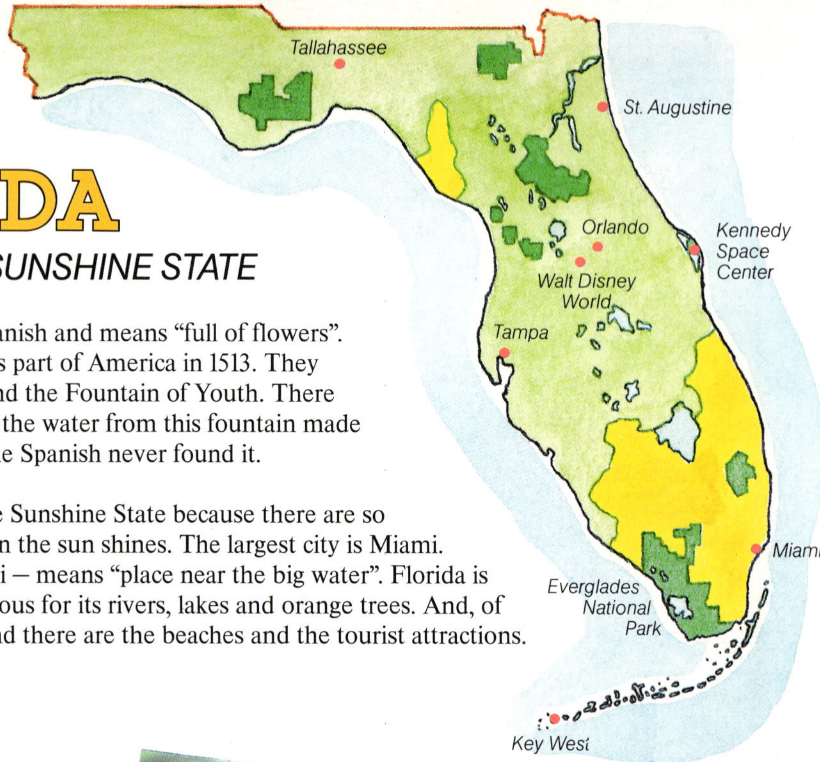

The name "Florida" is Spanish and means "full of flowers". The Spanish landed in this part of America in 1513. They came to look for gold – and the Fountain of Youth. There was an Indian legend that the water from this fountain made you young for ever. But the Spanish never found it.

Americans call Florida the Sunshine State because there are so many days in Florida when the sun shines. The largest city is Miami. Its Indian name – mayami – means "place near the big water". Florida is a very beautiful state, famous for its rivers, lakes and orange trees. And, of course, there is the sea, and there are the beaches and the tourist attractions.

The Kennedy Space Center is on the east coast at Cape Canaveral, about fifty miles from Orlando. In 1969 the first people flew from here to the moon. What people notice first at the Space Center is how big everything is. Visitors can go on a bus tour and see the launching pads, and they can go to the astronauts' training centre. There is a rocket museum where you can learn about the history of space travel.

Walt Disney World is a few miles south of Orlando. It is so big that you can easily spend several days there. You can meet Mickey Mouse, ride on a Mississippi river boat, fly to Mars, go fishing, canoeing, riding – and much more.

10 A

The Epcot Center is a part of Disney World. Here you can see examples of future technology. You can see life in an underwater city of the future. Or you can travel back into the past. And you can visit different "countries", too. You can have a meal in France, for example, or a coffee in Italy.

The Everglades National Park is in the southwest of Florida. It is one of the largest and most interesting national parks in America. You can sail along the rivers in a boat and see hundreds of birds and wild animals – even alligators.

St. Augustine is in the northeast of Florida. It is the oldest town in America. The Spanish founded it in 1565. America's oldest house is here, too.

The southernmost point of the U.S.A. is Key West. From here it is only about 100 miles to Cuba. The road between Miami and Key West goes over 25 islands and 42 bridges. It is over 100 miles long. The longest bridge is Seven Mile Bridge. You can drive for seven miles over the sea.

The Prince of the Sun and the Princess of the Sea

Before white people arrived in America, it was the home of many Indian nations. The Yamasee Indians, for example, told this story of how Florida began:

Many, many years ago the Big Chief of the Sea had a beautiful young daughter. One day she was swimming in the sea when she saw a young man on the beach. He was looking at the sun, and the sun was shining on him. He was the Prince of the Sun. The Big Chief's daughter fell in love with this young man. So she swam to her eight-armed magic dragon and said, "Go and fetch the young man from the Land of the Sun and bring him down to the Land of the Sea."

The dragon swam away and left the sea where the Prince of the Sun could not see it. Then it went towards the young man, caught him, and took him to the home of the Big Chief. And when the Prince of the Sun saw the Princess of the Sea, he fell in love with her, too.

The Big Chief of the Sea was very happy when he saw the young Prince, and he had an idea. "The Prince of the Sun and my daughter, the Princess of the Sea, must marry. Then the Sun and the Sea will be together." The Big Chief also decided to give his daughter and the Prince a new land as their home. He went to the fish in the sea and said to them, "You must all help to make a new land, and then add this new land to the coast of the old land."

So the fish started to collect shells and stones and sand and they made a new land. Then they added it to the coast of the old land. But they also made lots of rivers and lakes in the new land so that the Big Chief could easily visit his daughter and her husband. The Prince of the Sun and the Princess of the Sea lived in the land very happily.

Today the name of that land of Sun and Sea is Florida.

1 *Look at "The Prince of the Sun and the Princess of the Sea" on page 130 again. Some of these sentences are wrong. Try to correct them.*

1. Florida has always been the home of white people.
2. The Princess of the Sea fell in love with the Prince of the Sun.
3. The magic dragon had six arms.
4. The magic dragon said to the Prince: "Come with me."
5. The Prince of the Sun did not like the Princess of the Sea.
6. The Big Chief wanted to give them a new land as their home.
7. The Big Chief made the new land without any help.
8. He could not visit his daughter in the new land.

[2] Video games, ice-cream and homework

Nick Minardi is playing video games with Amy at the Connors' house. *Complete these sentences.*

Nick: I must go now, Amy.

Amy: – Oh, Nick. Let's play one more game.

Nick: I'd like to. But if I (not go) now, I (be) late for supper.

Amy: – And your dad (be) angry if you (be) late again. Right?

Nick: Right. But if it (be) all right with Dad, I (can come) back later.

Amy: – Great. You (can try) some of my ice-cream if Jonathan (not eat) it all at supper.

Nick: I hope he doesn't. And after our game we can do our homework together. If I (help) you with Spanish, you (can explain) that math to me.

Amy: – But Nick, I've done all *my* homework. . . . Well, OK, I (help) you with your math if you really (find) it so difficult.

[3] Plans for a day in Manhattan

Cathy and Diane, two friends from New Rochelle, are planning a visit to New York.

Look at the pictures, find suitable verbs and complete the sentences.

Cathy:
1. If we . . . the Statue of Liberty early in the morning, there . . . too many other tourists.
2. If it . . . , we . . . a museum.
3. We . . . some hamburgers for lunch if we . . . hungry.

Diane:

4. We . . . the bus if taxis . . . too expensive.
5. If I . . . something nice, I . . . a souvenir for my grandpa.
6. And if we . . . enough time, we . . . for a walk in Central Park.

[4] *Complete these sentences about the Connors and the Minardis.*

1. If the British Connors have got enough money, ...
2. Amy and her family will go fishing next weekend if . . . .
3. If Amy saves her pocket-money, ...
4. If the Connors go to Florida this summer, ...
5. The Minardis will drive for four days if . . . .
6. If they've got time, ...

[5] Nick Minardi wants to go to the coast tomorrow. He is talking to his friend Mike here.

Use "if" or "when" and complete these sentences. Then put the boxes 3-6 in the correct order.

Remember: If I go to the coast, . . . = Es ist nicht sicher, ob ich gehe.
When I go to the coast, . . . = Ich gehe bestimmt.

1. . . . the weather is nice tomorrow, I'll go to the coast.	2. That's a good idea. I'll come with you. I'll go for a swim . . . we get there.	Sure. But I'll have enough time to lie on beaches . . . I'm an old man.
After my swim I'll play football . . . I find enough players.	You'll be tired . . . we get home.	And I'll lie on the beach . . . it's warm enough.

[6] **Sorry?**

Kirsten Bleck from Berlin is at a party in Miami with her American friend Betsy. The music is loud and Kirsten cannot understand people, so Betsy is helping her.

Complete Betsy's sentences.

1. *Patti:* I go to Girl Scout camp every summer.
2. *Al:* What do you like most about Miami?
3. *Margie:* The beaches here are fantastic.
4. *Mary-Anne:* My mom is having a backyard picnic today.
5. *Steve:* Have you seen that German film at the Odeon?
6. *Joanna:* I've never met anybody from Germany before.
7. *Mike:* When did you start to learn English?
8. *Tony:* Would you like to come to my party next week?

1. Patti says . . .
2. Al wants to know . . . *Go on.*

7 Grandpa's wedding

Imagine you are Amy Connor and you want to write to Kevin about your grandfather's wedding.

Look at the pictures and tell the story. You can begin like this:

Dear Kev,
I must tell you about Grandpa's wedding in Miami. It was great. We arrived . . .

8 WORDS WORDS WORDS

cold, watch, park, flat, spend, save, fit, train, left

All these English words mean two different things. Can you make sentences with them?

Example: I've got a bad *cold.*
It's *cold* in here. Can you shut the window, please?

9 Revision: word order

A long way from New Rochelle to Denver . . .
Make sentences.

1. the oil and the brakes/Mr Minardi/checked/they/started/before
2. Nick/while/listened/they/to the radio programme/were driving
3. was dark/drove/they/it/till
4. looked for/when/near the road/they/a motel/were tired/they
5. at the motel/had/till/they/a hot shower/and/watched TV/went to bed/they
6. arrived at/when/their relatives' house in Denver/nobody/they/was there
7. "to the mountains/for a few days/they've gone"/said the neighbour

[10] Interpreting on holiday

Susanne Beckmann is in Florence for a week with her parents. They have met Mr and Mrs Henderson from America. But Susanne's parents do not speak English – and the Hendersons do not know any German!

Can you help Susanne to interpret?

Mr Henderson:
We were in Germany last week. We enjoyed it very much. Too bad that we couldn't stay any longer, but we've only got three weeks for all of Europe.
Susanne: . . .
Frau Beckmann:
Ist das nicht zu kurz, wenn man sich alle Sehenswürdigkeiten anschauen will?
Susanne: . . .
Mrs Henderson:
Well, of course we haven't seen as much as we'd like to. But things are so expensive over here that we can't stay any longer.
Susanne: . . .
Herr Beckmann:
Ich finde, acht Tage in Florenz sind schon genug. Dieser schreckliche Verkehr, der Lärm Tag und Nacht – und dann muß man so viele Kirchen und Museen besichtigen . . .
Frau Beckmann:
Also bitte, Walter. Wir haben hier viele schöne und interessante Dinge gesehen. Und das Essen in Italien ist fantastisch.
Susanne: My father thinks (that) . . .
My mother says (that) . . .
Herr Beckmann:
Übrigens, sag doch den Hendersons, daß wir vorhaben, nächstes Jahr unseren Urlaub in Amerika zu verbringen. Wenn die Hendersons uns ihre Adresse geben, werden wir sie vielleicht besuchen.
Susanne: . . .

○ 11 Kirsten's letter

Amy Connor has met Kirsten Bleck in Florida. Kirsten is spending her summer holidays with the Calderons. She has written a letter about Florida to her English teacher. Amy would like to know what Kirsten has written.

Can you help Kirsten with the translation?

Jetzt weiß ich, warum die Amerikaner Florida "The Sunshine State" nennen: Die Sonne scheint wirklich jeden Tag. Aber manchmal ist es zu heiß, und ich muß sehr viel Eis essen! Das amerikanische Eis ist viel besser als unseres. Wußten Sie, daß es in Florida Apfelsinenbäume gibt? Morgens holen wir immer einige Apfelsinen aus dem Garten und machen [einen] frischen Orangensaft zum Frühstück.

Die Calderons haben mir schon viel von Florida gezeigt. Der Everglades National Park ist wunderschön: Man kann mit einem Boot durch den Park fahren und viele Vögel und wilde Tiere sehen. Es gibt sogar Alligatoren dort – stellen Sie sich vor, einige sind 6 Meter lang! Letzte Woche besuchten wir Disney World. (Das ist ein riesiger Park mit vielen Touristenattraktionen.) Wir haben eine Menge Geld für Popcorn und Eis ausgegeben. Ich fand es langweilig. Mickey Mouse und Donald Duck finde ich in den Filmen und Comics interessanter und lustiger.

Familie Calderon verbringt viel Zeit draußen. Wir machen oft Picknicks (*have picnics*) – in Florida gibt es sehr viele Picknick-Tische und sogar Grills (*grills*) neben den Straßen. Da machen die Amerikaner meistens Steaks oder Hamburger, mit viel Ketchup natürlich. Also, wie Sie sehen, finde ich Florida prima. Wenn ich einen Job als Daisy Duck in Disney World kriege, bleibe ich vielleicht in Amerika und gehe nie wieder zur Schule.

12 Listening comprehension: The Magic Kingdom

[1] Bedingungssätze (Conditional sentences)

Nebensatz mit *if* (*if*-clause)	Hauptsatz (main clause)
If the Minardis **go** to Colorado, If they**'ve got** time, If Nick **doesn't go** to Colorado, If Amy **saves** her pocket-money, *Mrs Connor:* If you **see** the Minardis,	they**'ll visit** Nancy in Denver. they**'ll go** to other places, too. he **won't see** the new baby. she **can go** to Girl Scout camp. **invite** them to our picnic.
Im Nebensatz mit *if* steht das *simple present.* Der Nebensatz drückt eine Bedingung aus.	Im Hauptsatz stehen: – das *will-future, can* + Infinitiv, *must* + Infinitiv oder ein anderes Hilfsverb, – ein Imperativ. Der Hauptsatz drückt aus, was geschieht, wenn die Bedingung erfüllt wird.

Der Hauptsatz kann – wie im Deutschen – auch vor dem Nebensatz stehen:

We **won't go** out this afternoon if the weather **is** bad.

Zwischen dem Haupt- und dem Nebensatz braucht im Englischen kein Komma zu stehen.

⚠ *if* = wenn (= falls); *when* = (dann) wenn, wenn (= sobald)

If my cousin visits me next week, we'll go to the zoo together. (Es ist nicht sicher, ob sie kommt.)
When my cousin visits me next week, we'll go to the zoo together. (Die Kusine kommt bestimmt.)

[2] Die indirekte Rede mit dem einleitenden Verb im Präsens
(Reported speech with the introductory verb in the present tense)

		direkte Rede	indirekte Rede
a		"**I've got** something to tell **you** all. **I'm going to** get married."	*Amy:* Grandpa says (that) **he has got** something to tell **us** all. **He's going to** get married. Opa sagt, daß er uns etwas mitzuteilen **habe/hat**. Er **werde/wird** heiraten.
b		"**What's the weather like** in Florida?" "**Did he enjoy his** vacation?"	*Amy:* Mom asks **what the weather is like** in Florida. Mom asks **if you enjoyed your** vacation.

In der indirekten Rede berichtet man, was jemand gesagt oder geschrieben hat. Die indirekte Rede wird durch Verben wie *say, ask (if), think, want to know* usw. eingeleitet. Wenn das einleitende Verb im *simple present (she says, he thinks)* steht, verwendet man in der indirekten Rede die gleichen Zeiten wie in der direkten Rede. Konjunktivformen wie „er habe", „sie werde" werden im Englischen nicht gebraucht. Personalpronomen und Possessivpronomen müssen – genauso wie im Deutschen – verändert werden (z.B. I → *she/he*; my → *her/his*).

⚠ Im Englischen steht vor der indirekten Rede kein Komma. „That" kann man weglassen.

Beachte die Wortstellung S-V(-O) in der indirekten Rede:

What's the weather like? → She asks what the weather is like.
Did you enjoy your holiday? → He asks if you enjoyed your holiday.

A game: Lucky hands

For this game you need a dice.

	**3** Ich kann mein Buch nicht finden.	**6** Kann ich heute neben Susi sitzen?	**2** Ich habe meine Aufgaben nicht gemacht.
	**8** Können wir den Text nicht noch einmal lesen?	**1** Darf ich anfangen?	**5** Ich habe die Stelle noch nicht gefunden.
	**10** Lernen wir morgen die Lieder in Unit 6?	**3** Ich verstehe den dritten Satz nicht.	**6** Wie heißt der letzte Satz auf deutsch?
	**6** Auf welcher Seite sind wir?	**7** Müssen wir auch die Nummer 5 machen?	**3** Ich kann das nicht auf englisch sagen.
	**4** Wie buchstabiert man das Wort ‚spaghetti'?	**3** Warum kann man das nicht sagen?	**5** Können Sie das bitte noch einmal erklären?
	**5** Ich bin noch nicht mit der Übung fertig.	**1** Ich finde die Cassette toll.	**9** Hat jemand mein Lineal gesehen?

1. Make 2 groups in your class. Both groups must choose a pupil as "lucky hand". The "lucky hands" throw the dice. The group with the highest number starts the game.
2. The "lucky hand" throws the dice and says the across number (e.g. "four across"), then she or he throws the dice again and says the down number (e.g. "five down").
3. The first pupil with the correct English sentence scores the points in the box (here: four points) for her or his group.
4. Now the other "lucky hand" throws the dice and says the across and down numbers.
5. The first group with 50 points wins the game.

(10) Ich habe die Tafel gestern sauber gemacht.	(7) Darf ich heute früher gehen? Ich habe Geburtstag.	(2) Der Wievielte ist heute?
(8) Was war die Antwort auf Frage 10?	(1) Wo ist mein Workbook?	(4) Kann ich Sandras Rolle lesen?
(9) Kannst du nicht lauter sprechen? Ich kann dich nicht verstehen.	(3) Wieviel Zeit haben wir für die Arbeit?	(2) Kann ich den nächsten Satz machen?
(7) Was haben wir für die nächste Stunde auf?	(3) Wie viele Fragen müssen wir bilden?	(2) Diese Geschichte ist langweilig.
(4) Darf ich die Wörter an die Tafel schreiben?	(2) Müssen wir alle Wörter auf Seite 120 lernen?	(8) Das tut mir leid. Das war mein Fehler.
(3) Sind meine Sätze richtig?	(6) Was ist an (with) meinem Satz falsch?	(7) Welche Zeit (tense) muß ich benutzen?

The English alphabet ['ælfəbet]

a [eɪ]	d [di:]	g [dʒi:]	j [dʒeɪ]	m [em]	p [pi:]	s [es]	v [vi:]	y [waɪ]
b [bi:]	e [i:]	h [eɪtʃ]	k [keɪ]	n [en]	q [kju:]	t [ti:]	w ['dʌblju:]	z [zed]
c [si:]	f [ef]	i [aɪ]	l [el]	o [əʊ]	r [ɑ:]	u [ju:]	x [eks]	

English sounds

i:	tea, we, sweets	ʊ	book, put, would	p	pen, pupil, cup	s	six, December, yes, Miss
ɑ:	class, car, half	ə	again, sister, terrible	b	bike, table, Bob	z	zoo, present, his
ɔ:	or, small, four	eɪ	eight, name, play	t	ten, bottle, sit	ʃ	she, station, English
u:	two, blue, ruler	aɪ	my, time, night	d	dog, window, record	tʃ	children, teacher, watch
ɜ:	work, her, first	ɔɪ	boy, toilet	k	car, packet, book	dʒ	Jim, cages, village
ɪ	in, big, party	əʊ	only, road, yellow	g	good, finger, dog	ŋ	painting, long, think
e	yes, pen, bread	aʊ	now, house	l	like, old, small	θ	three, bathroom, month
æ	black, cat, plan	ɪə	here, we're, near	r	ruler, children, dry	ð	the, father, with
ʌ	rubber, bus, come	eə	there, repair, wear	v	very, November, save	j	yes, you, new, argue
ɒ	on, dog, watch	ʊə	you're, poor, tourist	w	we, what, one, quarter	ʒ	television, usually

' = Betonung; der Betonungsstrich steht immer **vor** der betonten Silbe, z. B. idea [aɪ'dɪə]
Die Silben eines Wortes kann man auch durch Striche angeben, z. B. idea [-'-]
‿ = zwei Wörter werden beim Sprechen aneinandergebunden, z. B. an idea [ən‿aɪ'dɪə]

Grammatical terms

adjective ['ædʒɪktɪv]	Adjektiv
adverb (of manner) ['ædvɜ:b‿əv 'mænə]	Adverb (der Art und Weise)
adverbial (of place/time) [əd'vɜ:bɪəl]	adverbiale Bestimmung (des Ortes/der Zeit)
clause [klɔ:z]	Gliedsatz, Teilsatz
comparative [kəm'pærətɪv]	Komparativ, erste Steigerungsform
comparison of adjectives/adverbs [kəm'pærɪsn]	Steigerung der Adjektive/Adverbien
conditional sentence [kən'dɪʃnəl 'sentəns]	Bedingungssatz(gefüge)
future ['fju:tʃə]	Futur
– going to-future	– Futur mit „going to"
– will-future	– Futur mit „will"
if-clause [klɔ:z]	if-Satz, Bedingungssatz
introductory verb [ɪntrə'dʌktrɪ 'vɜ:b]	einleitendes Verb
irregular verb [ɪ'regjʊlə 'vɜ:b]	unregelmäßiges Verb
main clause ['meɪn 'klɔ:z]	Hauptsatz
past participle ['pɑ:st 'pɑ:tɪsɪpl]	Partizip Perfekt
past progressive ['pɑ:st prə'gresɪv]	Verlaufsform der Vergangenheit
past tense ['pɑ:st 'tens]	Zeitform der Vergangenheit, Präteritum
possessive pronoun [pə'zesɪv 'prəʊnaʊn]	nominal gebrauchtes Possessivpronomen
preposition [prepə'zɪʃn]	Präposition
present perfect ['preznt 'pɜ:fɪkt]	Present perfect (Perfekt)
present tense ['preznt 'tens]	Zeitform der Gegenwart, Präsens
prop-word ['prɒpwɜ:d]	Stützwort
regular verb ['regjʊlə 'vɜ:b]	regelmäßiges Verb
reported speech [rɪ'pɔ:tɪd 'spi:tʃ]	indirekte Rede
simple past ['sɪmpl 'pɑ:st]	einfache Form der Vergangenheit
superlative [su:'pɜ:lətɪv]	Superlativ, zweite Steigerungsform
tense [tens]	Tempus, grammatische Zeit(form)

Names

Families

Beckham ['bekəm]
Bennett ['benɪt]
Buxton ['bʌkstn]
Calderon [kældə'rɒn]
Davis ['deɪvɪs]
Duncan ['dʌŋkən]
Evans ['evnz]
Fenwick ['fenwɪk]
Goodman ['gʊdmən]
Harris ['hærɪs]
Henderson ['hendəsn]
Henley ['henlɪ]
Hopper ['hɒpə]
Jackson ['dʒæksn]
Kelly ['kelɪ]
Lee [li:]
MacDonald [mək'dɒnəld]
McPherson [mək'fɜ:sn]
Minardi [mɪ'nɑ:dɪ]
Murphy ['mɜ:fɪ]
Parker ['pɑ:kə]
Price [praɪs]
Rider ['raɪdə]
Sharp [ʃɑ:p]
Walsh [wɔ:lʃ]
Warren ['wɒrən]
Whittle ['wɪtl]
Williams ['wɪljəmz]

Girls/women

Agatha ['ægəθə]
Alison ['ælɪsn]
Amy ['eɪmɪ]
Angela ['ændʒələ]
Anita [ə'ni:tə]
Bettina [bə'ti:nə]
Caroline ['kærəlaɪn]
Diana [daɪ'ænə]
Diane [daɪ'æn]
Elizabeth [ɪ'lɪzəbəθ]
Ellen ['elən]
Fiona [fɪ'əʊnə]
Helen ['helən]
Hilda ['hɪldə]
Iris ['aɪərɪs]
Jo-Ann [dʒəʊ'æn]
Julia ['dʒu:lɪə]
Kathy ['kæθɪ]
Kelly ['kelɪ]
Lucy ['lu:sɪ]
Maria [mə'rɪə]
Martha ['mɑ:θə]
Martina [mɑ:'ti:nə]
Nancy ['nænsɪ]
Nicola ['nɪkələ]
Penny ['penɪ]
Ruth [ru:θ]
Tanya ['tænjə]
Tracy ['treɪsɪ]
Wendy ['wendɪ]

Boys/men

Alex ['ælɪks]
Andrew ['ændru:]
Arthur ['ɑ:θə]
Brian ['braɪən]
Charles [tʃɑ:lz]
Chris(topher) ['krɪstəfə]
Derek ['derɪk]
Ernie ['ɜ:nɪ]
Fred(erick) ['fredrɪk]
Gary ['gærɪ]
Jake [dʒeɪk]
Jeremy ['dʒerəmɪ]
Jonathan ['dʒɒnəθən]
Keith [ki:θ]
Michael ['maɪkl]
Phil(ip) ['fɪlɪp]
Richard ['rɪtʃəd]
Roger ['rɒdʒə]
Rory ['rɔ:rɪ]
Steve [sti:v]
Thomas ['tɒməs]
Wayne [weɪn]

Place names

Alaska [ə'læskə]
Amsterdam [æmstə'dæm]
Atlantic Ocean [ət'læntɪk‿'əʊʃn]
Aylesbury ['eɪlzbərɪ]
Bath [bɑ:θ]
Berlin [bɜ:'lɪn]
Beverley Hills ['bevəlɪ 'hɪlz]
Bordeaux [bɔ:'dəʊ]
Bristol ['brɪstl]
Buckinghamshire ['bʌkɪŋəmʃə]
Camberwell Green ['kæmbəwəl 'gri:n]
Cambridge ['keɪmbrɪdʒ]
Cape Canaveral ['keɪp kə'nævərəl]
Cologne [kə'ləʊn]
Colorado [kɒlə'rɑ:dəʊ]
Dartmoor ['dɑ:tmʊə]
Denver ['denvə]
Devon ['devn]
Everglades ['evəgleɪdz]
Exeter ['eksɪtə]
Falmouth ['fælməθ]
Florence ['flɒrəns]
Florida ['flɒrɪdə]
Frankfurt ['fræŋkfət]
Great Yarmouth [greɪt 'jɑ:məθ]
Gulf of Mexico ['gʌlf‿əv 'meksɪkəʊ]
Hamburg ['hæmbɜ:g]
Haverhill ['heɪvrɪl]
Hitchin ['hɪtʃɪn]
Key West ['ki: 'west]
Land's End [lænz‿'end]
Little Missenden ['lɪtl 'mɪsndən]
Liverpool ['lɪvəpu:l]
Lizard Point ['lɪzəd 'pɔɪnt]
Los Angeles [lɒs‿'ændʒɪlɪz]
Luton ['lu:tn]
Malaga ['mæləgə]
Miami [maɪ'æmɪ]
Mississippi [mɪsɪ'sɪpɪ]
Mousehole ['maʊzl]
Munich ['mju:nɪk]
Newcastle ['nju:kɑ:sl]
New Rochelle [nju: 'rɒ'ʃel]
Newquay ['nju:ki:]
Norfolk Broads ['nɔ:fək 'brɔ:dz]
Norwich ['nɒrɪtʃ]
Orlando [ɔ:'lændəʊ]
Pennsylvania [pensɪl'veɪnjə]
Penzance [pen'zæns]
Plymouth ['plɪməθ]
Potter Heigham ['pɒtə 'heɪəm]
(River) Tamar ['rɪvə 'teɪmə]
(River) Thames [temz]
Royston ['rɔɪstn]
Southwold ['saʊθwəʊld]
St. Albans [snt‿'ɔ:lbənz]
Stanmore ['stænmɔ:]
St. Augustine [snt‿ɔ:'gʌstɪn]
Stevenage ['sti:vnɪdʒ]
St. Ives [snt‿'aɪvz]
Suffolk ['sʌfək]
Tallahassee [tælə'hæsɪ]
Tampa ['tæmpə]
Truro ['trʊərəʊ]

Amersham Road ['æməʃəm 'rəʊd]
Albert Road ['ælbət 'rəʊd]
Blake House ['bleɪk 'haʊs]
Bluebell Farm ['blu:bel 'fɑ:m]
Central Park ['sentrəl 'pɑ:k]
Elm Hill ['elm 'hɪl]
Epcot Center ['epkət 'sentə]
Grange Farm ['greɪndʒ 'fɑ:m]
Hanover Street ['hænəvə stri:t]
Heathrow ['hi:θ'rəʊ]
Kennedy Space Center ['kenədɪ 'speɪs 'sentə]
Longleat House ['lɒŋli:t 'haʊs]
Oxford Street ['ɒksfəd stri:t]
Seven Mile Bridge ['sevn 'maɪl 'brɪdʒ]
Swan Lane ['swɒn 'leɪn]

Other names

Apollo [ə'pɒləʊ]
Austin ['ɒstɪn]
Charlie Chaplin ['tʃɑ:lɪ 'tʃæplɪn]
Crystal Palace ['krɪstl 'pælɪs]
(Enid) Blyton ['i:nɪd 'blaɪtn]
Daisy Duck ['deɪzɪ 'dʌk]
Everton ['evətn]
Growler ['graʊlə]
Humphrey ['hʌmfrɪ]
Jumbo ['dʒʌmbəʊ]
King Kong ['kɪŋ 'kɒŋ]
Mars [mɑ:z]
Noah ['nəʊə]
Odeon ['əʊdjən]
Oliver Twist ['ɒlɪvə 'twɪst]
Oxfam ['ɒksfæm]
Penny Red ['penɪ 'red]
Robinson Crusoe ['rɒbɪnsn 'kru:səʊ]
Rolling Stones ['rəʊlɪŋ 'stəʊnz]
Spagat [spə'gɑ:t]
Turbo ['tɜ:bəʊ]
(Walt) Disney ['wɒlt 'dɪznɪ]
West Ham ['west 'hæm]
William Penn ['wɪljəm 'pen]
Yamasee ['jæməsi:]

Vocabulary

Hinweise zur Arbeit mit dem Vocabulary

Im folgenden Wörterverzeichnis (Vocabulary) sind die **neuen Wörter aus jeder Unit** Deines Englischbuches aufgeführt. Neue **grammatische Fachausdrücke** und **Eigennamen** stehen gesammelt auf den Seiten 138 und 139.
Die **fett** gedruckten Wörter gehören zum produktiven, die normal gedruckten zum rezeptiven Wortschatz. In Bundesländern, in denen nicht zwischen einem produktiven und einem rezeptiven Wortschatz unterschieden wird, sind alle Wörter als Lernwortschatz gleich zu behandeln.
Die *kursiv* gedruckten Wörter auf den Seiten 152, 155 und 166 sind aus fakultativen Stücken. Sie werden in folgenden Units nicht als bekannt vorausgesetzt.
Die rote Unterstreichung bei einigen Wörtern (z.B. address) soll Dich auf die richtige **Schreibung** besonders hinweisen.
Bei einigen Wörtern, die von Deutschen oft falsch ausgesprochen werden, ist das Betonungszeichen oder ein bestimmter Laut rot gedruckt, damit Du gleich siehst, worauf Du bei der **Aussprache** achten mußt. Eine Erklärung aller verwendeten **Lautschriftzeichen** findest Du auf Seite 138.

Die folgende Liste enthält einige englische Wörter aus den Bänden 1 und 2 Deines Englischbuches, die nicht im Vokabular aufgeführt sind. Alle diese Wörter werden auch im Deutschen verwendet, so daß sie gar nicht neu für Dich sind. Nur bei der englischen Aussprache mußt Du manchmal aufpassen:

baby [ˈbeɪbɪ], babysitter, basketball [ˈbɑːskɪtbɔːl], computer, cornflakes [ˈkɔːnfleɪks], cowboy, disc jockey [ˈdɪsk dʒɒkɪ], disco [ˈdɪskəʊ], fan [fæn], film, fit, golf [gɒlf], hamburger [ˈhæmbɜːgə], hockey, jeans [dʒiːnz], motel [məʊˈtel], pink, pizza [ˈpiːtsə], pony [ˈpəʊnɪ], popcorn, pop music, pop song, pullover [ˈpʊləʊvə], reporter [rɪˈpɔːtə], safari park [səˈfɑːrɪ pɑːk], squash [skwɒʃ], steak [steɪk], taxi [ˈtæksɪ], team, teenager, tennis, text, toast [təʊst], T-shirt, video [ˈvɪdɪəʊ], volleyball [ˈvɒlɪbɔːl]

Im Vokabular werden folgende **Abkürzungen** verwendet:
sb. = somebody, sth. = something; jd. = jemand, jm. = jemandem, jn. = jemanden
adj. = adjective, adv. = adverb, n. = noun, sing. = singular, pl. = plural

Introduction

1	(to) **hope** [həʊp]	hoffen	I *hope* Sally can come to my party. = Hoffentlich/Ich hoffe, ...
	(to) **remember** (sb./sth.) [rɪˈmembə]	sich (an jn./etwas) erinnern; sich (etwas) merken, daran denken	*Do* you *remember* Merlin the magician? He can do magic, but he can't *remember* phone numbers. *Remember:* The plural of 'mouse' is 'mice'.
2	(to) **teach** [tiːtʃ]	unterrichten, lehren, beibringen	Miss Green is a teacher. She *teaches* at Park School in Hatfield. She *teaches* music and French.
3	It's all right for Liz.	*hier:* Liz ist gut dran. Liz hat's gut.	

Revision Unit 1

1A1	in the **country** [ˈkʌntrɪ]	auf dem Land	Aunt Mary and Uncle Ernie don't live in the town. They live *in the country.*
	wood(s) [wʊdz]	Wald	Sandra sometimes takes Wag for a walk *in the wood(s).*
	field [fiːld]	Feld, Wiese, Weide; (Sport-)Platz	Uncle Ernie works *in the fields* from seven in the morning till lunch time.

in the country = auf dem Land
in the field(s) = auf dem Feld
in the street = auf der Straße

on the beach = am Strand
on the coast = an der Küste
on the (River) Thames = an der Themse

1A2	farmer [ˈfɑːmə]	Bauer, Bäuerin; Farmer/in	What's your Aunt Mary's job? – She's *a farmer.*
	cow [kaʊ]	Kuh	
	bull [bʊl]	Bulle, Stier	
	horse [hɔːs]	Pferd	
	a few [əˈfjuː]	ein paar, einige (wenige)	There are lots of comics but only *a few* books on the shelf.
	pig [pɪg]	Schwein	
	chicken [ˈtʃɪkɪn]	Huhn; (Brat-)Hähnchen	Aunt Mary feeds the *chickens* every morning. Uncle Ernie likes *chicken* for lunch.
1A3	(to) **drive** [draɪv]	(Auto) fahren	
	(to) **ride** (a horse); (to) **ride** (a bike) [raɪd]	(auf einem Pferd) reiten; (rad)fahren	This woman *is riding* a horse. She *isn't riding* a bike.

German **"fahren"**

Mr and Mrs Connor often **go** to London **by car**. Mrs Connor usually **drives**.

Do you **drive** to work, Mr Singh? – No, I **go by bike**. I can **ride** to my shop in five minutes.

1A4	They're smelly. [ˈsmelɪ]	Sie stinken. Sie riechen schlecht.	*It's smelly* in here. Open the window, please.
	dirty [ˈdɜːtɪ]	schmutzig, dreckig	The car is *dirty.* We must wash it.
1A5	(to) **happen** [ˈhæpn]	geschehen, passieren	It's so loud outside. What*'s happening*? = Was ist los?
1A6	(to) milk [mɪlk]	melken	Farmers must *milk* their cows every day.
	milk [mɪlk]	Milch	English people usually drink their tea with *milk.*
	enough [ɪˈnʌf]	genug	Liz hasn't got *enough* money for a new record-player.
	cowshed [ˈkaʊʃed]	Kuhstall	
	all the winter	den ganzen Winter	You can't sleep *all the* time! Don't spend *all your* pocket-money on sweets.
	You're right/wrong.	Du hast recht/unrecht.	*You're wrong.* There are 30 days in November, not 31. Liz says there are 30 days in November. *She's right.*
1A7	(to) **have breakfast**	frühstücken	
	(to) **go to bed**	ins Bett gehen	It's ten o'clock. Time *to go to bed.*

essen ◄——— (to) **have** ———► **trinken**

It's 7.30. The Kings **are having breakfast**. They usually **have breakfast** at 7.30 and they always **have toast for breakfast**.

What do you usually **have for lunch** on Sundays? / **have for your evening meal**?

Can I **have a drink**, please? Let's **have a cup of tea**. I always **have milk for breakfast**, I don't **have tea or coffee**.

1T	**exciting** [ɪkˈsaɪtɪŋ]	aufregend, spannend	A book can be *exciting*, interesting or boring.
	How do you like ...?	Wie gefällt dir ...? Wie findest du ...?	*How do you like* my idea? – I think it's great. *How do you like* it in the country? – It's boring.
	supermarket [ˈsuːpəmɑːkɪt]	Supermarkt	Some things are very cheap *at supermarkets.*
1Ex 2	some more	noch einige, noch etwas	Make *some more* questions with 'do' or 'does'.
	like these [laɪk]	wie diese	Sally would like to live on a farm *like* her uncle's.
	(to) **guess** [ges]	(er)raten	How old are you? – *Guess!* – 12? – No, I'm 14.
5	That's nice of you.	Das ist nett von dir.	
8	phrase [freɪz]	(zusammenhängende) (Rede-)Wendung; Wortgruppe	'That's nice of you' and 'a bottle of lemonade' are *phrases.*
	Let me see, ... [ˈlet mɪ ˈsiː]	Warte mal! Laß mich mal überlegen!	*Let me see,* what can we do tonight?

13	(an) **address** [ə'dres]	(eine) Adresse, Anschrift	What's your *address*? – 15 Smith Road, Dover.
	This is how you do it.	So/Auf diese Weise macht man es.	*This is how* you start a letter in English: Dear Kevin, ...
	Thank you very much.	Vielen Dank.	*Thank you very much* for the present.
	(to) **get** (to a place) [get]	(hin)kommen, gelangen (zu/nach)	How can I *get to* the town centre, please? You can *get from* Bonn *to* Berlin by train. Mr Dean often *gets* home late.
	weather ['weðə]	Wetter	The *weather* is nice today. It's warm.
	(an) **envelope** ['envələʊp]	(ein) Briefumschlag	Can you give me an *envelope* for this letter, please?
	postcode ['pəʊstkəʊd]	*britische Postleitzahl*	The *postcode* always comes after the name of the town: CARDIFF *CF3 1NQ*
	important [ɪm'pɔːtnt]	wichtig; bedeutend	It's *important* to learn English.

Unit 2

2A1	BMX ['biːem'eks] (= Bicycle Motocross) ['baɪsɪkl 'məʊtəkrɒs]	BMX („Fahrrad-Querfeldein-Rennen")	Lots of children have got *BMX* bikes. *'Bicycle'* is another word for 'bike'.
	a lot (of ...) [ə 'lɒt]	viele, viel, eine Menge	*a lot of* children = lots of children *a lot of* money = lots of money
	(the) **air** [ðɪ‿'eə]	(die) Luft	The *air* is often very dirty in big towns.
	(to) do tricks [trɪks]	Kunststücke/Tricks vorführen	A magician can *do* magic *tricks*. Be careful, it's a *trick*.
	(to) **have a race** [reɪs]	ein Rennen veranstalten	Let's *have a race* on our bikes after school.
2A2	**clothes** *(pl.)* [kləʊðz, kləʊz = 1 Silbe]	Kleidung, Kleidungsstücke	These *clothes* are very nice. 
	special ['speʃl]	besondere(r, s); Sonder-	Today is a *special* day. It's my birthday.
	(to) **protect** sb. (from sth.) [prə'tekt]	jn. (vor etwas) (be)schützen	Trees can *protect* you *from* the sun.
	rider ['raɪdə]	(Rad-)Fahrer/in; Reiter/in	German **"jeder"** **Everybody** knows that Oxford Street is in London. **Every tourist** wants to go there.
	everybody ['evrɪbɒdɪ]	jeder(mann), alle	
	helmet ['helmɪt]	Helm	When you ride a moped, you must wear a *helmet*.
	(to) **fall (off** the bike) [fɔːl‿'ɒf]	(herunter)fallen (vom Fahrrad)	Don't *fall off* (your bike), Kevin. Be careful, Sandra. Don't *fall* into the lake.
	without [wɪ'ðaʊt]	ohne	You can't play football *without* a ball!
	dangerous ['deɪndʒərəs]	gefährlich	Tigers are *dangerous* animals. 
2A3	**wheel** [wiːl]	Rad *(am Fahrrad, Auto usw.)*	A bike has got two *wheels*, a car has got four.
	tyre ['taɪə]	Reifen	A lot of cars have got special *tyres* for the winter.
	low [ləʊ]	niedrig, tief	Sandra's bedroom has got a *low* ceiling.
	saddle ['sædl]	Sattel	You sit on a *saddle* on a bike or a horse.
	high [haɪ]	hoch	How *high* is your house?
	handlebars *(pl.)* ['hændlbɑːz]	Lenkstange	The *handlebars* of a BMX bike are very high.
	brake [breɪk]	Bremse	When you want to stop your bike, you use your *brakes*.
	bell [bel]	Klingel; Glocke	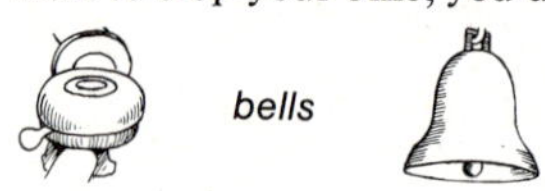 *bells*
	light [laɪt]	Licht, Lampe	
	pedal ['pedl]	Pedal	
2A4	(race) track [træk]	(Renn-)Bahn, Rennstrecke, Piste	
	bend [bend]	Kurve, Biegung	Be careful when you come to our house. We live *on a* dangerous *bend*.
	even ['iːvn]	sogar, selbst	Our town is very beautiful, *even* in the winter.
	mud [mʌd]	Schlamm, Matsch	

2A5	**last** Saturday [lɑːst]	(am) letzten Samstag	
	(to) **be**: I **was**; you **were**; he **was**; … [wɒz, wəz], [wɜː, wə]	sein: ich war, ich bin gewesen; du warst, du bist gewesen; er …	Dave *was* at the swimming-pool last weekend. Lots of his friends *were* there, too.
	meeting [ˈmiːtɪŋ]	Treffen, Versammlung; *hier:* Veranstaltung	The photo club *meetings* are in Room 10 on Mondays now. The *race meeting* on Saturday was very exciting.
	starter [ˈstɑːtə]	Starter/in, Schiedsrichter/in *(bei Wettrennen)*	
2A6	a week **ago** [əˈgəʊ]	vor einer Woche	My sister was here *two minutes/two days/a week/a year ago.*
2A7	**yesterday** [ˈjestədɪ, ˈjestədeɪ]	gestern	Today is Wednesday. So *yesterday* was Tuesday.
	last night	gestern abend; letzte Nacht	My parents were at a friend's house *last night.*
2A8	(the) **oil** [ðɪ‿ˈɔɪl]	(das) Öl	
2A9	**Did** Dave **help? – Yes, he did./No, he didn't.** [dɪd], [ˈdɪdnt]	Half Dave?/Hat Dave geholfen? – Ja./Nein.	
A10	**round** the track [raʊnd]	um die Rennstrecke (herum); *hier:* die Rennstrecke entlang	Mr Hill runs *round* the park every morning.
	(to) **shout** [ʃaʊt]	(laut) rufen, schreien	
	(to) **need** [niːd]	brauchen, benötigen	 "Do you *need* help?"
A11	(to) ride: I **rode** [rəʊd]	fahren: ich fuhr/bin gefahren	I often *ride* my bike. Yesterday I *rode* 20 miles in the country.
	towards the bend [təˈwɔːdz]	auf die Kurve zu, in Richtung auf die Kurve	Sandra is running *towards* Liz and Liz is running *towards* Sandra. 
	in front of Dave [ɪn ˈfrʌnt‿əv]	vor Dave	

in front of the house

behind the house

in, inside the house

outside the house

round the table

between the children

near the cat

next to the cat

at the table

on the table

under the table

over the table

German **"vor"**

The bus stops **in front of our house.** *(place)*
"Carter" **comes before "Connor"** in the list. *(In what order?)*

Sandra's grandmother died **two years ago.**
I usually go to bed **before ten** (o'clock).
Hurry up. It's ten minutes **to ten.**
} *(time)*

(to) overtake [--ˈ-]: I overtook [--ˈ-]	überholen: ich überholte/habe überholt	I tried to *overtake* two other bikes. But then I *overtook* only one because there was a dangerous bend.
(to) brake [breɪk]	bremsen	
suddenly [ˈsʌdnlɪ]	plötzlich	When you brake *suddenly*, you can fall off your bike.

	(to) **crash** (into) [kræʃ]	zusammenstoßen (mit), hineinfahren (in); verunglücken	The car *crashed into* a bus, and the bus *crashed into* a tree. On the next bend another car *crashed.* It was terrible.
	(to) fall: I **fell** [fel]	fallen: ich fiel/bin gefallen	*Did* you *fall* off your bike? – Yes, I *fell* into the mud.
2 A 12	(an) **accident** [ˈæksɪdənt]	(ein) Unfall; (ein) Versehen	I'm always careful when I ride my bike. I don't want *to have an accident.*
	Dave **didn't** overtake.	Dave überholte nicht/hat nicht überholt.	I'm sorry, but I *didn't* know what the homework was.
2 A 13	(to) say: I **said** [sed]	sagen: ich sagte/habe gesagt	Sorry, what *did* you *say*? – I *said*, "I must go now".
	foot [fʊt], *pl.* **feet** [fiːt]	Fuß	
	(to) **look for** sth./sb.	etwas/jn. suchen	Mr Hill *is looking for* his Underground ticket, but he can't find it.
	against Grove School [əˈgenst]	gegen die Grove-Schule	Kevin's football team often plays *against* teams from little towns or villages round Hatfield.
2 T	**ready** [ˈredɪ]	bereit, fertig; *hier:* startbereit	Lunch is *ready.* Are you *ready* (to start)?
	Go!	Los!	Starter: "Riders ready, pedals ready – *Go*!"
	… **when** 2F started.	…, als Klasse 2F startete.	Tina was at home **when** (= als) the accident happened. **When** (= Wann?) did the accident happen? **When** (= Wenn) you see an accident, you must phone the police.
	fast [fɑːst]	schnell	
	face [feɪs]	Gesicht	
	(to) **jump** [dʒʌmp]	springen	
	(It wasn't) **me**.	Ich (war's nicht).	Did you eat my sweets? – No, *it wasn't me.* Who can give the answer? – *Me.*
	finish line [ˈ-- -]	Ziellinie	
	(to) finish	*hier:* ins Ziel kommen	Liz was third over the finish line, but Tim never *finished.*
2 Ex 2	unlucky day [ʌnˈlʌkɪ]	Unglückstag	Many people say Friday 13th is an *unlucky day.*
	driver [ˈdraɪvə]	(Auto-)Fahrer/in; Lokführer/in	(car) *driver*, bus *driver*, taxi *driver*; train *driver*
	(an) ambulance [ˈæmbjʊləns]	(ein) Krankenwagen	An *ambulance* takes people to hospital.
	ambulance man	Sanitäter	
3	(to) **put**, is pu<u>tt</u>ing [pʊt]	stellen, legen, setzen, (etwas wohin) tun	*Put* the plates/books on the table, please. I can't *put* the model plane together. Don't *put* milk in my tea, please.
	(the) **order** [ðɪ‿ˈɔːdə]	(die) Reihenfolge, (An-)Ordnung	Put the words *in the right order.* = *hier:* Bring …
4	**for** four weeks [fə ˈfɔː ˈwiːks]	vier Wochen (lang)	Yesterday the children played on the beach *for hours.* [fər‿ˈaʊəz] = stundenlang My mum was in hospital *for a long time.* = lange Zeit
9	**th<u>e</u>n** [ðen]	zu der Zeit, damals	I was at Tina's house last week. She wasn't ill *then.* ⚠ *th<u>e</u>n* [ðen] = dann, damals (more) *th<u>a</u>n* [ðən] = (mehr) als
13	traffic lights *(pl.)* [ˈ-- -]	(Verkehrs-)Ampel	You must wait *at the traffic lights* till they're green.
	traffic [ˈtræfɪk]	Verkehr	
15	**What** are they **like?**	Wie sind sie? Wie sehen sie aus?	"*What*'s the book *like*?" – "It's great." *What*'s Sandra *like*? – She's tall and very lively. ⚠ *How*'s Sandra? – She's ill at the moment. *What does* Sandra *like*? – She likes pop music.
	the **only** [ðɪ‿ˈəʊnlɪ]	der/die/das einzige	Mr Singh's shop is *the only* pet shop in Hatfield.
16	a mixed bag [mɪkst]	eine bunte Mischung	
p. 27	**sign** [saɪn]	Zeichen; (Hinweis-)Schild	 a *sign*  a *road sign* = Verkehrszeichen

Unit 3

3A1	This is **the way** you do it.	So/Auf diese Weise macht man es.	Do you know a good *way* to learn new words? – Oh, you can do it *in many* different *ways*.
	hand [hænd]	Hand	
	(to) **brush** [brʌʃ]	bürsten	
	tooth [tu:θ], *pl.* **teeth** [ti:θ]	Zahn	⚠ tooth – teeth, foot – feet, mouse – mice man – men, woman – women, child – children
	hair *(sing.)* [heə]	Haar, Haare	⚠ Your *hair* is too long. = Deine Haare sind zu lang.
	shoe [ʃu:]	Schuh	
3A2	**saucer** [ˈsɔ:sə]	Untertasse	A cup usually stands on a *saucer*. 
	(to) **land** [lænd]	landen *(Flugzeug)*, anlegen *(Schiff)*	When did you arrive in Hamburg? – We *landed* at 7.30.
	knife [naɪf], *pl.* **knives** [naɪvz]	Messer	Terry, why can't you eat with *a knife and fork*?
	fork [fɔ:k]	Gabel	
	spoon [spu:n]	Löffel	
3A3	(to) **show** [ʃəʊ]	zeigen	Can you *show* me the way to the Underground station, please?
3A4	**bread** [bred]	Brot	You need *bread* and *butter* for a sandwich. ⚠ *Niemals:* ~~a bread~~
	butter [ˈbʌtə]	Butter	
	jam [dʒæm]	Marmelade, Konfitüre	
	(to) be thirsty [ˈθɜ:stɪ]	durstig sein, Durst haben	The children *were thirsty* after the race.
	(a boiled) **egg** [ˈbɔɪld‿ˈeg]	(ein gekochtes) Ei	
	roll [rəʊl]	Brötchen, Semmel	 I have bread/toast/rolls/muesli [ˈmju:zlɪ] butter/jam/an egg/a yoghurt/cornflakes coffee/tea/cocoa/milk/orange juice for breakfast.
	fresh [freʃ]	frisch	
	carrot [ˈkærət]	Karotte, Möhre, Mohrrübe	
	yoghurt [ˈjɒgət]	Joghurt	
	cocoa [ˈkəʊkəʊ]	Kakao	
3A6	**lovely** [ˈlʌvlɪ]	schön, herrlich, hübsch	a *lovely* day/meal/film/party/picture; *lovely* hair
	(to) take: I **took** [tʊk]	nehmen: ich nahm/habe genommen	*Did* you *take* my pencil out of my pencil-case? – Yes, and I *took* the biro, too.
	picnic [ˈpɪknɪk]	Picknick	Let's *have a picnic* on Bluebell Farm.
	(to) go: I **went** [went]	gehen; fahren: ich ging/bin gegangen; ich fuhr/bin gefahren	Ruth and her friends often *go* to a disco. They *went* there last week, too.
	I've got: I **had** [hæd]	ich habe: ich hatte/habe gehabt	**Has** Mrs Bell **got** a Ford? – No, she **hasn't got** a Ford. She **has got** an Austin. **Did** she **have** an Austin in 1980? – No, she **didn't have** an Austin. She **had** a Ford.
	full of cars [ˈfʊl‿əv]	voll mit/von Autos, voller Autos	
	(to) find: I **found** [faʊnd]	finden: ich fand/habe gefunden	
	(to) make: I **made** [meɪd]	machen: ich machte/habe gemacht	Dave and Tom often *make* models. They *made* a model train last weekend.
	(to) drink: I **drank** [dræŋk]	trinken: ich trank/habe getrunken	Mr Hill usually *drinks* tea for breakfast, but he *drank* coffee yesterday.
	(to) stand: I **stood** [stʊd]	stehen: ich stand/habe gestanden	The bus is very full. So we must *stand*. We *stood* yesterday, too.
	(to) see: I **saw** [sɔ:]	sehen: ich sah/habe gesehen	Can you *see* that big bird? Yesterday I *saw* three of those birds.
	(to) have lunch: I **had** lunch	(zu) Mittag essen: ich aß (zu) Mittag/habe (zu) Mittag gegessen	Kevin *has* lunch at school. He *didn't have* lunch at school last year. He sometimes *had* sandwiches.
	(to) eat: I **ate** [et, eɪt]	essen: ich aß/habe gegessen	Pete *eats* too much. Yesterday he *ate* nine sandwiches.

3 A 8	**country** ['kʌntrɪ]	Land; Staat	Germany and Great Britain are *countries.*
	chips [tʃɪps]	Pommes frites, „Fritten“	⚠ (Kartoffel-)Chips = *crisps*
	ham salad ['hæm 'sæləd]	Schinken mit Salat	
	sausage ['sɒsɪdʒ]	Wurst, Würstchen	Peanut's favourite meal is *sausages.*
	beans [bi:nz]	Bohnen	There's only one tin of *beans* in the cupboard.
	(an) omelette ['ɒmlɪt]	(ein) Omelett	
	cheese [tʃi:z]	Käse	
	roast beef ['rəʊst 'bi:f]	Rinderbraten, Roastbeef	
	potato, *pl.* **potatoes** [pə'teɪtəʊ]	Kartoffel	
	fish (⚠ *sing.* and *pl.*) [fɪʃ]	Fisch, Fische	
3 A 9	(to) have tea	Abendbrot essen, zu Abend essen	
	hot [hɒt]	heiß; warm *(z.B. Mahlzeit oder Wasser)*	*'Hot'* means 'very, very warm': a *hot* day/meal; *hot and cold* water
3 A 10	**Before** they leave, …	Bevor/Ehe sie weggehen, …	Don't try to run *before* you can walk. (Redensart)
	(to) **write** sth. **down** [raɪt 'daʊn]: I **wrote down** [rəʊt 'daʊn]	etwas aufschreiben, notieren: ich schrieb auf/habe aufgeschrieben	There are some new words on the board. *Write* them *down* in your exercise books, please. Last week I *wrote* a letter to my pen-friend.
3 A 11	**fruit** [fru:t]	Obst, Früchte	
	banana [bə'nɑ:nə]	Banane	
	(an) **apple** ['æpl]	(ein) Apfel	
	tomato, *pl.* tomatoes [tə'mɑ:təʊ]	Tomate	
	chocolate ['tʃɒklət]	Schokolade	Kevin is crazy about *chocolate* biscuits.
	sugar ['ʃʊgə]	Zucker	Do you take milk or *sugar* in your tea? – Milk, please.
3 A 12	They do**n't** need **any** bread. ['enɪ]	Sie brauchen kein Brot.	
	salt [sɔ:lt]	Salz	
	Do they need **any** cheese?	Brauchen sie Käse? (⚠ *„any“* unübersetzt)	
	And oranges? Do they need **any**?	Und Apfelsinen? Brauchen sie welche?	
3 A 13	**something** ['sʌmθɪŋ]	etwas	
	soup [su:p]	Suppe	
3 T	spaghetti *(sing.)* [spə'getɪ]	Spaghetti	⚠ This *spaghetti* is very nice. I like it. = Diese Spaghetti sind …
	factory ['fæktərɪ]	Fabrik	Tom's parents work *in a factory.*
	(to) **fill** sth. (with sth.) [fɪl]	etwas füllen, voll machen (mit etwas)	*'To fill'* means 'to make full': Kevin *filled* his pockets *with* apples.
	sauce [sɔ:s]	Soße (⚠ *nicht:* Bratensoße)	Sandra's favourite meal is spaghetti with *tomato sauce.*
	chewing gum ['tʃu:ɪŋ gʌm]	Kaugummi	Two packets of *chewing gum*, please.
	… **after** they visited us.	…, nachdem sie uns besucht hatten.	Sally went to the cinema *after* she visited us.
	machine [mə'ʃi:n]	Maschine	*Machines* can help us to do our work.
	(to) be **angry** (with sb.) ['æŋgrɪ]	wütend, böse, zornig sein (auf jn.)	Are you still *angry with* me? Let's be friends again.
	miss [mɪs]	*häufige Anrede für eine Lehrerin in Großbritannien*	Can I go to the toilet, *miss*? / sir?
	(an) elephant ['elɪfənt]	(ein) Elefant	How do you know when an *elephant* is in your sandwich? – You can't lift it.

Mr Hill usually **has breakfast** at 7 o'clock.
Carol didn't **have lunch** at school last year.
What's for lunch? = Was gibt's zum Mittagessen?
It's 5 o'clock. Liz **is having sandwiches for tea**.
I **had my evening meal** at 7 last night.

+	?	–
something ['--] = etwas	**anything?** ['---] = irgend (etwas)?	**not … anything** = nichts
somebody ['--] = jemand	**anybody?** ['---] = (irgend) jemand?	**not … anybody** = niemand
somewhere ['--] = irgendwo(hin)	**anywhere?** ['---] = irgendwo(hin)?	**not … anywhere** = nirgends, nirgendwohin

3 Ex 1	(to) play a trick (on sb.)	(jm.) einen Streich spielen	Lots of children *play tricks on* their teachers.
	(to) **decide** (to do sth.) [dɪˈsaɪd]	beschließen (etwas zu tun), (sich) entscheiden	Mr Hill wanted to go on holiday to Germany last year, but then he *decided* to stay in England.
4	We had a nice time.	Wir hatten eine schöne Zeit/viel Spaß.	
6	**stone** [stəʊn]	Stein	There's a *stone* wall at the end of the garden.
9	Here's five pounds.	Hier sind fünf Pfund.	
11	**comfortable** [ˈkʌmftəbl]	bequem, gemütlich	I like this chair. It's very *comfortable.*
	(an) **advert** [ˈædvɜːt]	(eine) Anzeige, Annonce, Reklame	There are lots of *adverts* in the newspaper on Sundays.

Unit 4

4 A 1	**finger** [ˈfɪŋgə]	Finger	
	thumb [θʌm]	Daumen	
	Keep moving. [kiːp ˈmuːvɪŋ]	Mach(t) immer weiter!	
	(to) **move** [muːv]	(sich) bewegen	
	merry [ˈmerɪ]	froh, fröhlich	
	bright [braɪt]	hell, leuchtend; *im Lied:* fröhlich, munter	
	arm [ɑːm]	Arm	Liz can't move **her** left arm. It's broken. = … **den/ihren** linken Arm … In some countries, people carry things on **their** heads. = … auf **dem** Kopf. Wash **your** hands before lunch, please. = … dir **die** Hände … Kevin washed **his** hair last night. = … sich **die** Haare …
	leg [leg]	Bein	
	nod (of the head) [nɒd]	Kopfnicken	
	head [hed]	Kopf	
	(to) **stand up** [stænd ˈʌp]: I **stood up** [stʊd ˈʌp]	*(von einem Platz)* aufstehen; aufrecht stehen: ich stand auf/bin aufgestanden	You can't sit here. Please *stand up.* ⚠ morgens aus dem Bett aufstehen = *(to) get up* Mr Hill *gets up* at half past six every day.
4 A 2	**time(s)** [taɪmz]	Mal, mal	The Kings visit Bluebell Farm about *four times* a year. Let's play table-tennis *this time*, we played football *last time.* We can play football *next time* again.
	clean [kliːn]	sauber	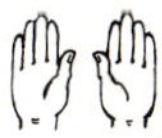 clean hands 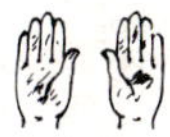 dirty hands
	eye [aɪ]	Auge	
	nose [nəʊz]	Nase	
	mouth [maʊθ]	Mund	Please don't speak with *your mouth* full.
	neck [nek]	Hals	
	ear [ɪə]	Ohr	
4 A 3	(to) **have a bath** [bɑːθ]	*(in der Wanne)* baden, ein Bad nehmen	(to) **have**  Sally **is having a bath**.
	(to) **have a shower**	(sich) duschen	Go upstairs and **have a shower/a wash**. Why not **have a party** on Sunday? We **had** a great bike **race** yesterday. Let's **have a picnic** tomorrow. It's five o'clock. The youth club **is having a meeting**. We **had a** history **lesson** at 10 today. Merlin **had a nice time** at the disco last night.
	shower [ˈʃaʊə]	Dusche, Brause; (Regen-) Schauer	
	(to) **have a wash** [wɒʃ]	sich waschen	
	(to) be **in a hurry** [ˈhʌrɪ]	in Eile sein, es eilig haben	
	(to) **come out** [kʌm ˈaʊt]	herauskommen, hinauskommen	
4 A 4	(the) fast**est** [ˈfɑːstɪst]	(der/die/das) schnellste; am schnellsten	Sandra is *the fastest* girl in her class.
4 A 5	(to) **win** [wɪn]: I **won** [wʌn]	gewinnen: ich gewann/habe gewonnen	Janet *won* the BMX race last weekend. But she *didn't win* any money, of course.
	(not) **as** fast **as** [æz … æz, əz … əz]	(nicht) so schnell wie	Liz is *as* old *as* Sandra, but she *isn't as* old *as* Sally.

4 A 6	**better** ['betə]	besser	My calculator is *better* than Peter's, but Anne's is *the best.*
	worse (than) [wɜ:s]	schlechter (als); schlimmer (als)	My cold is still bad, but it was *worse* yesterday.
	(the) worst [wɜ:st]	(der/die/das) schlechteste, schlimmste; am schlechtesten, schlimmsten	What are the best/*worst* pop groups at the moment?
	taller than **me**	größer als ich	
4 A 7	**more** exciting (than) [mɔ:]	aufregender, spannender (als)	A good book can be *more exciting than* a film on TV.
	(the) most exciting [məʊst]	(der/die/das) aufregendste, spannendste; am aufregendsten, spannendsten	 "*Which of you* was it?"
4 A 8	**Whose bike** is this? = **Whose** is this bike? [hu:z]	Wessen Fahrrad ist das? Wem gehört dieses Fahrrad?	
4 A 9	**Which bike** is Tom's? = **Which** is Tom's bike? [wɪtʃ]	Welches Fahrrad gehört Tom? Welches ist Toms Fahrrad?	
4 A 10	the blue **one** *(sing.),* the blue **ones** *(pl.)*	der/die/das blaue, die blauen	We've got three BMX bikes – two blue *ones* and a red *one.*
4 A 11	**funny** ['fʌnɪ]	komisch, seltsam	That's *funny.* I can't find my pen anywhere.
	both (of them) [bəʊθ]	(sie) beide, (alle) beide	*Both of us* like pop music. *Both (these) boys* have got black hair. Which do you want, fish or sausages? – I like *both.*
4 A 12	a **headache** ['hedeɪk]	Kopfschmerzen, Kopfweh	
	a **temperature** ['temprətʃə]	Fieber, (erhöhte) Temperatur	
	(to) **ache,** is **aching** [eɪk]	weh tun, schmerzen	
	What's **wrong with** Kevin?	Was fehlt Kevin? Was hat Kevin?	
	a bad cold	ein starker Schnupfen	
	(a) **stomach ache** ['stʌmək eɪk]	Magenschmerzen, Bauchschmerzen, Bauchweh	
	a sore throat [θrəʊt]	Halsschmerzen, Halsweh	
	sore [sɔ:]	wund, rauh, entzündet	
4 A 13	She **mustn't** get up. ['mʌsnt] = She **must not** get up.	Sie darf nicht aufstehen.	Hurry up. We *mustn't* be late.
	(to) **feel** [fi:l]: I **felt** [felt]	(sich) fühlen: ich fühlte (mich)/habe (mich) gefühlt	People say you're only as old as you *feel.* ⚠ *(to) feel: I felt – (to) fall: I fell*
	already [ɔ:l'redɪ]	schon, bereits	You can't be hungry *already,* Kevin – it's too soon after lunch!
	He **needn't** stay. ['ni:dnt] = He **need not** stay.	Er braucht nicht (zu) bleiben. Er muß nicht bleiben.	I can do the exercise. You *needn't* help me. ⚠ '(to) need' (= benötigen) needs 'do': I *don't need* any help with the exercise.

What's wrong with you?

I've got
- a (terrible/bad) headache.
- (a) toothache.
- a (high) temperature.
- a (terrible/bad) cold.
- (a) stomach ache.
- a sore throat/foot.

My head/stomach/left arm **is aching**.
There's nothing wrong with me.

needn't – mustn't – can't

You **needn't** drive so fast. We aren't in a hurry.
You **mustn't** drive too fast. It's dangerous.
I **can't** drive fast because I've got a very old car.

	medicine ['medsn]	Medizin, Arznei	You must sometimes take *medicine* when you're ill.
	(I feel/I'm) **well.**	(Ich bin) wohlauf/gesund. (Mir geht's) gut.	Yesterday I felt ill, but today I'm (feeling) *well* again. How are you? – Very *well*, thanks.
	fine [faɪn]	gut, fein, schön	How are you? – I'm *fine* (= all right), thanks. What a *fine* (= lovely) summer morning!
4 T	virus ['vaɪərəs]	Virus, Krankheitserreger	
	Scottish ['skɒtɪʃ]	schottisch, aus Schottland	Dr McPherson isn't English, she's *Scottish*.
	Let's see.	Schauen wir mal. Wollen mal sehen.	I'm feeling terrible, doctor. – Well, *let's see* what's wrong with you.
	(to) **do a test** [test]	einen Test/eine Arbeit schreiben, eine Prüfung machen	Liz *is doing a* French *test* today. How much time have we got for the *test*? Can we practise for the *test* in the next lesson?
	I see.	Ich verstehe. Aha! Ach so!	Julia's English is so good because her mother is English. – Oh, *I see.* I didn't know that.
	Wait a minute.	Einen Augenblick! Moment mal!	*Wait a minute.* You can't go on my bike.
	(to) mean: I **meant** [ment]	meinen (= sagen wollen, im Sinn haben): ich meinte/habe gemeint	Do you see what I *mean*? Miss Green said Tuesday, but she *meant* Thursday. ⚠ ich meine (= ich denke/glaube) = *I think*
	(to) hear: I **heard** [hɜːd]	hören: ich hörte/habe gehört	I *heard* that Tina was ill yesterday.
4 Ex 1	**mistake** [mɪ'steɪk]	Fehler, Irrtum	I think there's a *mistake* on the board. Can I correct it? Try not *to make* too many *mistakes* in the test.
3	**What** a question!	Was für eine Frage!	*What a* good idea! *What* lovely music! ⚠ *Niemals:* ~~What for ...!~~
4	(to) make comparisons [kəm'pærɪsnz]	Vergleiche machen, vergleichen	
	200 mph = 200 miles per hour ['maɪlz pər_'aʊə]	200 Meilen pro Stunde (= ca. 320 km/h)	Our car is very fast. It does 150 *mph*.
5	altogether [ɔːltə'geðə]	insgesamt, alles zusammen	The record is £2.99, and the book is £2.50. That's £5.49 *altogether*.
11	**part** (of) [pɑːt]	(ein) Teil (von); Gegend	 "Is this a *part* of your bike?" Cornwall is a beautiful *part* of England.
12	**What do you think about ...?**	Was hältst du von ...? Wie findest du ...?	*What do you think about* pop music? – I think it's great.
	opinion [ə'pɪnjən]	Meinung	*In my opinion* all sport is boring. = Meiner Meinung nach ... What's your *opinion*?
	(to) **imagine** [ɪ'mædʒɪn]	sich (etwas) vorstellen; sich (etwas) einbilden	*Imagine* it's your friend's birthday. What do you say? Nick *imagines* that people don't like him.
4 S	**(the) most** [məʊst]	(der/die/das) meiste, die meisten; am meisten	⚠ *most* people/words = *die meisten* Leute/Wörter *most of* my friends = *die meisten* meiner Freunde

Some more irregular simple past forms

Infinitive	Simple past			Infinitive	Simple past	
(to) buy	I **bought**	[bɔːt]	kaufen	(to) put	I **put** [pʊt]	stellen, legen, setzen
(to) come	I **came**	[keɪm]	kommen	(to) run	I **ran** [ræn]	rennen, laufen
(to) do	I **did**	[dɪd]	tun, machen	(to) shut	I **shut** [ʃʌt]	schließen, zumachen
(to) fly	I **flew**	[fluː]	fliegen	(to) sit	I **sat** [sæt]	sitzen; sich setzen
(to) get	I **got**	[gɒt]	bekommen; gelangen	(to) sleep	I **slept** [slept]	schlafen
(to) give	I **gave**	[geɪv]	geben; schenken	(to) swim	I **swam** [swæm]	schwimmen
(to) know	I **knew**	[njuː]	kennen; wissen	(to) think	I **thought** [θɔːt]	meinen, denken
(to) leave	I **left**	[left]	weggehen; verlassen	(to) understand	I **understood** [ʌndə'stʊd]	verstehen, begreifen
(to) lie	I **lay**	[leɪ]	liegen			

Unit 5

5 A 1

(to like) **very much**	sehr (gern mögen)
member (of) [ˈmembə]	Mitglied (in, von)
in town	in der (Innen-)Stadt
(to) **leave school**	von der Schule abgehen, die Schulzeit beenden
player [ˈpleɪə]	Spieler, Spielerin
international [ɪntəˈnæʃnəl]	international
(to) like sth. **better/best**	etwas lieber/am liebsten mögen
things **like that**	so etwas, solche Sachen
like that	so

Your new pullover is very nice. I *like* it *very much.*
Kevin *would like* to go to Sandra's party *very much.*
Mr Hill plays football, but he isn't a *member* of a club.

town – hospital – church – school (⚠ ohne „the"!)
I bought a new pullover **in town** yesterday.
Carol is **in hospital**. She's very ill.
I sometimes go **to church** on Sundays.
Dave isn't at home. He's **at school**.

I *like* the town *better* than the country.

A car *like that* must be very expensive. →

Don't talk *like that.*

5 A 2

(to) **do sports**	Sport treiben
I'm **interested in** sport. [ˈɪntrɪstɪd]	Ich bin an Sport interessiert. Ich interessiere mich für Sport.
weightlifting [ˈweɪtlɪftɪŋ]	Gewichtheben
skiing [ˈskiːɪŋ]	Skilaufen, Skifahren
riding [ˈraɪdɪŋ]	Reiten
gymnastics [dʒɪmˈnæstɪks]	Turnen, Gymnastik
ice-skating [ˈaɪsskeɪtɪŋ]	Eislauf(en), Schlittschuhlaufen
cycling [ˈsaɪklɪŋ]	Radfahren, Radsport
running [ˈrʌnɪŋ]	Laufen, Rennen
swimming [ˈswɪmɪŋ]	Schwimmen
judo [ˈdʒuːdəʊ]	Judo
handball [ˈ– –]	Handball

Do you *do* any *sports*? – Yes, I play hockey.
⚠ (to) be *interested* (in) = *interessiert* sein (an)
an *interesting* book = ein *interessantes* Buch

5 A 3

I'm **good/bad at** skiing.	Ich bin gut/schlecht im Skilaufen. Ich kann gut/schlecht Ski laufen.
quick [kwɪk]	schnell
weak [wiːk]	schwach
slow [sləʊ]	langsam

"Excuse me, what's the *quickest* way to the station?" – "Run."

The shelf is too *weak* for all the books. It's not strong enough.
Quick! Hurry up! Don't be so *slow*!

Prepositions at the end of questions

I'm **good at** [ət] tennis. But what are you **good at** [æt]? = Worin …? In was …?
Dave **looked at** [ət] the track. But what did Kevin **look at** [æt]? = Was …?
Liz is **waiting for** [fə] the bus. But what's Peter **waiting for** [fɔː]? = Worauf …? Auf was …?
Carol is **listening to** [tə] some cassettes. But what's Tina **listening to** [tuː]? = Was …?
Our last test was **about** irregular verbs. But what's the next test **about**? = Worüber …? Über was …?
I'm **from** [frəm] Hamburg. Where are you **from** [frɒm]? = Woher …? Von wo …?
Exercise 3 is **on** page 61. But what page is exercise 4 **on**? = Auf welcher Seite …?

5 A 4

almost [ˈɔːlməʊst]	fast, beinahe
(to) **lose** [luːz]: **I lost** [lɒst]	verlieren: ich verlor/habe verloren

It's three minutes to ten.

It's *almost* ten.
I hope England *doesn't lose* the match against Germany.
I think I *lost* my watch at the swimming-pool.

	(to) **beat** [bi:t]: I **beat** [bi:t]	schlagen, besiegen: ich schlug/habe geschlagen	Mrs Connor *beat* her husband at tennis on Saturday.
	confident ['kɒnfɪdənt]	(selbst)sicher, selbstbewußt; zuversichtlich	Sally is *confident* that she can beat Martina. She's a very *confident* player.
	easy ['i:zɪ]	leicht, einfach	That was an *easy* question. It was *easy* to answer.
	nervous ['nɜ:vəs], more nervous	ängstlich, aufgeregt, nervös	Jane is often *nervous* before a test. 
5A5	She played nervous**ly**. *(adv.)* ['nɜ:vəslɪ]	Sie spielte nervös.	In the last lesson Jane answered her teacher's questions *nervously.*
	set [set]	Satz *(Tennis usw.)*	
	as (always) [æz, əz]	wie (immer)	

as ◄—— German **"wie"** ——► **like**

Tim is late, **as always**.
As you can imagine, I'm very angry with him.
In England, **as in Germany**, people watch lots of TV.

Like all children, Timmy loves sweets.
My sister sings **like a bird**.
We need somebody **like your brother** in our football team.

5A6	She played **well**. *(adv.)* [wel]	Sie spielte gut.	My English is *good*, but I don't speak French very *well.* I hope you sleep *well.*
	net [net]	Netz	
	fast *(adj./adv.)*	schnell	Mrs Bell has got a *fast* car. It goes *fast.*
	hard *(adj./adv.)* [hɑ:d]	schwer; hart; heftig, mit aller Kraft	It's a *hard* job. You must work *hard.* Sally tried *hard* to beat Martina, but Martina won.
5A7	100 kilos (of) ['ki:ləʊz]	100 Kilo	Mrs Bell bought two *kilos* of apples yesterday.
5A8	disabled [dɪs'eɪbld]	(körper)behindert	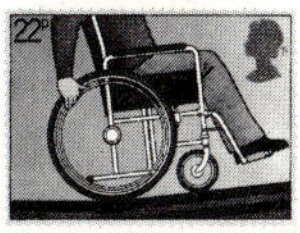 1981 was the International Year of *Disabled* People. This stamp shows a man in a *wheelchair.*
	wheelchair ['wi:ltʃeə]	Rollstuhl	
	(to) **enjoy** sth. [ɪn'dʒɔɪ]	etwas genießen, Spaß an etwas haben, etwas gern haben/tun	She *enjoys* swimming. = Sie schwimmt gern. Schwimmen macht ihr Spaß. I (very much) *enjoyed* the book/film. = Das Buch/Der Film hat mir (sehr) gefallen. I *enjoyed* the meal. = Das Essen hat mir gut geschmeckt.
	(to) **take part in** sth. [pɑ:t]	an etwas teilnehmen, bei etwas mitmachen	Kevin plays for Sandfield Youth Club. But he can't *take part in* their match on Saturday because he's ill.
	(to) train (sb.) [treɪn]	(jn.) trainieren; jn. ausbilden	Sally *trained* hard for the tennis match against Martina. Her sport teacher *trained* her very well.
	competition [kɒmpə'tɪʃn]	Wettbewerb, Wettkampf; Konkurrenz	There's a swimming *competition* at our school next month.
	successful [sək'sesfəl]	erfolgreich	Sandra did that job very *successfully.* She was *more successful* than last time.
	prize [praɪz]	Preis, Gewinn	Liz won a *prize* at the BMX race last weekend.
5A10	**notice** ['nəʊtɪs]	Anschlag; Mitteilung, Hinweis(schild)	There are some new *notices* on the *notice board* of the youth club.
	(to) choose [tʃu:z]: I **chose** [tʃəʊz]	(aus)wählen, aussuchen: ich wählte aus/habe ausgewählt	*Choose* between these two pullovers. →  Dave and Sally *chose* a book for Sandra's birthday.
	I'm going to write.	Ich werde/will schreiben. Ich habe vor/habe die Absicht zu schreiben.	What *are* you *going to* do at the weekend? *Are* you *going to* be at home? – No, I*'m not. I'm going to* be at a friend's house.
5A11	chess [tʃes]	Schach	
	(an) instrument ['ɪnstrəmənt]	(ein) Instrument	Dave plays the guitar, but he's going to learn a new *instrument* this year.

5 T	She did 50 metres in 61 seconds.	Sie schaffte 50 Meter in 61 Sekunden.	
	metre [ˈmiːtə]	Meter	⚠ **English plural = German singular** 50 metre<u>s</u>, 20 kilometre<u>s</u>, 10 kilo<u>s</u>, 5 pound<u>s</u>
	holiday(s) [ˈhɒlədɪz, ˈhɒlədeɪz]	Ferien, Urlaub	We went to the coast in the summer *holidays.* It was a lovely *holiday.*
	difficult [ˈdɪfɪkəlt]	schwierig, schwer	Our English tests aren't easy. They're always *difficult.*
	regular [ˈregjʊlə]	regelmäßig	The verb 'listen' is *regular* because you make the simple past with '-ed'. Take this medicine *regularly* three times a day. 
	polio [ˈpəʊlɪəʊ]	Kinderlähmung, Polio	
	marathon [ˈmærəθən]	Marathon	
5 Ex 4	(to) **break** [breɪk]: I **broke** [brəʊk]	(zer)brechen; kaputtmachen, kaputtgehen: ich zerbrach/habe zerbrochen	John fell off his bike yesterday and *broke* his arm. The plate fell and *broke.* Please be careful. Don't *break* my guitar.
	good for sore throats	gut gegen Halsschmerzen	
7	**careful** [ˈkeəfl]	sorgfältig, sorgsam	Be *more careful* with your work next time.
	price [praɪs]	(Kauf-)Preis	What's the *price* of the car? = How much is the car? ⚠ Preis in einem Wettbewerb = *prize* [praɪz]
	card [kɑːd]	(Spiel-, Post-)Karte	Let's play *cards* tonight. I like *card* games.

German **"Karte"**

cards

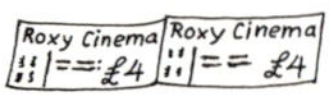

cinema tickets

a birthday card

a train ticket

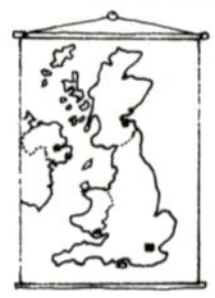

a map of the British Isles

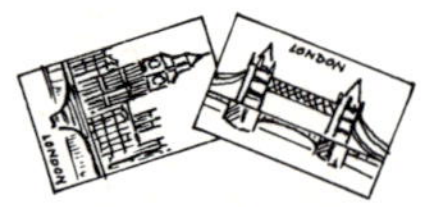

postcards of London

8	**plan** [plæn]	Plan, Vorhaben	What are your *plans* for the weekend? – I'm going to visit a friend.
9	(to) put sth. in	etwas einsetzen	*Put in* the right words. = Fill in the right words.
	(to) **park** [pɑːk]	parken	We can *park* (the car) in front of the shop.
10	(to) **love** [lʌv]	lieben, sehr mögen, sehr gern haben	Derek *loves* Susan very much. Do you like pop music? – Like it? I *love* it!
	quite [kwaɪt]	ziemlich; ganz	There were *quite* a lot of people at Sandra's party. I *quite* like your new jeans. – Well, they're *quite* new.
11	(to) be last/first	der letzte/erste sein, als letzter/erster (an)kommen	
	(to) be missing	fehlen	Who *is missing* today? – Oh, Martin isn't here.
	underlined [ʌndəˈlaɪnd]	unterstrichen	In the sentence 'I'm <u>not</u> silly!' the word 'not' is *underlined.*
°12	*(to) translate* [trænzˈleɪt]	übersetzen	Please *translate* this text from German *into* English.
13	boss [bɒs]	Chef/in, Boß	Mr Dean's *boss* is a woman.
p. 67	junior [ˈdʒuːnɪə]	Junioren-, Jugend-	Martina is in the *junior* team at her sports club.
	(an) adult [ˈædʌlt]	(ein) Erwachsener	*Junior* tickets are 50p and *adult* tickets are £1.50.

Some more irregular simple past forms

Infinitive	Simple past		Infinitive	Simple past	
(to) catch	I caught [kɔːt]	fangen, erwischen	(to) sing	I sang [sæŋ]	singen
(to) draw	I drew [druː]	zeichnen	(to) speak	I **spoke** [spəʊk]	sprechen
(to) drive	I **drove** [drəʊv]	(Auto) fahren	(to) spell	I **spelt** [spelt]	buchstabieren, schreiben
(to) feed	I fed [fed]	füttern	(to) spend	I **spent** [spent]	*(Geld)* ausgeben
(to) meet	I **met** [met]	(sich) treffen, begegnen	(to) teach	I taught [tɔːt]	unterrichten, lehren
(to) read	I **read** [red]	(vor)lesen	(to) tell	I **told** [təʊld]	sagen, nennen; erzählen, berichten
(to) sell	I **sold** [səʊld]	verkaufen			
(to) shine	it shone [ʃɒn]	scheinen *(Sonne)*	(to) wear	I **wore** [wɔː]	tragen, anhaben

Unit 6

6 A 1	**north** (of) [nɔːθ]	nördlich (von); Nord-; (nach) Norden	
	south (of) [saʊθ]	südlich (von); Süd-; (nach) Süden	

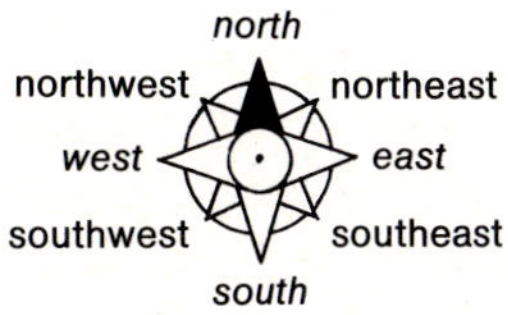

Newcastle is *north* of York. It's in the *north* of England.
Some birds fly *south* in winter. = They fly towards the *south*.
Wales is (to the) *west* of England.
My aunt lives in *East* London.

	flat [flæt], **flatter**	flach, eben	The Norfolk Broads are the *flattest* part of England.
	canal [kəˈnæl]	Kanal *(für Schiffe)*	There are lots of *canals* in Amsterdam.
	(to) hire sth. [ˈhaɪə]	*(Boot, Auto, Saal)* mieten	My sister *hired* a car for a week.
	boat [bəʊt]	Boot; Schiff	There were lots of *boats* on the water.
	several [ˈsevrəl]	mehrere; verschiedene	I've got *several* books about animals.
	also [ˈɔːlsəʊ]	auch	Dave was at Sandra's house yesterday, and Kevin was there, too. = Kevin was *also* there. Yesterday it was *not only* cold *but also* wet.
	your own canoe [əʊn]	dein/Ihr/Euer eigenes Kanu, ein eigenes Kanu	I've got *my own* room. ⚠ *Niemals:* ~~an own room~~
	canoe [kəˈnuː]	Paddelboot; Kanu	 a canoe
6 A 2	(to) **go on a trip** [trɪp]	eine Reise/Fahrt machen, einen Ausflug machen	The Kings *went on a trip* to London last Sunday. When are we going to have our next *class trip*?
	during the holidays [ˈdjʊərɪŋ]	während der Ferien, in den Ferien	We went to the mountains *during* the summer holidays.
	Easter [ˈiːstə]	Ostern; Oster-	*At Easter* children in Germany look for *Easter* eggs.
	(to) camp [kæmp]	zelten, campen	
	(to) load [ləʊd]	(auf)laden; beladen	Mrs Bell *is loading* some boxes *into* her car. = She*'s loading* her car *with* some boxes. 
	(to) unload [ʌnˈləʊd]	ausladen, abladen	Can you help me to *unload* these things, please?
	coach [kəʊtʃ]	Reisebus	When does the *coach* to London leave, please?
	at last [ət ˈlɑːst]	endlich, schließlich	We waited a long time, and *at last* the train came. ⚠ *at least* = mindestens; zumindest

You can go …

by plane

by car

by bus

by coach

by train

by Underground

by bike

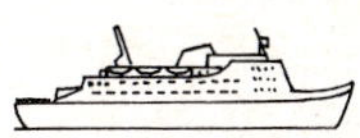
by boat

6 A 5	(to) give: I gave – I've **given** [ˈgɪvn]	geben: ich gab/habe gegeben – ich habe gegeben	I don't think you*'ve given* me my book back. – Of course I have. I *gave* it to your brother yesterday. He's going to *give* it to you.
	(to) **put** sth. **up** [pʊt‿ʌp]: I **put up** – I've **put up**	etwas aufbauen, aufstellen; aufhängen, anbringen: ich baute auf/habe aufgebaut – ich habe aufgebaut	You can *put up* a tent/a bookshelf. / a poster/some pictures.
	wood [wʊd]	Holz	We get *wood* from trees. ⚠ [ʊ]: wood, foot, took – [uː]: food, spoon, pool
	fire [ˈfaɪə]	Feuer, Brand	Let's *make a fire* in the garden. A *fire* broke out during the night.

Some irregular verbs where the simple past and the past participle are the same

Infinitive	Simple past	Present perfect	
(to) buy	I bought	I've **bought** [ɔː]	kaufen
(to) catch	I caught	I've caught [ɔː]	fangen, erwischen
(to) feed	I fed	I've fed	füttern
(to) find	I found	I've **found**	finden
(to) get	I got	I've **got**	bekommen; gelangen
(to) have (an accident/lunch)	I had	I've **had**	haben; essen
I've got	I had	I've **had**	ich habe, ich besitze
(to) hear	I heard	I've **heard** [ɜː]	hören
(to) lose	I lost	I've **lost**	verlieren
(to) make	I made	I've **made**	machen, bauen
(to) put	I put	I've **put**	stellen, legen, setzen
(to) read	I read	I've **read** [e]	(vor)lesen
(to) say	I said	I've **said** [e]	sagen
(to) sell	I sold	I've **sold**	verkaufen
(to) shut	I shut	I've **shut** [ʌ]	schließen, zumachen
(to) sleep	I slept	I've **slept**	schlafen
(to) spend	I spent	I've **spent**	*(Geld)* ausgeben
(to) tell	I told	I've **told**	sagen, nennen; erzählen, berichten
(to) win	I won	I've **won** [ʌ]	gewinnen

6A6	**not … yet** [jet]	noch nicht	Have you still got my book? – Yes, I have*n't* read it *yet*. Has anybody cleaned the windows? – No, *not yet*.
	canister [ˈkænɪstə]	Kanister	
6A7	**… yet?**	… schon …?	Has Sandra arrived *yet*? – No, not yet.
	(to) **return** [rɪˈtɜːn]	zurückkommen, zurückgehen	*'To return'* means 'to come or go back'.
6A8	**just** [dʒʌst]	gerade (eben), soeben	Aunt Mary has *just* phoned.
6A9	**ever** [ˈevə]	je(mals), schon (irgendwann) mal	Have you *ever* milked a cow? – No, never. I have*n't ever* played tennis. = I've never … ⚠ immer = *always*
	(to) be: I was – I've **been** [biːn, bɪn]	sein: ich war, ich bin gewesen – ich bin gewesen	I*'ve been*, you*'ve been*, he/she *has been*, we*'ve been*, you*'ve been*, they*'ve been*
	I've **been to** Norwich.	Ich bin (schon) in Norwich gewesen. Ich war (schon mal) in Norwich.	
	before [bɪˈfɔː]	zuvor, vorher, schon einmal	

I've been here **before** (= zuvor, schon mal).
⚠ *before* am Satzende
Wash your hands **before** (= vor) **lunch**.
Wash your hands **before** (= bevor) **we eat**.

6A10	(to) **bring** [brɪŋ]: I **brought** [brɔːt] – I've **brought** [brɔːt]	(mit-, her)bringen: ich brachte/habe gebracht – ich habe gebracht	
	folk song [ˈfəʊk sɒŋ]	Volkslied; Folksong	
	(to) sing: I sang – I've sung [sʌŋ]	singen: ich sang/habe gesungen – ich habe gesungen	What *did* you *sing*? – We *sang* 'Old Mac Donald had a farm'. – Again? You*'ve sung* that song so often, you must be crazy about it.
	ghost [gəʊst]	Geist, Gespenst	
	(to) **believe** (in sth.) [bɪˈliːv]	(an etwas) glauben	Lots of people *don't believe in* ghosts. It's true. You can *believe* me.
	dark [dɑːk]	dunkel, finster	During the night it's *dark* outside.
	moon [muːn]	Mond	Look, there's a full *moon* tonight.
	star [stɑː]	Stern	
	strange [streɪndʒ]	seltsam, sonderbar; fremd	What *strange* clothes you're wearing! I know London well, but this street is *strange* to me.

6 T	**nobody** ['nəʊbədɪ]	niemand	*Nobody* ever writes to me.
	son [sʌn]	Sohn	
	out *(adv.)* [aʊt]	hinaus, heraus; draußen	Let's go *out* into the garden. We can play *out* there.
	(to) see: I saw – I've **seen** [siːn]	sehen: ich sah/habe gesehen – ich habe gesehen	What film *did* you *see* last night? – We *saw* "Ghost train". *Have* you ever *seen* it? – No, I haven't.
	(to) go by [gəʊ 'baɪ]	vergehen, vorübergehen	Two years *went by* and nothing happened.
	dead [ded]	tot	
	(to) **offer** ['ɒfə]	anbieten	Can I *offer* you a cup of tea? Mum *has offered* to help me with my homework.
	(to) **knock** [nɒk]	(an)klopfen; schlagen, stoßen	Please *knock* (on the door) before you go into the room. Be careful. Don't *knock* your head.
	grave [greɪv]	Grab	
	person ['pɜːsn]; *pl.* **people**	Person, Mensch; *Pl.* Leute	
	empty ['emptɪ]	leer	
	(to) **be frightened** (of sb./sth.) ['fraɪtnd]	Angst haben (vor jm./etwas), sich (vor jm./etwas) fürchten	
	hall [hɔːl]	Flur, Diele; Halle, Saal	
	scream [skriːm]	Schrei, Aufschrei	
	on the first night	in der ersten Nacht	
	land [lænd]	(festes) Land; Grund und Boden	Mary and Ernie have got a lot of *land*. We were happy to go *on land* after a week at sea. ⚠ ein Land, Staat = *a country* auf dem Land = *in the country*
	(to) pull down [pʊl 'daʊn]	abreißen, niederreißen	Yesterday they *pulled down* the old school in our street. It's a pity.

In a house or flat:

hall	window
living-room	door
dining-room	wall
bedroom	floor
bathroom	ceiling
toilet	stairs
kitchen	balcony

Prepositions in adverbials of time

allgemeine Tageszeit			näher bestimmte Tageszeit
	in the morning	–	**on** Monday morning(s)
	in the afternoon	–	**on** that afternoon
	in the evening	–	**on** a cold evening in November
	⚠ **at** night	–	**on** the first night

p. 76 ○ **Some British folk songs**

everywhere ['evrɪweə]	überall	*ladies* ['leɪdɪz]	(meine) Damen
duck [dʌk]	Ente	*chorus* ['kɔːrəs]	Refrain
goose [guːs], *pl. geese* [giːs]	Gans	*(to) roll along* [rəʊl]	*hier:* weiterziehen
(to) mow [məʊ]	mähen	*o'er* ['əʊə]	= *over*
meadow ['medəʊ]	Wiese	*Farewell.* [feə'wel]	Leb(t) wohl!

6 Ex 1	(to) happen **to** sb.	mit jm. passieren	What*'s happened to* the dog? I can't find her.
2	(to) **worry** (about) ['wʌrɪ]	sich Sorgen machen (wegen)	Please *don't worry about* me. I'm all right. *Don't worry.* = Mach dir keine Sorgen! Ist schon gut!
3	**worried** (about), **more worried**	besorgt (um), beunruhigt (wegen)	Sandra is *worried about* her grandfather. He's very ill.
	farmhouse ['--]	Bauernhaus	
11	**I'd love to** come.	Ich würde sehr gern kommen.	Can you come to my party? – Yes, *I'd love to (come).* *I'd love* a cup of tea. = Ich hätte (liebend) gern eine Tasse Tee.
	I'm afraid [ə'freɪd]	leider	I must go now, *I'm afraid. I'm afraid* I can't stay.
	(to) **invite** [ɪn'vaɪt]	einladen	Sandra *invited* Kevin and Dave *to* her birthday party.
13	**like this**	so, auf diese Weise; folgendermaßen	Start your letter *like this:* "Dear Terry, I was happy to hear from you …"
14	mixed [mɪkst]	gemischt, vermischt	I'd like a packet of *mixed* biscuits, please.
p. 83	cathedral [kə'θiːdrəl]	Kathedrale, Dom	Lots of tourists visit Cologne[1] *Cathedral* every year.
	Information Centre [ɪnfə'meɪʃn]	Auskunft, Verkehrsbüro	
	market ['mɑːkɪt]	Markt	Some things are quite cheap *at our market.*

[1]Cologne [kə'ləʊn] *Köln*

Some more irregular past participles

Infinitive	Simple past	Present perfect	
(to) break	I broke	I've **broken** [ˈbrəʊkən]	(zer)brechen; kaputtmachen
(to) choose	I chose	I've **chosen** [ˈtʃəʊzn]	(aus)wählen, aussuchen
• (to) do	I did	I've **done** [dʌn]	tun, machen
• (to) eat	I ate	I've **eaten** [ˈi:tn]	essen
• (to) fly	I flew	I've **flown** [fləʊn]	fliegen
• (to) go	I went	I've **gone** [gɒn]]	gehen; fahren
(to) show	I showed	I've **shown** [ʃəʊn]	zeigen
(to) take	I took	I've **taken** [ˈteɪkən]	(mit)nehmen; (hin-, weg)bringen

Unit 7

7A1	wardrobe [ˈwɔ:drəʊb]	Kleiderschrank
	skirt [skɜ:t]	Rock
	trousers *(pl.)* [ˈtraʊzəz]	(lange) Hose, Hosen
	dress [dres]	Kleid
	shirt [ʃɜ:t]	(Ober-)Hemd
	blouse [blaʊz]	Bluse
	tie [taɪ]	Krawatte, Schlips
	jacket [ˈdʒækɪt]	Jacke, Jackett (⚠ *nicht:* Strickjacke)
	shorts *(pl.)* [ʃɔ:ts]	Shorts, kurze Hose(n)
	sock [sɒk]	Socke, Strumpf

A *wardrobe* is a cupboard for clothes.

⚠ s**h**irt = **H**emd
s**k**irt = Roc**k**

7A2	(to) **grow** [grəʊ]: I **grew** [gru:] – I've **grown** [grəʊn]	wachsen: ich wuchs/bin gewachsen – ich bin gewachsen
	(to) **fit** [fɪt]	*(in der Größe)* passen
	tight [taɪt]	eng(anliegend), stramm
	fat [fæt], **fatter**	dick *(Mensch oder Tier)*

Orange trees *grow* only in hot countries.
My little brother *has grown* a lot. He's almost as big as me now.
The jacket *doesn't fit* me, but the coat *fits* very well.
The brown shoes are too *tight* for me.
I'm too *fat* for these jeans – I mustn't eat so much.

7A3	**cheque** [tʃek]	(Bank-)Scheck
	size [saɪz]	Größe
	The blouse suits you. [su:ts]	Die Bluse steht dir.

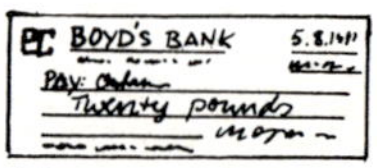

a cheque for £20

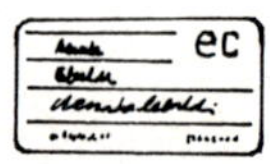

a cheque card

What size (shoes) *do* you *take?*
= Welche (Schuh-)Größe hast du/haben Sie?

7A4	(to) try sth. on [traɪ‿ˈɒn]	etwas anprobieren
	(to) **pay** (for sth.) [peɪ]: I **paid** [peɪd] – I've **paid** [peɪd]	(etwas) bezahlen: ich bezahlte/habe bezahlt – ich habe bezahlt
	I pay for **my own** clothes.	*hier:* Ich bezahle meine Kleidung selbst.

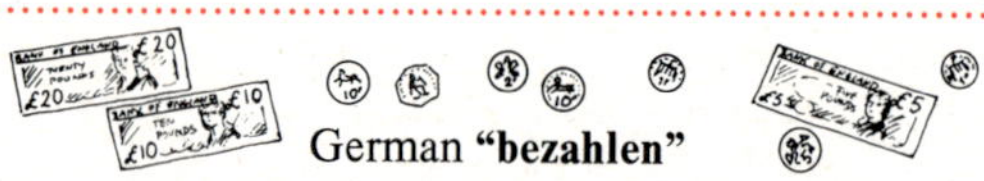

German **"bezahlen"**

I can't **pay for the tickets**/the meal/these clothes.
I **pay £5** a week for guitar lessons.
I can't **pay you** much for your work, I'm afraid.

7A5	(to) **put** sth. **on** [pʊt‿ˈɒn]:	*(Kleidung)* anziehen
	Mum **has given** it (= my blouse) **to** people from the church.	Mutti hat sie (= meine Bluse) Leuten von der Kirche gegeben.
	Oxfam [ˈɒksfæm]	*brit. Hilfsorganisation zur Bekämpfung der Hungersnot*
	toy [tɔɪ]; **toys**	Spielzeug; Spielsachen

Andrew's new shirt is super. He **showed** it **to his mother** (= seiner Mutter) yesterday.
Mrs King bought the cinema tickets and **gave** them **to the children** (= den Kindern).
On Monday Liz sold her old Rolling Stones records. She **sold** them **to a friend** (= einem Freund).

In Britain people often take their old clothes to *Oxfam shops.*

toys

7 A 7	(to) **collect** [kə'lekt]	*hier:* abholen; einsammeln	Mrs Bell sometimes *collects* Sandra from school in her car.

Clothes

You can wear/put on/try on

a coat	a hat	a dress
a uniform	a (T-)shirt	a skirt
a jacket	a blouse	jeans
(some) socks	a pullover	(some) trousers
(some) shoes	a tie	(some) shorts

7 A 8	**coat** [kəʊt] **hat** [hæt]	Mantel, Jacke Hut	
	It's **worth** lots of money. [wɜːθ]	Es ist viel Geld wert.	
	Just imagine. [dʒʌst‿ɪ'mædʒɪn]	Denk dir nur! Stell dir mal vor!	
	Have you done anything **to** help?	Hast du etwas getan, um zu helfen?	⚠ Kein Komma vor *to*!
7 T	(to) **throw** sth. (away) [θrəʊ‿ə'weɪ] I **threw** [θruː] – I've **thrown** [θrəʊn]	etwas (weg)werfen: ich warf/habe geworfen – ich habe geworfen	

Throw the book **away**. = **Throw away** the book.
I've **put** my coat **on**. = I've **put on** my coat.
Can I **try** the jeans **on**? = Can I **try on** the jeans?
Write the words **down**. = **Write down** the words.
⚠ Aber nur: **Throw** it **away**. I've **put** it **on**.
Can I **try** them **on**? **Write** them **down**.

	catalogue ['kætəlɒg]	Katalog	
	I haven't heard of that street.	Ich habe von dieser Straße noch nicht gehört.	⚠ von jm. hören, Nachricht erhalten = *(to) hear from sb.* Have you *heard from* your aunt? – Yes, she has written to me.
	at 22 Albert Road	in der Albertstraße Nr. 22	Mary Sharp lives *at* 22 Albert Road. (*at* + Hausnummer) Mary Sharp lives *in* Albert Road. (*in* + Straßenname)
	(to) find out [faɪnd‿'aʊt]	herausfinden, erfahren	Please *find out* when our train leaves. How *did* you *find out* her name?
	Well!	Na so was! Du meine Güte! Wirklich!?	Mum, I won the race this afternoon! – *Well!*
7 Ex 2	some **information** *(sing.)* [ɪnfə'meɪʃn]	Information(en), Auskunft	I'd like *some information* about holidays in Scotland, please. ⚠ *Niemals:* ~~some informations~~ *oder:* ~~an information~~

English singular = German plural

Here's some interesting **information** about the Norfolk Broads. Have you seen it?
This new **furniture** is very nice. Was it expensive?
Your **hair** is too long.
That's too much **homework** for tomorrow!
The **spaghetti** is ready.
The **U.S.A.** is very big. It's the fourth biggest country in the world.

3	**unhappy** [ʌn'hæpɪ]	unglücklich, traurig	*'Unhappy'* is the opposite of 'happy'.
	(un)tidy [(ʌn)'taɪdɪ]	(un)ordentlich, (un)aufgeräumt	When your room is *untidy,* you must tidy it up.
5	style [staɪl]	Stil, Mode; Art, Weise	The new clothes shop sells trousers in all sizes and *styles*.
	It **looks** nice.	Es sieht schön aus.	What *does* the missing girl *look* like? – She's very tall with dark hair.
6	the **airport** [ðɪ‿'eəpɔːt]	der Flughafen	An *airport* is a place where planes can land.
13	**over there** [əʊvə 'ðeə]	dort drüben, da drüben	 This bike *here* is old. That bike *over there* is new. → 
	yesterday's lesson	die gestrige Stunde, die Stunde gestern	
	the day before yesterday	vorgestern	
	even worse	(sogar) noch schlimmer	
	maths [mæθs]	Mathe(matik)	

yesterday's – today's – tomorrow's

There was an exciting story in **yesterday's paper**.
But **today's paper** is also very interesting.
Tomorrow's paper can't be as interesting as **today's**.

7 S	**in** 1980	(im Jahre) 1980	The first men walked on the moon *in 1969*. = ... *in the year 1969.*

Some more irregular past participles

Infinitive	Simple past	Present perfect	
(to) beat	I beat	I've **beaten** ['bi:tn]	schlagen, besiegen
(to) come	I came	I've **come** [kʌm]	kommen
(to) draw	I drew	I've drawn [drɔ:n]	zeichnen
(to) drink	I drank	I've **drunk** [drʌŋk]	trinken
(to) drive	I drove	I've **driven** ['drɪvn]	(Auto) fahren
(to) fall	I fell	I've **fallen** ['fɔ:lən]	fallen
(to) feel	I felt	I've **felt** [felt]	(sich) fühlen
(to) know	I knew	I've **known** [nəʊn]	kennen; wissen
(to) leave	I left	I've **left** [left]	weggehen, abfahren; verlassen
(to) lie	I lay	I've **lain** [leɪn]	liegen
(to) mean	I meant	I've **meant** [ment]	bedeuten; meinen
(to) meet	I met	I've **met** [met]	(sich) treffen, kennenlernen
(to) overtake	I overtook	I've overtaken [əʊvə'teɪkən]	überholen
(to) ride	I rode	I've **ridden** ['rɪdn]	reiten; (rad)fahren
(to) run	I ran	I've **run** [rʌn]	rennen, laufen
(to) shine	it shone	it has shone [ʃɒn]	scheinen *(Sonne)*
(to) sit	I sat	I've **sat** [sæt]	sitzen; sich setzen
(to) speak	I spoke	I've **spoken** ['spəʊkən]	sprechen
(to) spell	I spelt	I've **spelt** [spelt]	buchstabieren, schreiben
(to) stand (up)	I stood (up)	I've **stood** (up) [stʊd]	(auf)stehen
(to) swim	I swam	I've **swum** [swʌm]	schwimmen
(to) teach	I taught	I've taught [tɔ:t]	unterrichten, lehren
(to) think	I thought	I've **thought** [θɔ:t]	meinen, denken
(to) understand	I understood	I've **understood** [ʌndə'stʊd]	verstehen, begreifen
(to) wear	I wore	I've **worn** [wɔ:n]	*(Kleidung)* tragen, anhaben
(to) write (down)	I wrote (down)	I've **written** (down) ['rɪtn]	(auf)schreiben

Unit 8

8 A 1	Noah's ark ['nəʊəz‿'ɑ:k]	die Arche Noah
	bear [beə]	Bär
	camel ['kæml]	Kamel
	chimp [tʃɪmp]	Schimpanse
	giraffe [dʒɪ'rɑ:f]	Giraffe
	gorilla [gə'rɪlə]	Gorilla
	hippo ['hɪpəʊ], *pl.* hippos	Flußpferd, Nilpferd
	kangaroo [kæŋgə'ru:]	Känguruh
	lion ['laɪən]	Löwe
	monkey ['mʌŋkɪ]	Affe
	parrot ['pærət]	Papagei
	penguin ['peŋgwɪn]	Pinguin
	polar bear ['pəʊlə'beə]	Eisbär
	sea lion ['si: laɪən]	Seelöwe
	zebra ['zebrə]	Zebra

Pets

Farm animals

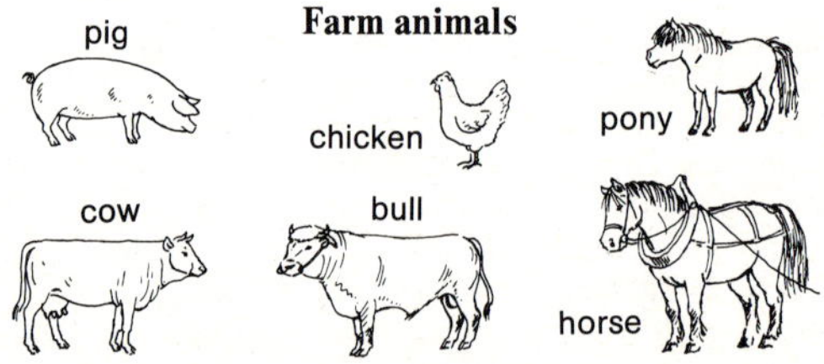

8 A 2	(to go) **in**	hinein(gehen)
	two by two	zu zweit, paarweise
	hurrah! [hʊ'rɑ:]	hurra!
	for to get out of the rain	*hier:* um aus dem Regen zu kommen
	rain [reɪn]	Regen

Come *in*! = Come into the room.

Park School has won the race – *hurrah!*

⚠ Always use *to* (not: *for to*) in your own English:
The animals went into the ark *to* get out of the rain.

Rain, rain, go away, come again another day. (rhyme)

8A4	**probably** *(adv.)* ['prɒbəblɪ]	wahrscheinlich	Mike has *probably* told Susan about the accident. It's *probable* because he usually tells everybody everything.
	zoo [zuː]	Zoo	Let's go to the *zoo* and watch the monkeys.

Places in town

bank	Bank(haus)	**market**	Markt(platz)	**sports centre**	Sportzentrum
café	Café, Restaurant	**museum**	Museum	**square**	Platz
cathedral	Dom, Kathedrale	**offices**	Büros	**stadium**	Stadion
church	Kirche	**park**	Park	**station**	Bahnhof
cinema	Kino	**pedestrian precinct**	Fußgängerzone	**supermarket**	Supermarkt
disco	Diskothek	**police station**	Polizeiwache	**swimming pool**	Schwimmbad
factory	Fabrik	**post office**	Post(amt)	**Tourist Information Centre**	Verkehrsamt
hospital	Krankenhaus	**restaurant**	Restaurant	**town centre**	Stadtmitte, City
hotel	Hotel	**school**	Schule	**zoo**	Zoo
library	Bibliothek	**shops**	Geschäfte, Läden		

8A5	**early** ['ɜːlɪ]	früh, (früh)zeitig	We're ten minutes *early/late*. = zu früh/zu spät
	yours [jɔːz]	der/die/das deine; deiner, deine, deines	
	(an) **ice-cream** ['aɪs'kriːm]	(ein) (Speise-)Eis, Eiskrem	

mine	= meine(r, s)
yours	= deine(r, s), Ihre(r, s)
his	= seine(r, s)
hers	= ihre(r, s)
ours	= unsere(r, s)
yours	= eure(r, s)
theirs	= ihre(r, s)

"They're *mine*!"

8A6	What's on the sign? (⚠ *nicht:* ~~What stands ...?~~)	Was steht auf dem Schild (geschrieben)?	
8A7	keeper ['kiːpə]	Wärter/in, Wächter/in	
	(to) **look after** sb./sth.	sich um jn./etwas kümmern, auf jn. aufpassen	A zoo keeper *looks after* animals in a zoo.
	for the first time	zum ersten Mal	Ellen and Wayne have never met before. They've just met *for the first time*.
	(to) **hide** [haɪd]: I **hid** [hɪd] – I've **hidden** ['hɪdn]	(sich) verstecken: ich versteckte/habe versteckt – ich habe versteckt	*Don't hide* Carol's bike again, Tina. When you *hide*, nobody can see you.
8A8	It'll be hard work. ['ɪtl] = It **will** be hard work. [wɪl]	Es wird (eine) harte Arbeit sein.	
	She **won't** die. [wəʊnt] = She **will not** die.	Sie wird nicht sterben.	

The sun *will* shine tomorrow.
It *won't* rain.

⚠ Ich *will nicht* sterben. = I *don't want* to die.

8A9	feeding-time ['---]	Fütterungszeit	
	... **pm** [ˌpiːˈem]	... Uhr nachmittags/abends	

Roxy Cinema
KING KONG
5.00 pm
9.00 pm

'King Kong' is at 5 (o'clock) in the afternoon and at 9 (o'clock) in the evening.

8A10	... **as** they walked to the zoo.	..., als/während sie zum Zoo gingen.	
	(to) **suppose** [sə'pəʊz]	annehmen, vermuten	Anne isn't at school today. I *suppose* she's ill.
	(to) **die out**	aussterben	Dinosaurs ['daɪnəsɔːz] *died out* millions of years ago.
	future ['fjuːtʃə]	Zukunft	Who can tell what'll happen *in the future*? Be more careful *in future*. = künftig, ab jetzt
	danger ['deɪndʒə]	Gefahr	Terry drives dangerously. He's a *danger* to all of us. A lot of trees are *in danger* because there are too many cars.
8T	**not long ago**	vor kurzem	I saw a very funny film *not long ago*.
	century ['sentʃərɪ]	Jahrhundert	We're living in the 20th *century*. a *sixteenth-century* house = ein Haus aus dem 16. Jahrhundert
	wild [waɪld]	wild; ausgelassen; stürmisch	A dog is a pet; lions are *wild* animals.

	free [fri:]	frei; kostenlos	Birds don't like cages. They all want to be *free.* They want to move *freely.* The disco tonight is *free.*
	only one week old	erst eine Woche alt	
	large [lɑ:dʒ]	groß, umfangreich	

German **"groß"**

a **big** or **large** town/house/room/field/family
a **big** mistake, my **big** sister (= my older sister)
a **tall** man/tree (= hoch aufragend)
How **tall** are you? – I'm 1.60 metres (**tall**).

⚠ die großen Ferien = the **summer** holidays
A, B, C = **capital** letters   a, b, c = small letters

	gate [geɪt]	Tor	Please shut the *gate* or the cows will get out of the field.
	steering wheel ['stɪərɪŋ wi:l]	Steuer(rad), Lenkrad	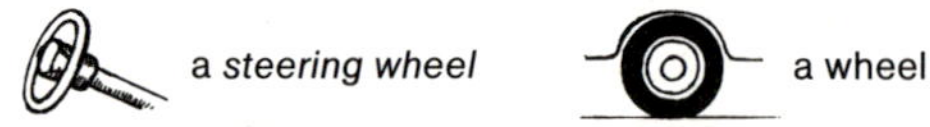
	petrol ['petrəl]	Benzin (⚠ *nicht:* Petroleum)	Let's go to London. – OK, but we must buy some *petrol* first.
	There were **no more** lions.	Da waren keine Löwen mehr.	
	handbook ['--]	Handbuch	A *handbook* can help you to repair your car.
	wolf [wʊlf], *pl.* wolves [wʊlvz]	Wolf	A *wolf* is a wild animal. It looks like a big dog.
	handbrake ['--]	Handbremse	
	(to) release (the brake) [rɪ'li:s]	(die Bremse) lösen; los-, freilassen	*Release the handbrake* before you start to drive.
	proper ['prɒpə]	richtig, passend, geeignet	The *proper* place for your clothes is in the wardrobe. It's too noisy. I can't hear *properly.*
8 Ex 2	crane [kreɪn]	Kran	People use a *crane* to lift big things.
4	**bus stop** ['bʌs stɒp]	Bushaltestelle	You wait for a bus *at a bus stop.*
	hairstyle ['heəstaɪl]	Frisur	
	(to) **let** sb. **do** sth. [let]: **I let** – I've **let**	jn. etwas tun lassen; zulassen, daß jd. etwas tut: ich ließ/habe gelassen – ich habe gelassen	*Let* me *use* your bike, please. Miss Green *let* her pupils *go* home ten minutes earlier today.
7	racing driver ['reɪsɪŋ draɪvə]	Rennfahrer/in	
8	(to) **go out** (with sb.)	(mit jm.) ausgehen	Let's *go out* tonight. I'd love to go to the cinema.
10	**message** ['mesɪdʒ]	Nachricht, Botschaft	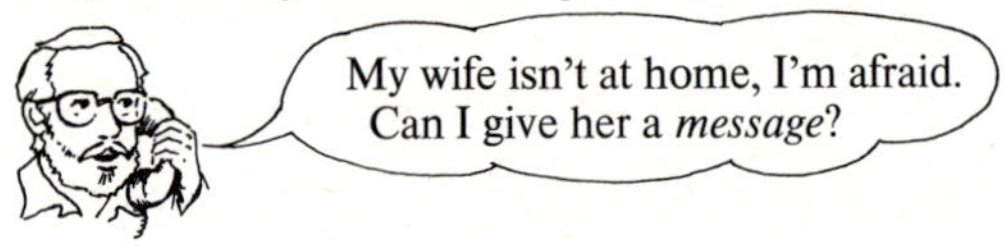
	usual ['ju:ʒʊəl], **more usual**	üblich, gewöhnlich	
p. 110	**for sale** [fə 'seɪl]	zu verkaufen	
	reward [rɪ'wɔ:d]	Belohnung; Finderlohn	The police offered a *reward* of £50 for information about the missing girl.
	wanted ['wɒntɪd]	gesucht	
	Dear Sir or Madam, …	Sehr geehrte Damen und Herren, …	*Dear* Mrs Price, … = 1. Liebe Frau Price, … 2. Sehr geehrte Frau Price, …
	madam ['mædəm]	meine Dame *(höfliche Anrede für eine Frau)*	Can I help you, *madam*? / sir?
	(to) **make a phone call** ['fəʊn kɔ:l]	einen Anruf machen, ein Telefongespräch führen	Kevin is going *to make a phone call to* New York. He wants to phone his cousin in New York.
	(to) answer the phone	ans Telefon gehen, sich am Telefon melden	I phoned Sandra this afternoon, but nobody *answered (the phone).*

Unit 9

9A1	(to) **begin** [bɪ'gɪn]: I **began** [bɪ'gæn] – I've **begun** [bɪ'gʌn]	beginnen, anfangen: ich begann/habe begonnen – ich habe begonnen	It's time *to begin* work. = … to start work. Look, it*'s beginning* to rain. 
	Denmark ['denmɑːk]	Dänemark	
9A2	**It's** (great) **fun.** [fʌn]	Es macht (viel) Spaß.	Cycling *is great fun.* We all enjoy it.
	countryside ['kʌntrɪsaɪd]	(ländliche) Gegend; Landschaft	The *countryside* round London is quite different from the *countryside* in the north of England.
9A3	**sand** [sænd]	Sand	
	ship [ʃɪp]	Schiff	
	(to) **sink** [sɪŋk]: I **sank** [sæŋk] – I've **sunk** [sʌŋk]	sinken, untergehen; versenken: ich sank/bin gesunken – ich bin gesunken	

Stumme Buchstaben

w:	wreck, answer	**d:**	sandwich
k:	knock, knife	**t:**	castle, mustn't
b:	climb, thumb	**h:**	ghost, wheel, hour
u:	guess, guitar	**l:**	folk song, half

	rock [rɒk]	Fels, Felsen	
	wreck [rek]	Wrack	
	on top (of sth.) [ɒn 'tɒp]	oben, zuoberst (auf etwas)	Put your exercise book *on top of* the others, please. I'd like some cake with fruit *on top.*
	cave [keɪv]	Höhle	Thousands of years ago people lived in *caves.*
	famous **as** smugglers' caves	berühmt als Schmugglerhöhlen	I use an old shoe box *as* a home for my mouse. My brother works *as* a bus driver in the summer holidays. ⚠ schneller *als* = faster *than*
	smuggler ['smʌglə]	Schmuggler/in	
	ruin ['ruːɪn]	Ruine	The house was *in ruins* after the fire. 
	tin mine ['tɪn maɪn]	Zinnmine, Zinnbergwerk	
	typical (of) ['tɪpɪkl]	typisch (für)	Pam arrived late again. That was *typical of* her.
	sight [saɪt]	*hier:* Anblick	After the fire, the house was a terrible *sight.*
	tunnel ['tʌnl]	Tunnel; *hier:* (Bergwerks-) Stollen	 a narrow street  ⚠ tight jeans
	narrow ['nærəʊ], **narrower**	eng, schmal	
	2000 feet [fiːt]	2000 Fuß (= 600 m)	My dad is *6 ft* (= *6 feet*) tall. (*1 foot* = ca. 30 cm)
	ground [graʊnd]	(Erd-)Boden	We can't sit down here. The *ground* is too wet. ⚠ Fußboden = *floor*
	half a mile [hɑːf]	eine halbe Meile	The train is *half an* hour late.
	(to) **work**	*hier:* in Betrieb sein, funktionieren	A few old tin mines in Cornwall *are* still *working* today. I can't phone Dave because our phone *isn't working.*
	(to) go on a guided tour ['gaɪdɪd 'tʊə]	eine Führung (mit)machen	Miss Green and her class *went on a guided tour* of Norwich at Easter.
	fishing ['fɪʃɪŋ]	Fischen, Fischerei; Fischer-	The old woman's son went out to sea in his *fishing* boat.
	life [laɪf], *pl.* **lives** [laɪvz]	(das) Leben	⚠ *Life* in Alaska is hard. = *Das Leben …* Three people lost *their lives* in the accident last night.
	(to) **send** [send]: I **sent** [sent] – I've **sent** [sent]	schicken, senden: ich schickte/habe geschickt – ich habe geschickt	*Did* you *send* Sarah an invitation? – Yes, I *sent* her one yesterday. I*'ve sent* invitations to all my friends.
9A4	Cornish ['kɔːnɪʃ]	kornisch, aus Cornwall; die kornische Sprache	Not many *Cornish* people speak *Cornish.*
	language ['læŋgwɪdʒ]	Sprache	I speak two *languages:* German and English.
9A5	tobacco [tə'bækəʊ]	Tabak	
	As the coast is near, …	Da/Weil die Küste nahe ist, …	
	Cornishman ['kɔːnɪʃmən]/ Cornishwoman	Einwohner/Einwohnerin von Cornwall	

As/Because (= Weil) it's raining, we can't play outside.
As (= Wie) you know, Scotland isn't a part of England.
As/When (= Als) I opened my eyes, I heard a funny sound.
As (= Als) a child, Mr Hill didn't like fish.
A man can't run **as** (= so) fast **as** (= wie) a horse.

	(to) **become** [bɪ'kʌm]: I **became** [bɪ'keɪm] – I've **become** [bɪ'kʌm]	werden: ich wurde/bin geworden – ich bin geworden	Mike Walker *became* a pop singer five years ago. He *has* now *become* a famous star. ⚠ Was willst du mal *werden*? = What do you want *to be* later?
	They **were(n't) allowed to** do it. [ə'laʊd]	Sie durften es (nicht) machen.	Jill's brother *wasn't allowed to* drive a car last year. Now he's 17 and he *can* drive one.

⚠"False friends"

(to) **become**	**bekommen**	**rock**	**Rock**	**floor**	**Flur**	**chips**	**Chips**	**cakes**	**Kekse**
werden	(to) get	Felsen	skirt	Fußboden	hall	Pommes frites	crisps	Kuchen	biscuits

9A6	wrecker ['rekə]	Strandräuber *(der Schiffe durch falsche Lichtsignale zum Stranden brachte)*	
	storm [stɔ:m]	Sturm; Gewitter	
	sailor ['seɪlə]	Seemann, Matrose	
	They **could(n't)** see. [kʊd, 'kʊdnt]	Sie konnten (nicht) sehen.	
	(to) **follow** ['fɒləʊ]	folgen; verfolgen, nachfolgen	
	(to) **hit** sth./sb., is **hitting** [hɪt]: I **hit** [hɪt] – I've **hit** [hɪt]	etwas/jn. schlagen, treffen; gegen etwas stoßen: ich schlug/habe geschlagen – ich habe geschlagen	
	onto the ship ['ɒntʊ, 'ɒntə]	auf das Schiff (hinauf)	

Some short forms

couldn't = could not, **can't** = cannot
isn't, aren't, wasn't, weren't, hasn't, haven't
doesn't, don't, didn't
wouldn't, ⚠ **won't** [wəʊnt] = will not
mustn't ['mʌsnt], **needn't**

I'm	= I am	**here's**	= here is
I've	= I have	**that's**	= that is
I'll	= I will	**how's**	= how is
I'd (like)	= I would (like)	**where's**	= where is
you're	= you are	**what'll**	= what will
she's	= she is	**that'll**	= that will

9A7	**While** I'm writing, ... [waɪl]	Während ich schreibe, ...	
	wind [wɪnd]	Wind	
	(to) **blow** [bləʊ]: I **blew** [blu:] – I've **blown** [bləʊn]	blasen, wehen: ich blies/habe geblasen – ich habe geblasen	The wind *is blowing* hard today. Yesterday it *blew* from the north, too.
	on deck [ɒn 'dek]	auf Deck, an Deck	
	captain ['kæptɪn]	Kapitän (eines Schiffes); Mannschaftskapitän	On a ship, the *captain* is the most important person. Mr Hill is usually the *captain* of the teachers' football team.
	(to) **save** [seɪv]	retten	The doctors couldn't *save* the old man's life. He died yesterday.
	(to) drown [draʊn]	ertrinken, ertränken	Six people *drowned* when the boat sank.

German **"während"**

while vor Sätzen: **While** I was on holiday | I broke my leg.
during vor Nomen: **During** my holidays | I broke my leg.

9A9	lifeline ['laɪflaɪn]	Rettungsleine	
	(an) **invention** [ɪn'venʃn]	(eine) Erfindung	The telephone is a great *invention*. 
	They **had to** swim.	Sie mußten schwimmen.	Sandra *must* do a maths test today. Yesterday she *had to* work for the test.
	They **didn't have to** swim.	Sie mußten nicht schwimmen.	
	safe [seɪf]	sicher, gefahrlos	Put your money in a *safe* place. The children can play *safely* in the garden. ⚠ Ich bin *sicher*, daß sie kommt. = I'm *sure* she'll come.

Be careful how you pronounce your new words.

safe [-f] – to **save** [-v], the **sand** [æ] – to **send** [e], to **sink** [s-] – to **think** [θ-], I **sank** [-ŋk] – I **sang** [-ŋ], to **work** [ɜ:] – to **walk** [ɔ:], their **lives** [aɪ] – she **lives** [ɪ], I **send** [-d] – I **sent** [-t], I **hit** [-t] – I **hid** [-d]

9 A 10	(to) **get into trouble** [ˈtrʌbl]	in Schwierigkeiten geraten, Probleme bekommen	Don't drive too fast. We don't want *to get into trouble* with the police.
	lifeboat [ˈlaɪfbəʊt]	Rettungsboot	A *lifeboat* can save people's lives when a ship is sinking.
9 T	beggar [ˈbegə]	Bettler/in	
	waggon [ˈwægən]	Pferdewagen, Planwagen	a *waggon* 
	(to) **roll** [rəʊl]	rollen	There was nobody in the car when it *rolled* out into the street.
	(to) **sail** [seɪl]	*(mit einem Schiff)* fahren; segeln	You can *sail* across the Atlantic in five days.
	noise [nɔɪz]	Lärm, Geräusch	Don't *make* so much *noise*, please. = Don't be so noisy. I think I heard a *noise* somewhere.
	(to) **leave**	lassen; zurücklassen, liegen/stehen lassen	You can *leave* your bag in the classroom. Don't *leave* the door open. Shut it, please.
	cloud [klaʊd]	Wolke	 The sun is behind some *clouds*.
	down [daʊn]	herunter, hinunter; herab, hinab	
	gold [gəʊld]	Gold; gold(en)	
	up [ʌp]	herauf, hinauf	
	(to) **lock** [lɒk]	abschließen, zuschließen	
	path [pɑːθ], *pl.* **paths** [pɑːðz]	Pfad, Fußweg	
	fog [fɒg]	(dicker) Nebel	

⚠ Word order

down	the road	=	die Straße **hinunter**
up	the road	=	die Straße **hinauf**
along	the road	=	die Straße **entlang**
half	a mile	=	eine **halbe** Meile
worth	£10	=	10 Pfund **wert**
all	the time	=	die **ganze** Zeit
both	her dogs	=	ihre **beiden** Hunde

Unit 10

10 A 1	suburb ['sʌbɜːb]	Vorstadt, Vorort, Randbezirk	We don't live in the town centre; we live *in a suburb.*
	They can't wait.	*hier:* Sie können es kaum noch erwarten.	
	… **until** they go back. [ən'tɪl]	…, bis sie wieder hinfahren.	till – *Aber:* until full – *Aber:* successful, beautiful all – *Aber:* almost, already, also, always
	motorhome *(AE[1])* ['məʊtəhəʊm]	Wohnmobil, Campingbus	
	(to) **go** fish**ing** ['fɪʃɪŋ]	fischen, angeln (gehen)	Jack *has gone fishing* in his fishing boat. He *goes fishing* every weekend.
	(to) **go** walk**ing**	wandern	On Sundays I usually *go walking* along the coast.

You can **go** canoe**ing**/cycl**ing**/fish**ing**/ice-skat**ing**/rid**ing**/runn**ing**/ski**ing**/swimm**ing**/walk**ing**.

	(to) **cut**, is **cutting** [kʌt]: I **cut** – I've **cut**	(ab)schneiden: ich schnitt/habe geschnitten – ich habe geschnitten	You *cut* bread with a knife. ⚠ I*'ve cut* my finger. = Ich habe mir in den Finger geschnitten.
	… **so that** she can go. ['səʊ ðət]	…, damit/so daß sie gehen kann.	Please speak louder *so that* everybody can hear you.
	Girl Scout camp *(AE)* ['gɜːl skaʊt 'kæmp]	(amerikanisches) Ferienlager für Pfadfinderinnen	
10 A 2	**neighbour** ['neɪbə]	Nachbar/in	Who sits next to you at school? Who is your *neighbour*?
	backyard *(AE)* ['bæk'jɑːd]	Garten hinter dem Haus	Where's Jonathan? – He's playing ball *in the backyard.*
	vacation *(AE)* [və'keɪʃn]	Ferien, Urlaub	= holidays *(BE[2])* *Amy:* Only two days till *summer vacation* starts. *Kevin:* Only two days till *the summer holidays* start.
	If we've got time, … [ɪf]	Wenn/Falls wir Zeit haben, …	⚠ *If* (= Falls) I get home before 8, I'll phone you. *When* (= Dann wenn/Sobald) I get home, I'll phone you.
	ketchup ['ketʃəp]	Ketchup	My favourite meal? Chips – with lots of *ketchup.*
	girlfriend ['gɜːlfrend]	Freundin *(eines Jungen oder Mannes)*	Do you know Mr Hill's *girlfriend*? Her name is Angela. ⚠ Angelas *Freundin* Sue = Angela's *friend* Sue
	Grandpa, grandpa ['grænpɑː]	Opa, Großvater	Have you got a grandfather? – Yes, my *grandpa* lives in York.
10 A 3	tradition [trə'dɪʃn]	Tradition	We've got a nice *tradition* in our family. Dad cooks the meals at the weekend.
	waffle ['wɒfl]	Waffel	You can find lots of German food in the U.S.A. – schnitzels, sauerkraut and *waffles*, for example.
	(to) **ring** [rɪŋ]: I **rang** [ræŋ] – **I've rung** [rʌŋ]	klingeln, läuten; anrufen: ich klingelte/habe geklingelt – ich habe geklingelt	*The phone rang* when I was leaving the house. It was my girlfriend Mary. Why don't pigs find it easy to ride a bike? – Because they've got no thumb *to ring the bell.*
	Amy Connor **speaking.**	(Hier) Amy Connor. *(am Telefon)*	Tim answered the phone and said, "Hallo, *Tim Price speaking.*"
	Hi. [haɪ]	Hallo!	Hallo, Dave. – *Hi*, Sandra.
	How's everything?	Wie geht's denn so?	*How's everything* at home, Mary? – Fine, thanks.

Making a phone call:

Hallo, **this is** Kevin Connor.
Can I **speak to** Susan, please?
Can I **give** you **a message**?
Can I **phone** her **later**?
My **phone number** is …
Is it OK if I **phone again** at 6 o'clock?
Sorry, I've got **the wrong number**.

Answering the phone:

Hallo, Hatfield 72809, Rod Cox **speaking**.
I'm afraid Susan isn't here.
Can I **take a message**?
Can Susan **phone** you **later**?
What's your **number**?
Can you **phone again** later?
Sorry, you've got **the wrong number**.

[1] *AE = American English* [2] *BE = British English*

	Mom, mom *(AE)* [mɑːm]	Mutti, Mama, Mami	= Mum, mum *(BE)*
	(to) **get married** (to sb.) ['mærɪd]	(sich ver)heiraten (mit jm.), (jn.) heiraten	Lucy wants *to get married*, but she doesn't want *to get married to* you!
	wedding ['wedɪŋ]	Hochzeit	My parents had a really big *wedding* with 100 guests.
0 A 4	(It's) too bad.	(Es ist) schade.	It's a pity you can't come to my party, Sandra. – And *it's too bad* you can't come to mine!
	(to) leave **for** …	abfahren nach …	Miss Green has gone. She *left for* London an hour ago.
	(to) **say hello** (to sb.)	(jm.) guten Tag sagen; (jn.) grüßen	*Say hello to* Kevin from me if you see him. (In British English you can write *hallo* or *hello,* but in American English you can only write *hello.*)
p. 128	**sunshine** ['sʌnʃaɪn]	Sonne(nschein)	**Talking about the weather** It's fine/nice/lovely/terrible / warm/hot/cold/wet today. The **sun** is shining. Come out into the **sunshine**. Look at the **clouds**. I think it'll rain soon. There'll be some **rain**/some **showers**/a **storm** this afternoon. A strong **wind** is blowing.
	Spanish *(adj., n.)* ['spænɪʃ]	spanisch; Spanier/in; Spanisch	
	flower ['flaʊə]	Blume, Blüte	
	Fountain of Youth ['faʊntɪn_əv 'juːθ]	Jungbrunnen	
	Indian ['ɪndɪən]	indianisch; Indianer/in	
	legend ['ledʒənd]	Legende, Sage	
	for ever [fər_'evə]	für immer, ewig	
	(to) **call** [kɔːl]	nennen; (an)rufen	Her name is Elizabeth, but we all *call* her Liz. ⚠ *What* do you call this in English? = *Wie* …? Please *call* the doctor. Sandra is ill.
	attraction [ə'trækʃn]	Attraktion, Anziehungspunkt	
	space [speɪs]	der (Welt-)Raum; Platz	To get to the moon you must fly through *space.* There isn't enough *space* in the car for six people.
	center *(AE)* ['sentə]	Zentrum	= centre *(BE)*
	(to) **notice** ['nəʊtɪs]	(be)merken, beachten	Jenny was too busy. So she *didn't notice* me.
	visitor ['vɪzɪtə]	Besucher/in, Gast	The Kings are visiting the Connors. So the Connors have got *visitors.*
	(to) go on a bus tour	eine Bus(rund)fahrt machen	
	launching pad ['lɔːntʃɪŋ pæd]	Abschußrampe *(für Raketen, Raumfahrzeuge)*	
	(an) astronaut ['æstrənɔːt]	(ein/e) Astronaut/in	In 1969 two American *astronauts* landed on the moon for the first time.
	training ['treɪnɪŋ]	Ausbildung, Schulung; Training	
	rocket ['rɒkɪt]	Rakete	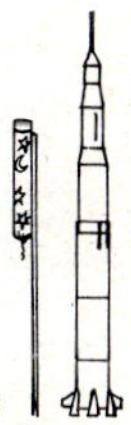 rockets
	travel ['trævl]	(das) Reisen	*Travel* is an exciting way to learn about people and places. Sandra is interested in *space travel* (= Raumfahrt).
	(to) **spend** [spend]	*(Zeit)* verbringen	I *spent* four hours at the shops yesterday. And I *spent* all my pocket-money.
p. 129	**future** *(adj.)* ['fjuːtʃə]	(zu)künftig	Helen and Steve are going to get married. So Helen is Steve's *future* wife.
	technology [tek'nɒlədʒɪ]	Technologie, Technik	20th-century *technology* has made life easier for most people.
	underwater ['ʌndə'wɔːtə]	Unterwasser-; unter Wasser	With an *underwater* camera you can take pictures *underwater.*
	past [pɑːst]	Vergangenheit	

The time

the past	second	week
the present	minute	month
the future	hour	year
	day	century

What time is it, please?
Excuse me, can you **tell me the time**, please?
It's **one o'clock/quarter past** one/**half past** one/**quarter to** two.
My watch **is right/is wrong/has stopped**.
I'm sorry **I'm late**./I hope **I'm** not too **early**.
It's time to eat/to go to bed/to go home/…

	(an) alligator ['ælɪgeɪtə]	(ein) Alligator, Krokodil(art)	 an *alligator*
	(to) found [faʊnd]	gründen, errichten	⚠ She *founded* a new school. = Sie *gründete* … She *found* the lost child. = Sie *fand* …
	southern ['sʌðən]	südlich, Süd-	Cornwall is the *southernmost* (= südlichste) part of England.
	point [pɔɪnt]	Punkt	
	Cuba ['kju:bə]	Kuba	
	bridge [brɪdʒ]	Brücke	
	You can drive for seven miles.	Man kann sieben Meilen (weit) fahren.	
10 T	**prince** [prɪns]	Prinz, Fürst	
	princess ['prɪnses]	Prinzessin, Fürstin	
	nation ['neɪʃn]	Nation, Volk; *hier:* Indianerstamm	In an Indian *nation,* the *chief* is the most important person.
	chief [tʃi:f]	Oberhaupt; Häuptling	⚠ Herrn Deans *Chef/in* = Mr Dean's *boss*
	daughter ['dɔ:tə]	Tochter	
	(to) fall in love (with sb.)	sich (in jn.) verlieben	
	eight-armed ['eɪt_'ɑ:md]	achtarmig, mit acht Armen	
	dragon ['drægən]	Drache	
	(to) **marry** ['mærɪ]	heiraten	Prince Charles *married* Princess Diana in 1981. They (got) *married* on July 29th.
	(to) **add** sth. (to sth.) [æd]	etwas (zu etwas) hinzufügen	The tea is too strong. I must *add* some hot water. Can I *add* something *to* what you've just said?
	shell [ʃel]	Muschel(schale)	You can sometimes find beautiful *shells* on the beach.
10 Ex [2]	*supper* ['sʌpə]	Abendessen, Abendbrot	The English Connors often *have* beans on toast *for supper.* They have it at 9 in the evening. The American Connors *have supper* when Mr and Mrs Connor come home from work at 5.30.
	If it's all right with Dad, …	Wenn es Vati recht ist, … Wenn Vati zustimmt, …	
	Spanish (adj., n.) ['spænɪʃ]	spanisch; Spanier/in; Spanisch	Do you know any *Spanish* words? – No, I don't. I can't speak *Spanish.*
	math (AE) [mæθ]	Mathe(matik)	= maths *(BE)*
	(to) explain sth. to sb.	jm. etwas erklären	Can you *explain to* me how the machine works? ⚠ *Niemals:* ~~Can you *explain* me …?~~
[3]	*(to) plan, is planning* [plæn]	planen	What are your plans for the weekend? – Oh, I *haven't planned* anything yet.
	suitable ['su:təbl]	passend, geeignet	Pullovers aren't *suitable* for hot weather.
	(to) go for a walk	einen Spaziergang machen, spazierengehen	You're tired? Well, if you *go for a walk,* you'll feel better.
	central ['sentrəl]	zentral (gelegen)	The Browns' flat is very near the centre of town. It's very *central.*
[5]	*(to) go for a swim*	schwimmen gehen	I don't want to go for a walk. Let's *go for a swim.*
	Sure. [ʃɔ:, ʃʊə]	Klar! Aber sicher!	May I borrow your knife? – *Sure.*
[10]	*interpreting*	(das) Dolmetschen	*Interpreting* can be very difficult.
	(to) interpret [ɪn'tɜ:prɪt]	dolmetschen	*Have* you ever *interpreted* for your parents on holiday?
	Europe ['jʊərəp]	Europa	
○11	*translation* [trænz'leɪʃn]	Übersetzung	Can you translate Penny's letter for me, please? – I can try, but I'm not very good at *translation.*

Countries

Britain (= England + Wales + Scotland)
Austria Cuba Denmark France
Germany India Italy Spain
the U.S.A. Yugoslavia

The family

grandmother	– grandfather	aunt	– uncle
mother	– father	cousin	– cousin
daughter	– son	sister	– brother

p. 136/7 ○ **A game: Lucky hands**

(to) throw the dice [daɪs]	würfeln	*(to) score (a point)* [skɔ:]	(einen Punkt) erzielen, bekommen

Alphabetical list of words (Books 1 + 2)

Die alphabetische Wortliste enthält den gesamten obligatorischen Wortschatz der Bände A1 und A2.
Fett gedruckte Wörter gehören zum produktiven, normal gedruckte zum rezeptiven Wortschatz. In Bundesländern, in denen keine Unterscheidung zwischen produktiv und rezeptiv verlangt wird, sind alle Wörter als produktiv anzusehen.
Die Fundstellenangaben beziehen sich auf Band A2, Wörter ohne Fundstellenangabe sind aus Band A1.

Intro 2 = Introduction, Abschnitt 2 · 1 A 1 = Unit 1, Acquisition, Abschnitt 1 · 2 T = Unit 2, Text · 3 Ex 4 = Unit 3, Exercise 4 · 4 S = Unit 4, Summary · 5 67 = Unit 5, page 67

adj. = adjective, adv. = adverb, sing. = singular, pl. = plural

Unregelmäßige *simple past-* und *past participle*-Formen erscheinen als getrennter Eintrag, von dem auf den Infinitiv des Verbs verwiesen wird, z. B. made → (to) make. Eine vollständige Liste aller unregelmäßigen Verbformen befindet sich auf den Seiten 181-182.

A

a	ein, eine
50p a week	50 Pence pro Woche
about	über
about	ungefähr, etwa; wegen
abroad	ins/im Ausland
accident 2 A 12	Unfall; Versehen
ache: (a) **stomach ache** 4 A 12	Magenschmerzen, Bauchschmerzen
(to) **ache** 4 A 12	weh tun, schmerzen
across	(quer) über, (quer) durch
activity	Projekt, Beschäftigung
(to) **add** (to) 10 T	hinzufügen (zu)
address 1 Ex 13	Adresse, Anschrift
adult 5 67	Erwachsene(r)
advert 3 Ex 11	Anzeige, Reklame
afraid: I'm afraid 6 Ex 11	leider
after	nach
after	hinter ... her
(to) **look after** 8 A 7	sich kümmern um, aufpassen auf
after 3 T	nachdem
afternoon	Nachmittag
Good afternoon.	Guten Tag!
in the afternoon(s)	am Nachmittag
on that afternoon 6 T	an jenem Nachmittag
this afternoon	heute nachmittag
again	wieder; noch (ein)mal
against 2 A 13	gegen
... ago 2 A 6	vor ...
not long ago 8 T	vor kurzem
(to) **agree** (with)	übereinstimmen (mit)
air 2 A 1	Luft
airport 7 Ex 6	Flughafen
all	alle; alles
all of you	ihr alle
all (the) winter 1 A 6	den ganzen Winter
all right	gut, in Ordnung
I'm all right.	Mir geht's gut.
It's all right for Liz. Intro 3	Liz ist gut dran. Liz hat's gut.
That's all right.	Schon gut. Macht nichts. Nichts zu danken.
alligator 10 129	Alligator
allowed: (to) **be allowed to** 9 A 5	(tun) dürfen
almost 5 A 4	fast, beinahe
along	entlang
already 4 A 13	schon, bereits
also 6 A 1	auch
not only ... but also 6 A 1	nicht nur ..., sondern auch
altogether 4 Ex 5	insgesamt, alles zusammen
always	immer
am	bin
ambulance 2 Ex 2	Krankenwagen
ambulance man 2 Ex 2	Sanitäter
America	Amerika
American	amerikanisch; Amerikaner/in
an	ein, eine
and	und
angry (with) 3 T	wütend, böse, zornig (auf)
animal	Tier
another	ein(e) andere(r, s); noch ein(e)
answer	Antwort
(to) **answer**	antworten, beantworten
(to) answer the (tele)phone 8 110	ans Telefon gehen
any: Do they need **any** cheese? 3 A 12	Brauchen sie Käse?
any? 3 A 12	(irgend)welche(r, s)?
not ... any 3 A 12	(gar) kein, keine; keins
anybody? 3 S	(irgend) jemand?
not ... anybody 3 S	niemand
anything? 3 S	(irgend) etwas?
Anything else?	Sonst noch etwas?
not ... anything 3 S	nichts
anywhere? 3 S	irgendwo(hin)?
not ... anywhere 3 S	nirgendwo(hin)
apple 3 A 11	Apfel
April	April
are	bist, sind, seid
(to) argue (about)	(sich) streiten, zanken (über/wegen)
ark: Noah's ark 8 A 1	die Arche Noah
arm 4 A 1	Arm
(to) **arrive**	ankommen, eintreffen
as (always) 5 A 5	wie (immer)
as 8 A 10	als, während
as 9 A 5	da, weil
(famous) **as** 9 A 3	(berühmt) als
(not) **as fast as** 4 A 5	(nicht) so schnell wie
(to) **ask**	fragen
(to) **ask a question**	eine Frage stellen
(to) **ask for**	bitten um
assistant	Verkäufer/in
astronaut 10 128	Astronaut/in
at: at Dave's/**my house**	bei Dave/mir (zu Hause)
at Easter 6 A 2	zu Ostern
at home	zu Hause
at last 6 A 2	endlich; schließlich
at least	mindestens; wenigstens, zumindest
at night 6 T	nachts, bei Nacht
at school	in der Schule
at the end	am Ende, am Schluß
at the moment	im Moment, im Augenblick; zur Zeit
at the weekend	am Wochenende
at 3 o'clock	um 3 Uhr
at 22 Albert Road 7 T	in der Albertstraße Nr. 22
at work	bei der Arbeit
good/bad at 5 A 3	gut/schlecht in
(to) **look at**	anschauen

ate → (to) **eat**	
attraction 10 128	Attraktion, Anziehungspunkt
August	August
aunt	Tante
Austria	Österreich
autumn	Herbst
in (the) autumn	im Herbst
away	weg, fort; entfernt
(to) **go away**	verreisen
(to) **throw away** 7 T	wegwerfen

B

back	zurück, wieder
backyard *(AE)* 10 A 2	Garten hinter dem Haus
bad	schlecht; schlimm
bad at 5 A 3	schlecht in
a bad cold 4 A 12	ein starker Schnupfen
(It's) too bad. 10 A 4	(Es ist) schade.
bag	Tasche, Beutel, Tüte
a mixed bag 2 Ex 16	eine bunte Mischung
balcony	Balkon
ball	Ball
banana 3 A 11	Banane
bank	Bank, Sparkasse
(to) bark	bellen
basket	Korb
bath 4 A 3	Bad
(to) **have a bath** 4 A 3	*(in der Wanne)* baden, ein Bad nehmen
bathroom	Bad(ezimmer)
(to) **be**	sein
(to) **be early** 8 A 5	zu früh kommen
(to) be frightened 6 T	Angst haben, sich fürchten
(to) **be fun** 9 A 2	Spaß machen
(to) be hungry	Hunger haben
(to) **be late**	zu spät kommen
(to) be lucky	Glück haben
(to) be missing 5 Ex 11	fehlen
(to) **be right** 1 A 6	recht haben
(to) be smelly 1 A 4	stinken
(to) be thirsty 3 A 4	Durst haben
(to) **be wrong** 1 A 6	nicht recht haben
What's on the sign? 8 A 6	Was steht auf dem Schild (geschrieben)?
beach	Strand
on the beach	am Strand
bean(s) 3 A 8	Bohne(n)
bear 8 A 1	Bär
(to) **beat** 5 A 4	schlagen, besiegen
beaten → (to) **beat**	
beautiful	(wunder)schön
became → (to) **become**	
because	weil
(to) **become** 9 A 5	werden
bed	Bett
in bed	im Bett
(to) **go to bed** 1 A 7	ins Bett gehen
bed and breakfast	Übernachtung mit Frühstück
bedroom	Schlafzimmer
beef: roast beef 3 A 8	Rinderbraten, Roastbeef
been → (to) **be**	
before	vor *(einem Zeitpunkt)*
before 3 A 10	bevor, ehe
before 6 A 9	vorher, schon einmal
began → (to) **begin**	
beggar 9 T	Bettler/in
(to) **begin** 9 A 1	beginnen, anfangen
begun → (to) **begin**	
behind	hinter
(to) **believe** (in) 6 A 10	glauben (an)
bell 2 A 3	Klingel; Glocke
bend 2 A 4	Kurve, Biegung
best	bester, beste, bestes
(to) like **best** 5 A 1	am liebsten mögen
better 4 A 6	besser
(to) like **better** 5 A 1	lieber mögen
between	zwischen
bicycle 2 A 1	Fahrrad
big	groß
bike	Fahrrad, Rad
by bike	mit dem Fahrrad
bird	Vogel
biro	Kugelschreiber, Kuli
birthday	Geburtstag
for sb.'s birthday	zum Geburtstag
Happy birthday (to you)!	Herzlichen Glückwunsch zum Geburtstag!
on your birthday	an deinem Geburtstag
When's your birthday?	Wann hast du Geburtstag?
biscuit	Keks
black	schwarz
blew → (to) **blow**	
blouse 7 A 1	Bluse
(to) **blow** 9 A 7	wehen, blasen
blown → (to) **blow**	
blue	blau
BMX (= Bicycle Motocross) 2 A 1	BMX
board	(Wand-)Tafel; Brett
boat 6 A 1	Boot; Schiff
by boat 6 A 2	mit dem Schiff
boiled 3 A 4	gekocht
book	Buch
boring	langweilig
(to) **borrow**	sich (aus)leihen, entleihen
boss 5 Ex 13	Chef/in, Boß
both 4 A 11	beide, beides
bottle	Flasche
bought → (to) **buy**	
box	Kiste, Schachtel
boy	Junge
brake 2 A 3	Bremse
(to) brake 2 A 11	bremsen
bread 3 A 4	Brot
(to) **break** 5 Ex 4	(zer)brechen; kaputtmachen, kaputtgehen
breakfast	Frühstück
for breakfast	zum Frühstück
(to) **have breakfast** 1 A 7	frühstücken
bridge 10 129	Brücke
bright 4 A 1	hell, leuchtend
(to) **bring** 6 A 10	(mit-, her)bringen
(Great) Britain	Großbritannien
British	britisch; Brite, Britin
broke → (to) **break**	
broken	kaputt; zer-, gebrochen
broken → (to) **break**	
brother	Bruder
brought → (to) **bring**	
brown	braun
(to) **brush** 3 A 1	bürsten
budgie	Wellensittich
bull 1 A 2	Bulle, Stier
bus	Bus
by bus	mit dem Bus
bus stop 8 Ex 4	Bushaltestelle
busy	beschäftigt
but	aber
not only ... but also 6 A 1	nicht nur ..., sondern auch
butter 3 A 4	Butter
(to) **buy**	kaufen
by: (to) **go by bike,** etc.	mit dem Rad usw. fahren
(to) go by 6 T	vergehen, vorübergehen
two by two 8 A 2	zu zweit, paarweise
Bye.	Wiedersehen! Tschüs!

C

café	Café; kleines Restaurant
cage	Käfig
cake	Kuchen
calculator	Taschenrechner
calendar	Kalender
call: (tele)phone call 8 110	Anruf, Telefongespräch

(to) **call** 10 128	nennen; (an)rufen
What do you call ...? 10 128	Wie nennt man ...?
came → (to) **come**	
camel 8 A 1	Kamel
camera	Fotoapparat, Kamera
camp 10 A 1	Lager
(to) camp 6 A 2	zelten, campen
camping	Camping, Zelten; Zelt-
camp site	Campingplatz, Zeltplatz
can	können, dürfen
can't = cannot	nicht können
canal 6 A 1	Kanal *(für Schiffe)*
canister 6 A 6	Kanister
canoe 6 A 1	Paddelboot; Kanu
capital	Hauptstadt
capital (letter)	Großbuchstabe
captain 9 A 7	Kapitän; Mannschaftskapitän
car	Auto, Wagen
by car	mit dem Auto
caravan	Wohnwagen
card 5 Ex 7	(Spiel-, Post-)Karte
careful	vorsichtig
careful 5 Ex 7	sorgfältig, sorgsam
carrot 3 A 4	Karotte, Möhre
(to) **carry**	tragen
cassette	Cassette
cassette-recorder	Cassettenrecorder
castle	Burg, Schloß
cat	Katze
catalogue 7 T	Katalog
(to) catch	fangen, erwischen
cathedral 6 83	Kathedrale, Dom
caught → (to) **catch**	
cave 9 A 3	Höhle
ceiling	Zimmerdecke
centre	(Stadt-)Mitte, (Stadt-)Zentrum; Sportzentrum
Information Centre 6 83	Auskunft, Verkehrsbüro
century 8 T	Jahrhundert
a sixteenth-century house 8 T	ein Haus aus dem 16. Jahrhundert
chair	Stuhl
cheap	billig
(to) check	(über)prüfen, kontrollieren
cheese 3 A 8	Käse
cheque 7 A 3	(Bank-)Scheck
chess 5 A 11	Schach
chewing gum 3 T	Kaugummi
chicken 1 A 2	Huhn; (Brat-)Hähnchen
chief 10 T	Oberhaupt; Häuptling
child, *pl.* **children**	Kind
chimp 8 A 1	Schimpanse
chips 3 A 8	Pommes frites

chocolate 3 A 11	Schokolade
(to) **choose** 5 A 10	(aus)wählen, aussuchen
chose → (to) **choose**	
chosen → (to) **choose**	
church	Kirche
(to) **go to church**	in die Kirche gehen
cinema	Kino
city	Stadt, Großstadt
class	Klasse
clean 4 A 2	sauber
(to) **clean**	putzen, reinigen
clever	klug, schlau
(to) climb	klettern, steigen
clock	(Wand-, Stand-, Turm-)Uhr
... o'clock	... Uhr
closed	geschlossen, zu
clothes *(pl.)* 2 A 2	Kleidung(sstücke)
cloud 9 T	Wolke
club	Verein, Klub
coach 6 A 2	Reisebus
by coach 6 A 2	mit dem Reisebus
coast	Küste
on the coast	an der Küste
coat 7 A 8	Mantel, Jacke
cocoa 3 A 4	Kakao
coffee	Kaffee
coin	Münze
cold	kalt
cold: (to) have a cold	Schnupfen haben, erkältet sein
a bad cold 4 A 12	ein starker Schnupfen
(to) **collect**	sammeln
(to) **collect** 7 A 7	abholen, einsammeln
colour	Farbe
What colour is/are ...?	Welche Farbe hat/haben ...?
combination exercise	Kombinationsübung, Zuordnungsübung
(to) **come**	kommen, mitkommen
Come here.	Komm(t) her!
(to) **come out** 4 A 3	herauskommen, hinauskommen
comfortable 3 Ex 11	bequem, gemütlich
comic	Comic-Heft
comparison 4 Ex 4	Vergleich
(to) make comparisons 4 Ex 4	Vergleiche machen, vergleichen
competition 5 A 8	Wettbewerb, Wettkampf; Konkurrenz
(to) complete	vervollständigen
confident 5 A 4	(selbst)sicher, selbstbewußt, zuversichtlich
(to) **cook**	kochen, zubereiten
Cornish 9 A 4	kornisch, aus Cornwall; die kornische Sprache
Cornishman/Cornishwoman 9 A 5	Einwohner/in von Cornwall

correct	richtig, korrekt
(to) correct	berichtigen, verbessern, korrigieren
could 9 A 6	konnte(n)
country 1 A 1	Land
in the country 1 A 1	auf dem Land
country 3 A 8	Land; Staat
countryside 9 A 2	(ländliche) Gegend, Landschaft
course: of course	natürlich
cousin	Vetter, Kusine
cow 1 A 2	Kuh
cowshed 1 A 6	Kuhstall
crane 8 Ex 2	Kran
(to) **crash (into)** 2 A 11	zusammenstoßen (mit), hineinfahren (in); verunglücken
crazy	verrückt, wahnsinnig
(to) be crazy about	ganz verrückt sein auf
crisps	Kartoffelchips
Cuba 10 129	Kuba
cup	Tasse
cupboard	Schrank
(to) **cut** 10 A 1	(ab)schneiden
cycling 5 A 2	Radfahren, Radsport

D

dad	Vati, Papa, Papi
danger 8 A 10	Gefahr
dangerous 2 A 2	gefährlich
dark 6 A 10	dunkel, finster
date	Datum
What date is it (today)?	Der Wievielte ist heute?
daughter 10 T	Tochter
day	Tag
the day before yesterday 7 Ex 13	vorgestern
dead 6 T	tot
dear	liebe, lieber, liebes
Dear Sir or Madam, ... 8 110	Sehr geehrte Damen und Herren, ...
December	Dezember
(to) **decide** 3 Ex 1	beschließen, (sich) entscheiden
deck: on deck 9 A 7	auf Deck, an Deck
deep	tief
Denmark 9 A 1	Dänemark
desk	Schreibtisch, Schülertisch
dialogue	Dialog
did → (to) **do**	
(to) **die**	sterben
(to) **die out** 8 A 10	aussterben
different (from)	verschieden, unterschiedlich; anders (als)

difficult 5 T	schwierig, schwer
dining-room	Eßzimmer
dirty 1 A 4	schmutzig, dreckig
disabled 5 A 8	(körper)behindert
dishes	Geschirr
(to) **do**	tun, machen
(to) do (50 metres) 5 T	(50 Meter) schaffen
(to) **do a test** 4 T	eine Arbeit schreiben, eine Prüfung machen
(to) **do homework**	die Hausaufgabe(n)/ Schularbeiten machen
(to) do magic	zaubern
(to) **do sports** 5 A 2	Sport treiben
(to) **do the housework**	die Haus(halts)arbeit machen
doctor	Arzt, Ärztin
dog	Hund
done → (to) **do**	
door	Tür
down 9 T	herunter, hinunter; herab, hinab
(to) pull down 6 T	abreißen, niederreißen
(to) **sit down**	sich setzen
(to) **write down** 3 A 10	aufschreiben
downstairs	unten *(im Haus)*; nach unten
Dr = Doctor	Dr. = Doktor
dragon 10 T	Drache
drank → (to) **drink**	
(to) draw	zeichnen
drawn → (to) draw	
dream	Traum
dress 7 A 1	Kleid
drew → (to) draw	
drink	Getränk
(to) **drink**	trinken
(to) **drive** 1 A 3	(Auto) fahren
driven → (to) **drive**	
driver 2 Ex 2	(Auto-)Fahrer/in; Lokführer/in
drove → (to) **drive**	
(to) drown 9 A 7	ertrinken, ertränken
drunk → (to) **drink**	
(to) dry the dishes	(Geschirr) abtrocknen
during 6 A 2	während

E

ear 4 A 2	Ohr
early 8 A 5	früh, (früh)zeitig
(to) **be early** 8 A 5	zu früh kommen
east (of)	östlich (von); Ost-; (nach) Osten
Easter 6 A 2	Ostern, Oster-
at Easter 6 A 2	zu Ostern
easy 5 A 4	leicht, einfach
(to) **eat**	essen
eaten → (to) **eat**	
e.g.	z. B. (= zum Beispiel)
egg 3 A 4	Ei
elephant 3 T	Elefant
else: Anything else?	Sonst noch etwas?
empty 6 T	leer
end: at the end	am Ende, am Schluß
England	England
English	englisch; Englisch; Engländer/in
in English	auf englisch
(to) **enjoy** 5 A 8	genießen, Spaß haben an, gern haben/tun
enough 1 A 6	genug
envelope 1 Ex 13	Briefumschlag
even 2 A 4	sogar, selbst
even worse 7 Ex 13	(sogar) noch schlimmer
evening	Abend
in the evening(s)	abends
on a cold evening 6 T	an einem kalten Abend
this evening	heute abend
ever 6 A 9	je(mals), schon mal
for ever 10 128	für immer, ewig
not ever 6 A 9	nie
every	jeder, jede, jedes
everybody 2 A 2	jeder(mann), alle
everything	alles
example	Beispiel
for example = e.g.	zum Beispiel = z. B.
exciting 1 T	aufregend, spannend
Excuse me, ...	Entschuldigen Sie, ...
exercise	Übung(saufgabe)
exercise book	Heft, Schulheft
expensive	teuer
(to) **explain**	erklären, erläutern
eye 4 A 2	Auge

F

face 2 T	Gesicht
factory 3 T	Fabrik
(to) **fall (off)** 2 A 2	(herunter)fallen
(to) fall in love (with) 10 T	sich verlieben (in)
fallen → (to) **fall**	
false	falsch, unecht
family	Familie
famous	berühmt
fantastic	phantastisch, toll
farm	Bauernhof, Farm
farmer 1 A 2	Bauer, Bäuerin; Farmer/in
farmhouse 6 Ex 3	Bauernhaus
fast *(adj./adv.)* 2 T; 5 A 6	schnell
fat 7 A 2	dick
father	Vater
favourite	Lieblings-
February	Februar
fed → (to) feed	
(to) feed	füttern
feeding-time 8 A 9	Fütterungszeit
(to) **feel** 4 A 13	(sich) fühlen
fell → (to) **fall**	
felt → (to) **feel**	
felt-tip	Filzstift
(to) **fetch**	holen; abholen
a few 1 A 2	ein paar, einige (wenige)
field 1 A 1	Feld, Wiese, Weide; (Sport-)Platz
in the field(s) 1 A 1	auf dem Feld
(to) **fill** (with) 3 T	füllen, voll machen (mit)
(to) fill in	einsetzen
(to) **find**	finden
(to) find out 7 T	herausfinden, erfahren
fine 4 A 13	gut, fein, schön
finger 4 A 1	Finger
(to) **finish**	enden, aufhören (mit); beenden, fertigmachen
(to) finish 2 T	ins Ziel kommen
finish line 2 T	Ziellinie
fire 6 A 5	Feuer, Brand
first	(zu)erst, zunächst
(to) be first 5 Ex 11	der erste sein, als erster (an)kommen
fish (*sing.* and *pl.*) 3 A 8	Fisch, Fische
fishing 9 A 3	Fischen, Fischerei; Fischer-
fishing: (to) go **fishing** 10 A 1	fischen, angeln (gehen)
(to) **fit** 7 A 2	*(in der Größe)* passen
flat	Wohnung
flat 6 A 1	flach, eben
flew → (to) **fly**	
floor	Fußboden
flower 10 128	Blume, Blüte
flown → (to) **fly**	
(to) **fly**	fliegen
fog 9 T	(dicker) Nebel
folk song 6 A 10	Volkslied, Folksong
(to) **follow** 9 A 6	folgen; verfolgen, nachfolgen
following	folgend
food	Essen, Lebensmittel, Nahrung; Futter
foot, *pl.* feet 2 A 13	Fuß
1 foot 9 A 3	1 Fuß *(= 30,5 cm)*

football	Fußball
for	für
for a long time 2 Ex 4	lange Zeit
for breakfast, etc.	zum Frühstück usw.
for ever 10 128	für immer, ewig
for example	zum Beispiel
for four weeks 2 Ex 4	vier Wochen (lang)
for hours 2 Ex 4	stundenlang
for sale 8 110	zu verkaufen
for sb.'s birthday	zum Geburtstag
for seven miles 10 129	sieben Meilen weit
for the first time 8 A 7	zum ersten Mal
(to) **ask for**	bitten um
(to) **leave for** … 10 A 4	abfahren nach …
(to) **look for** 2 A 13	suchen
(to) **pay for** 7 A 4	bezahlen
(to) **wait for**	warten auf
good for 5 Ex 4	gut gegen
fork 3 A 2	Gabel
form	Form
found → (to) **find**	
(to) found 10 129	gründen, errichten
fountain	Springbrunnen
France	Frankreich
free 8 T	frei; kostenlos
free time	Freizeit
French	französisch; Franzose, Französin; Französisch
fresh 3 A 4	frisch
Friday	Freitag
friend	Freund, Freundin
frightened: (to) **be frightened** (of) 6 T	Angst haben (vor), sich fürchten (vor)
from	aus; von
from now on	von jetzt an, ab jetzt
I'm from …	Ich bin/komme aus …
Where are you **from?**	Wo kommst du her?
in front of 2 A 11	vor
fruit 3 A 11	Obst, Früchte
full (of) 3 A 6	voll (mit/von)
fun: (to) **be fun** 9 A 2	Spaß machen
funny	lustig, komisch, witzig
funny 4 A 11	komisch, seltsam
furniture *(sing.)*	Möbel
future 8 A 10	Zukunft
in future 8 A 10	künftig, ab jetzt
future 10 129	(zu)künftig

G

game	Spiel
garage	Garage
garden	Garten
gate 8 T	Tor
gave → (to) **give**	
German	deutsch; Deutsche, Deutscher; Deutsch
Germany	Deutschland
(to) **get**	bekommen, kriegen
(to) **get** (to) 1 Ex 13	gelangen, (hin)kommen
(to) **get in** (the train)	(in den Zug) einsteigen
(to) **get into trouble** 9 A 10	in Schwierigkeiten geraten
(to) **get married** (to) 10 A 3	(sich ver)heiraten (mit)
(to) **get out** (of the train)	(aus dem Zug) aussteigen
(to) **get up**	aufstehen
ghost 6 A 10	Geist, Gespenst
giraffe 8 A 1	Giraffe
girl	Mädchen
girlfriend 10 A 2	Freundin *(eines Jungen oder Mannes)*
Girl Scout *(AE)* 10 A 1	Pfadfinderin *(in den USA)*
(to) **give**	geben; schenken
given → (to) **give**	
(to) **go**	gehen; fahren
Go! 2 T	Los!
(to) **go away**	verreisen
(to) go by 6 T	ver-, vorübergehen
(to) **go fishing,** etc. 10 A 1	fischen usw. gehen
(to) **go home**	nach Hause gehen
(to) **go in** 8 A 2	hineingehen
(to) go on	weitermachen
(to) go on a bus tour 10 128	eine Bus(rund)fahrt machen
(to) go on a guided tour 9 A 3	eine Führung (mit)machen
(to) **go on a trip** 6 A 2	eine Reise/Fahrt machen
(to) **go on holiday**	in Urlaub fahren, Ferien machen
(to) **go out** (with) 8 Ex 8	ausgehen (mit)
(to) **go to bed** 1 A 7	ins Bett gehen
(to) **go to school**	zur Schule gehen
I'm going to write. 5 A 10	Ich werde/will schreiben. Ich habe vor/habe die Absicht zu schreiben.
gold 9 T	Gold; gold(en)
gone → (to) **go**	
good	gut
good at 5 A 3	gut in, geschickt in
good for 5 Ex 4	gut gegen
Good afternoon.	Guten Tag!
Good morning.	Guten Morgen!/Tag!
Goodbye.	Auf Wiedersehen!
gorilla 8 A 1	Gorilla
got → (to) **get, have got**	
grandfather	Großvater
grandmother	Großmutter
grandpa 10 A 2	Opa, Großvater
grandparents	Großeltern
grass	Gras
grave 6 T	Grab
great	großartig, prima, toll
green	grün
grew → (to) **grow**	
grey	grau
ground 9 A 3	(Erd-)Boden
group	Gruppe
(to) **grow** 7 A 2	wachsen
grown → (to) **grow**	
(to) **guess** 1 Ex 2	(er)raten
guest	Gast
guest house	Pension, Gästehaus
guided: (to) go on a guided tour 9 A 3	eine Führung (mit)machen
guitar	Gitarre
(to) **play the guitar**	Gitarre spielen
gymnastics 5 A 2	Turnen, Gymnastik

H

had → **have got,** (to) **have**	
had to 9 A 9	mußte(n)
hair *(sing.)* 3 A 1	Haar, Haare
hairstyle 8 Ex 4	Frisur
half a mile 9 A 3	eine halbe Meile
half past ten	halb elf (= 10.30)
hall 6 T	Flur, Diele; Halle, Saal
Hallo.	= **Hello.**
ham 3 A 8	Schinken
ham salad 3 A 8	Schinken mit Salat
hamster	Hamster
hand 3 A 1	Hand
handball 5 A 2	Handball
handbook 8 T	Handbuch
handbrake 8 T	Handbremse
handlebars *(pl.)* 2 A 3	Lenkstange
(to) **happen** 1 A 5	geschehen, passieren
(to) **happen to** 6 Ex 1	passieren, geschehen mit
happy	glücklich, froh
Happy birthday (to you)!	Herzlichen Glückwunsch zum Geburtstag!
hard *(adj./adv.)* 5 A 6	schwer; hart; heftig, mit aller Kraft
hat 7 A 8	Hut
(to) **hate**	hassen, gar nicht mögen

(to) **have** 1 A 7	haben; essen, trinken
(to) **have a bath** 4 A 3	*(in der Wanne)* baden, ein Bad nehmen
Have a good time!	Viel Spaß! Viel Vergnügen!
(to) have a nice time 3 Ex 4	eine schöne Zeit/viel Spaß haben
(to) have a picnic 3 A 6	ein Picknick machen
(to) have a race 2 A 1	ein Rennen veranstalten
(to) **have a shower** 4 A 3	(sich) duschen
(to) **have a wash** 4 A 3	sich waschen
(to) **have breakfast** 1 A 7	frühstücken
(to) **have lunch** 3 A 9	(zu) Mittag essen
(to) **have tea** 3 A 9	Abendbrot essen, zu Abend essen
(to) **have to** 9 A 9	(tun) müssen
have got	haben, besitzen
he	er
head 4 A 1	Kopf
a **headache** 4 A 12	Kopfschmerzen, Kopfweh
(to) **hear**	hören
(to) hear of 7 T	hören von
heard → (to) **hear**	
Hello. 10 A 4	Hallo! (Guten) Tag!
(to) **say hello (to)** 10 A 4	grüßen
helmet 2 A 2	Helm
help	Hilfe
(to) **help** (with)	helfen (bei)
her	ihr, ihre; ihr, sie
here	hier
Come here.	Komm(t) her!
Here you are.	Hier bitte. Bitte sehr.
hers 8 A 5	ihre(r, s)
Hi. 10 A 3	Hallo!
hid → (to) **hide**	
hidden → (to) **hide**	
(to) **hide** (from) 8 A 7	(sich) verstecken (vor)
high 2 A 3	hoch
hill	Hügel, (kleiner) Berg
him	ihm, ihn
hippo 8 A 1	Flußpferd, Nilpferd
(to) hire 6 A 1	*(Boot, Auto, Saal)* mieten, leihen
his	sein, seine
his 8 A 5	seine(r, s)
history	Geschichte
(to) **hit** 9 A 6	schlagen, treffen
hobby	Hobby
holiday(s) 5 T	Ferien, Urlaub
(to) **go/be on holiday**	in Urlaub fahren/sein, Ferien machen/haben
home	Heim, Zuhause
at home	zu Hause, daheim
(to) **go home**	nach Hause gehen
homework: (to) **do homework**	die Hausaufgabe(n) machen
(to) **hope** Intro 1	hoffen
horse 1 A 2	Pferd
hospital	Krankenhaus, Klinik
in/to hospital 5 A 1	im/ins Krankenhaus
hostel: youth hostel	Jugendherberge
hot 3 A 9	heiß, warm
hotel	Hotel
hour	Stunde
for hours 2 Ex 4	stundenlang
house	Haus
at Dave**'s/my house**	bei Dave/mir zu Hause
housework: (to) **do the housework**	die Haus(halts)arbeit machen
how	wie
How are you?	Wie geht es dir?
How many?	Wie viele?
How much?	Wieviel?
How much is ...?	Was kostet ...?
How old are you?	Wie alt bist du?
huge	sehr groß, riesig
hungry	hungrig
(to) be hungry	Hunger haben
hurrah! 8 A 2	hurra!
hurry: (to) be **in a hurry** 4 A 3	in Eile sein, es eilig haben
(to) hurry up	sich beeilen
husband	(Ehe-)Mann

I

I	ich
ice-cream 8 A 5	(Speise-)Eis
ice-skating 5 A 2	Schlittschuhlaufen
idea	Idee, Einfall
if 10 A 2	wenn, falls
... if ...	..., ob ...
ill	krank
(to) **imagine** 4 Ex 12	sich vorstellen; sich einbilden
Just imagine. 7 A 8	Denk dir nur! Stell dir mal vor!
important 1 Ex 13	wichtig, bedeutend
in	in
in a hurry 4 A 3	in Eile
in a minute	gleich, sofort
in bed	im Bett
in different **ways** 3 A 1	auf verschiedene Weise(n)
in English	auf englisch
in future 8 A 10	künftig, ab jetzt
in January	im Januar
in my opinion 4 Ex 12	meiner Meinung nach
in 1980 7 S	(im Jahre) 1980
in ruins 9 A 3	zerstört
in the country 1 A 1	auf dem Land
in the field(s) 1 A 1	auf dem Feld
in the morning(s)	am Morgen, morgens
in the picture/photo	auf dem Bild/Foto
in (the) spring	im Frühling/Frühjahr
in the street	auf der Straße
in town 5 A 1	in der (Innen-)Stadt
interested in 5 A 2	interessiert an
(to go) **in** 8 A 2	hinein(gehen)
(to) **believe in** 6 A 10	glauben an
(to) fill in	einsetzen
(to) **get in** (the train)	(in den Zug) einsteigen
(to) put in 5 Ex 9	einsetzen
(to) **take part in** 5 A 8	teilnehmen an, mitmachen bei
India	Indien
Indian 10 128	indianisch, Indianer/in
information *(sing.)* 7 Ex 2	Information(en), Auskunft
Information Centre 6 83	Auskunft, Verkehrsbüro
in front of 2 A 11	vor
inside (the house)	innen/drinnen (im Haus); nach drinnen
instrument 5 A 11	Instrument
interested (in) 5 A 2	interessiert (an)
interesting	interessant
international 5 A 1	international
interview	Interview
into	in ... (hinein)
introduction	Einführung
invention 9 A 9	Erfindung
invitation	Einladung
(to) **invite** 6 Ex 11	einladen
is	ist
island	Insel
it	es (er, sie; ihn, sie)
Italy	Italien
its	sein, seine; ihr, ihre

J

jacket 7 A 1	Jacke, Jackett
jam 3 A 4	Marmelade, Konfitüre
January	Januar
Japanese	japanisch; Japaner, Japanerin; Japanisch
job	Beruf, Arbeit, Job; Aufgabe

judo 5 A 2	Judo
juice	Saft
July	Juli
(to) **jump** 2 T	springen
June	Juni
junior 5 67	Junioren-, Jugend-
just	nur, bloß
Just imagine. 7 A 8	Denk dir nur! Stell dir mal vor!
just 6 A 8	gerade (eben), soeben

K

kangaroo 8 A 1	Känguruh
Keep moving. 4 A 1	Mach(t) immer weiter!
keeper 8 A 7	Wärter/in, Wächter/in
ketchup 10 A 2	Ketchup
kilo 5 A 7	Kilo
kilometre	Kilometer
king	König
kit: a repair kit	Flickzeug
kitchen	Küche
knew → (to) **know**	
knife, *pl.* **knives** 3 A 2	Messer
(to) **knock** 6 T	(an)klopfen; schlagen, stoßen
(to) **know**	kennen; wissen
you know	weißt du, nämlich
known → (to) **know**	

L

ladder	Leiter
lain → (to) **lie**	
lake	(ein) See
lamp	Lampe
land 6 T	(festes) Land, Boden
(to) **land** 3 A 2	landen *(Flugzeug)*; anlegen *(Schiff)*
language 9 A 4	Sprache
large 8 T	groß, umfangreich
last 2 A 5	letzte(r, s)
last night 2 A 7	gestern abend; letzte Nacht
last Saturday 2 A 5	(am) letzten Samstag
(to) be last 5 Ex 11	der letzte sein, als letzter (an)kommen
at last 6 A 2	endlich, schließlich
late	spät
(to) **be late**	zu spät kommen
(to) **laugh**	lachen
launching pad 10 128	Abschußrampe *(für Raketen)*
lay → (to) **lie**	
lazy	faul, träge
(to) **learn**	lernen
least: at least	mindestens; wenigstens, zumindest
(to) **leave** (a place)	weggehen, abfahren (von); verlassen
(to) **leave for** … 10 A 4	abfahren nach …
(to) **leave school** 5 A 1	von der Schule abgehen
(to) **leave** 9 T	lassen; zurücklassen, liegen/stehen lassen
left	linke(r, s), nach links
on the left	links, auf der linken Seite
left → (to) **leave**	
leg 4 A 1	Bein
legend 10 128	Legende, Sage
lemonade	Limonade
lesson	Unterrichtsstunde
(to) **let** 8 Ex 4	(zu)lassen
Let me see, … 1 Ex 8	Warte mal! Laß mich mal überlegen!
let's = let us	laß(t) uns
Let's see. 4 T	Wollen mal sehen.
letter	Brief; Buchstabe
liberty	Freiheit
library	Bibliothek, Bücherei
(to) **lie**	liegen
life, *pl.* **lives** 9 A 3	(das) Leben
lifeboat 9 A 10	Rettungsboot
lifeline 9 A 9	Rettungsleine
(to) lift	heben, hochheben
light 2 A 3	Licht, Lampe
traffic lights *(pl.)* 2 Ex 13	(Verkehrs-)Ampel
like 1 Ex 2	wie
like this 6 Ex 13	so, auf diese Weise; folgendermaßen
like that 5 A 1	so
things **like that** 5 A 1	so etwas, solche Sachen
What's it like? 2 Ex 15	Wie ist es? Wie sieht es aus?
(to) **like**	mögen, gern haben
(to) like **better/ best** 5 A 1	lieber/am liebsten mögen
How do you like …? 1 T	Wie gefällt dir …? Wie findest du …?
I'd like	ich möchte (haben)
I'd like to	ich möchte (tun)
line	Zeile; Linie
lion 8 A 1	Löwe
list	Liste
(to) **listen** (to)	zu-, anhören
listening comprehension	Hörverstehen
little	klein, jung
(to) **live**	wohnen, leben
lively	lebhaft
living-room	Wohnzimmer
(to) load 6 A 2	(auf)laden, (be)laden
(to) **lock** 9 T	ab-, zuschließen
long	lang
not long ago 8 T	vor kurzem
(to) **look**	sehen, schauen
(to) **look after** 8 A 7	sich kümmern um, aufpassen auf
(to) **look at**	anschauen
(to) **look for** 2 A 13	suchen
(to) **look** 7 Ex 5	aussehen
(to) **lose** 5 A 4	verlieren
lost → (to) **lose**	
a lot (of …) 2 A 1	viele, viel, eine Menge
lots (of …)	viele, viel, eine Menge
loud	laut
Love, …	Viele liebe Grüße von …
(to) fall in love (with) 10 T	sich verlieben (in)
(to) **love** 5 Ex 10	lieben, sehr mögen, sehr gern haben
I'd love (to) 6 Ex 11	ich hätte (liebend) gern; ich würde sehr gern (tun)
lovely 3 A 6	schön, herrlich, hübsch
low 2 A 3	niedrig, tief
lucky: (to) be lucky	Glück haben
lunch	Mittagessen
for lunch	zum Mittagessen
(to) **have lunch** 3 A 9	(zu) Mittag essen
What's for lunch? 3 A 9	Was gibt's zum Mittagessen?

M

machine 3 T	Maschine
madam 8 110	meine Dame *(höfliche Anrede)*
Dear Sir or Madam, … 8 110	Sehr geehrte Damen und Herren, …
made → (to) **make**	
magazine	Zeitschrift, Illustrierte
magic	Zauberkunst, Magie
(to) do magic	zaubern
magician	Zauberer
(to) **make**	machen, bauen
(to) **make tea**	Tee kochen
man, *pl.* **men**	Mann
many	viele
map	Landkarte, Stadtplan
marathon 5 T	Marathon
March	März
market 6 83	Markt
(to) **marry** 10 T	heiraten
(to) **get married** (to) 10 A 3	(sich ver)heiraten (mit)
match	Spiel, Wettkampf
maths 7 Ex 13	Mathe(matik)
may	(tun) dürfen
May	Mai

me	mir, mich
(It wasn't) **me.** 2 T	Ich (war's nicht).
taller than **me** 4 A 6	größer als ich
meal	Mahlzeit, Essen
(to) **mean**	bedeuten
(to) **mean** 4 T	meinen (= sagen wollen)
meant → (to) **mean**	
mechanic	Mechaniker/in
medicine 4 A 13	Medizin, Arznei
(to) **meet**	(sich) treffen, kennenlernen
meeting 2 A 5	Treffen, Versammlung; Veranstaltung
member (of) 5 A 1	Mitglied (in, von)
merry 4 A 1	froh, fröhlich
message 8 Ex 10	Nachricht, Botschaft
met → (to) **meet**	
metre 5 T	Meter
mile	Meile
miles per hour = mph 4 Ex 4	Meilen pro Stunde
milk 1 A 6	Milch
(to) milk 1 A 6	melken
million	Million
mine 8 A 5	meine(r, s)
mine 9 A 3	Bergwerk
minute	Minute
in a minute	gleich, sofort
Wait a minute. 4 T	Einen Augenblick! Moment mal!
Miss ...	Fräulein/Frau ...
miss 3 T	*häufige Anrede für eine Lehrerin in Großbritannien*
missing	fehlend
(to) be missing 5 Ex 11	fehlen
mistake 4 Ex 1	Fehler, Irrtum
mixed 6 Ex 14	ge-, vermischt
a mixed bag 2 Ex 16	eine bunte Mischung
model	Modell, Modell-
modern	modern
mom *(AE)* 10 A 3	Mutti, Mama, Mami
moment	Moment, Augenblick
at the moment	im Moment, im Augenblick; zur Zeit
Monday	Montag
on Monday(s)	montags, am Montag
money	Geld
monkey 8 A 1	Affe
monster	Ungeheuer, Monster
month	Monat
moon 6 A 10	Mond
more (than)	mehr (als)
more exciting 4 A 7	aufregender

some more 1 Ex 2	noch einige/etwas
no more ... 8 T	keine ... mehr
morning	Morgen, Vormittag
Good morning.	Guten Morgen! Guten Tag!
in the morning(s)	am Morgen, morgens
on Monday morning(s) 6 T	am Montag morgen
this morning	heute morgen
tomorrow morning	morgen früh
(the) most 4 S	(der/die/das) meiste, die meisten; am meisten
(the) most exciting 4 A 7	(der/die/das) aufregendste; am aufregendsten
mother	Mutter
motorhome *(AE)* 10 A 1	Wohnmobil, Campingbus
mountain(s)	Berg; Gebirge
mouse, *pl.* mice	Maus
mouth 4 A 2	Mund
(to) **move** 4 A 1	(sich) bewegen
Keep moving. 4 A 1	Mach(t) immer weiter!
mph = miles per hour 4 Ex 4	Meilen pro Stunde
Mr ...	Herr ...
Mrs ...	Frau ...
much	viel
(to like) **very much** 5 A 1	sehr (gern mögen)
Thank you very much. 1 Ex 13	Vielen Dank.
mud 2 A 4	Schlamm, Matsch
mum	Mutti, Mama, Mami
museum	Museum
music	Musik
must	(tun) müssen
mustn't 4 A 13	nicht (tun) dürfen
my	mein, meine

N

name	Name
What's your name?	Wie ist dein Name? Wie heißt du?
narrow 9 A 3	eng, schmal
nation 10 T	Nation, Volk; Stamm
national	national, National-
near	in der Nähe von, nahe
neck 4 A 2	Hals
(to) **need** 2 A 10	brauchen, benötigen
needn't 4 A 13	nicht (zu tun) brauchen, nicht (tun) müssen
neighbour 10 A 2	Nachbar/in
nervous(ly) 5 A 4; 5 A 5	ängstlich, aufgeregt, nervös

net 5 A 6	Netz
never	nie, niemals
new	neu
newspaper	Zeitung
next	nächste(r, s)
next Monday	(am) nächsten Montag
next to	neben
nice	nett, schön, hübsch
night	Nacht, (später) Abend
at night 6 T	nachts, bei Nacht
last night 2 A 7	gestern abend; letzte Nacht
on the first night 6 T	in der ersten Nacht
no	nein; kein, keine
no more ... 8 T	keine ... mehr
Noah's ark 8 A 1	die Arche Noah
nobody 6 T	niemand
nod (of the head) 4 A 1	Kopfnicken
noise 9 T	Lärm, Geräusch
noisy	laut, lärmend
north (of) 6 A 1	nördlich (von); Nord-; (nach) Norden
nose 4 A 2	Nase
not	nicht
not ... any 3 A 12	(gar) kein, keine; keins
not ... anybody 3 S	niemand
not ... anything 3 S	nichts
not ... anywhere 3 S	nirgends, nirgendwohin
not ever 6 A 9	nie
not ... yet 6 A 6	noch nicht
note	(Geld-)Schein
nothing	nichts
notice 5 A 10	Anschlag; Mitteilung, Hinweis(schild)
(to) **notice** 10 128	(be)merken, beachten
November	November
now	jetzt, nun
number	Zahl, Nummer; Anzahl

O

0	null *(in Telefonnummern)*
... o'clock	... Uhr
October	Oktober
Odd man out!	Welches Wort paßt hier nicht?
of: bottle **of** lemonade	Flasche Limonade
both **of** them 4 A 11	sie beide, alle beide
(to) hear of 7 T	hören von
nice of you 1 Ex 5	nett von dir

the name **of** the street	der Name (von) der Straße
(to) **think of**	denken an
typical of 9 A 3	typisch für
of course	natürlich
off: (to) **fall off** 2 A 2	herunterfallen
(to) **offer** 6 T	anbieten
office	Büro
often	oft
oil 2 A 8	Öl
OK = okay	gut, in Ordnung
I'm OK.	Mir geht's gut.
old	alt
omelette 3 A 8	Omelett
on	auf; an
on a **visit to** …	bei einem Besuch in …
on holiday	auf Urlaub, in den Ferien
on Monday(s)	montags, am Montag
on Monday morning(s) 6 T	am Montag morgen
on my way to	auf dem Weg/unterwegs nach
on October 12th	am 12. Oktober
on the beach	am Strand
on the coast	an der Küste
on the first night 6 T	in der ersten Nacht
on the left/right	links/rechts
on the phone	am Telefon
on the radio; on TV	im Radio; im Fernsehen
on the River Thames 1 A 1	an der Themse
on your birthday	an deinem Geburtstag
(to) go on	weitermachen
(to) go on a bus tour 10 128	eine Bus(rund)fahrt machen
(to) go on a guided tour 9 A 3	eine Führung (mit)machen
(to) **go on a trip** 6 A 2	eine Reise/Fahrt machen, einen Ausflug machen
(to) **put on** 7 A 5	*(Kleidung)* anziehen
(to) try on 7 A 4	anprobieren
from now on	von jetzt an, ab jetzt
one: the blue **one**; the blue **ones** 4 A 10	der/die/das blaue; die blauen
only	nur
not only … but also 6 A 1	nicht nur …, sondern auch
only one week old 8 T	erst eine Woche alt
the **only** 2 Ex 15	der/die/das einzige, die einzigen
onto 9 A 6	auf … (hinauf)
open	offen, geöffnet, auf
(to) **open**	öffnen, aufmachen
opinion 4 Ex 12	Meinung
in my opinion 4 Ex 12	meiner Meinung nach
opposite (of)	Gegenteil (von)
or	oder
orange	orange(farben); Apfelsine, Orange
order 2 Ex 3	Reihenfolge, (An-)Ordnung
(the) other	(der/die/das) andere
our	unser, unsere
ours 8 A 5	unsere(r, s)
out *(adv.)* 6 T	hinaus, heraus; draußen
out of	aus (… heraus/hinaus)
(to) **come out** 4 A 3	herauskommen, hinauskommen
(to) **die out** 8 A 10	aussterben
(to) find out 7 T	herausfinden, erfahren
(to) **get out** (of the train)	(aus dem Zug) aussteigen
(to) **go out** (with) 8 Ex 8	ausgehen (mit)
outside (the house)	draußen (vor dem Haus); nach draußen
over	über
over there 7 Ex 13	dort drüben, da drüben
(to) overtake 2 A 11	überholen
overtaken → (to) overtake	
overtook → (to) overtake	
own 6 A 1	eigene(r, s)
I pay for **my own** clothes. 7 A 4	Ich bezahle meine Kleidung selbst.
owner	Besitzer, Besitzerin
Oxfam 7 A 5	*brit. Hilfsorganisation zur Bekämpfung der Hungersnot*

P

p = **pence** *(pl.)*	Pence
(to) **pack**	(ein)packen
packet	Paket, Päckchen; Packung
page	Seite *(im Buch)*
paid → (to) **pay**	
(to) **paint**	streichen, anstreichen; malen
palace	Palast, Schloß
paper = **newspaper**	Zeitung
parents	Eltern
park	Park
(to) **park** 5 Ex 9	parken
parrot 8 A 1	Papagei
part (of) 4 Ex 11	Teil (von); Gegend
(to) **take part** (in) 5 A 8	teilnehmen (an), mitmachen (bei)
part	Rolle *(eines Schauspielers)*
partner	Partner, Partnerin
party	Party, Fest, Fete
past 10 129	Vergangenheit
past: half past ten	halb elf (= 10.30)
path 9 T	Pfad, Fußweg
(to) **pay** (for) 7 A 4	(be)zahlen
pedal 2 A 3	Pedal
pedestrian	Fußgänger/in
pedestrian precinct	Fußgängerzone
pen	Füller; *auch:* Stift *(außer Bleistift)*
pence *(pl.)*	Pence
pencil	Bleistift
pencil-case	Federtasche, Federmäppchen
pen-friend	Brieffreund, Brieffreundin
penguin 8 A 1	Pinguin
people *(pl.)*	Leute, Menschen
perhaps	vielleicht
person 6 T	Person, Mensch
pet	Haustier, Tier
pet shop	Tierhandlung
petrol 8 T	Benzin
phone	= **telephone**
(to) **phone**	= (to) **telephone**
photo	Foto, Bild
in the photo	auf dem Foto
(to) **take photos**	fotografieren
phrase 1 Ex 8	Redewendung; Wortgruppe
piano	Klavier
picnic 3 A 6	Picknick
(to) have a picnic 3 A 6	ein Picknick machen
picture	Bild; Aufnahme, Foto
in the picture	auf dem Bild
(to) **take pictures**	fotografieren, Fotos/Bilder machen
pig 1 A 2	Schwein
pity: It's a pity.	Das ist schade.
place	Ort, Platz, Stelle
plan 5 Ex 8	Plan, Vorhaben
plane	Flugzeug
by plane	mit dem Flugzeug
plate	Teller
platform	Bahnsteig
(to) **play**	spielen
(to) play a trick (on) 3 Ex 1	(jm.) einen Streich spielen
player 5 A 1	Spieler, Spielerin
please	bitte
… **pm** 8 A 9	… Uhr nachmittags/abends
pocket	Tasche *(im Mantel usw.)*
pocket-money	Taschengeld

point 10 129	Punkt
polar bear 8 A 1	Eisbär
police *(pl.)*	Polizei
police station	Polizeiwache, Polizeirevier
polio 5 T	Kinderlähmung, Polio
poor	arm
popular (with)	beliebt (bei)
postcard	Postkarte
postcode 1 Ex 13	*britische Postleitzahl*
poster	Poster, Plakat
post office	Post(amt)
potato, *pl.* **potatoes** 3 A 8	Kartoffel
pound	Pfund *(britische Währung)*
(to) **practise**	üben, trainieren
precinct: pedestrian precint	Fußgängerzone
(to) prepare	vorbereiten, zubereiten
present	Geschenk
president	Präsident/in
price 5 Ex 7	(Kauf-)Preis
prince 10 T	Prinz, Fürst
princess 10 T	Prinzessin, Fürstin
prize 5 A 8	Preis, Gewinn
probably 8 A 4	wahrscheinlich
problem	Problem
programme	Sendung, Programm
(to) **pronounce**	aussprechen
proper 8 T	richtig, passend, geeignet
(to) **protect** (from) 2 A 2	(be)schützen (vor)
(to) pull down 6 T	abreißen, niederreißen
puncture	Reifenpanne
pupil	Schüler, Schülerin
(to) **put** 2 Ex 3	stellen, legen, setzen, (wohin) tun
(to) put in 5 Ex 9	einsetzen
(to) **put on** 7 A 5	*(Kleidung)* anziehen
(to) **put up** 6 A 5	aufbauen, aufstellen; aufhängen, anbringen
puzzle	Rätsel

Q

quarter past/to ten	viertel nach/vor zehn
queen	Königin
question	Frage
(to) **ask a question**	eine Frage stellen
quick 5 A 3	schnell
quiet	still, ruhig, leise
quite 5 Ex 10	ziemlich; ganz
quiz	Quiz

R

rabbit	Kaninchen
race 2 A 1	Rennen, (Wett-)Lauf
(to) **have a race** 2 A 1	ein Rennen veranstalten
racing driver 8 Ex 7	Rennfahrer/in
radio	Radio, Rundfunk
on the radio	im Radio
rain 8 A 2	Regen
(to) **rain**	regnen
ran → (to) **run**	
rang → (to) **ring**	
(to) **read**	(vor)lesen
ready 2 T	bereit, fertig
really	wirklich, tatsächlich
record	Schallplatte
record-player	Plattenspieler
red	rot
regular 5 T	regelmäßig
relative	Verwandte/r
(to) release (the brake) 8 T	(die Bremse) lösen; los-, freilassen
(to) **remember** Intro 1	sich erinnern (an); daran denken, sich merken
(to) **repair**	reparieren
a repair kit	Flickzeug
repair shop	Reparaturwerkstatt für Fahrräder
restaurant	Restaurant, Gaststätte
(to) **return** 6 A 7	zurückkommen, zurückgehen
reward 8 110	Belohnung; Finderlohn
rhyme	Reim, Vers
ridden → (to) **ride**	
(to) **ride** (a horse/ a bike) 1 A 3	(auf einem Pferd) reiten; (rad)fahren
rider 2 A 2	(Rad-)Fahrer/in; Reiter/in
riding 5 A 2	Reiten
right	richtig
all right	gut, in Ordnung
(to) **be right** 1 A 6	recht haben
My watch is right.	Meine Uhr geht richtig.
That's right.	Richtig! Stimmt!
right	rechte(r, s), nach rechts
on the right	rechts, auf der rechten Seite
(to) **ring** 10 A 3	klingeln, läuten; anrufen
river	Fluß
on the (River) Thames 1 A 1	an der Themse
road	(Land-)Straße
road sign 2 27	Verkehrszeichen
roast beef 3 A 8	Rinderbraten, Roastbeef
rock 9 A 3	Fels(en)
rocket 10 128	Rakete
rode → (to) **ride**	
role-play	Rollenspiel
roll 3 A 4	Brötchen, Semmel
(to) **roll** 9 T	rollen
room	Zimmer, Raum
round 2 A 10	um (... herum)
round	Kanon
rubber	Radiergummi; Gummi
ruin 9 A 3	Ruine
in ruins 9 A 3	zerstört
ruler	Lineal
(to) **run**	rennen, laufen
rung → (to) **ring**	
running 5 A 2	Laufen, Rennen

S

saddle 2 A 3	Sattel
safe 9 A 9	sicher, gefahrlos
said → (to) **say**	
(to) **sail** 9 T	segeln, fahren
sailor 9 A 6	Seemann, Matrose
salad 3 A 8	(angemachter) Salat
ham salad 3 A 8	Schinken mit Salat
sale: for sale 8 110	zu verkaufen
salt 3 A 12	Salz
the same	der-, die-, dasselbe
sand 9 A 3	Sand
sandwich	belegtes Butterbrot
sang → (to) sing	
sank → (to) **sink**	
sat → (to) **sit**	
Saturday	Samstag, Sonnabend
sauce 3 T	Soße
saucer 3 A 2	Untertasse
sausage 3 A 8	Wurst, Würstchen
(to) **save**	sparen
(to) **save** 9 A 7	retten
saw → (to) **see**	
(to) **say**	sagen
(to) **say hello (to)** 10 A 4	grüßen
school	Schule
at school	in der Schule
(to) **go to school**	zur Schule gehen
(to) leave school 5 A 1	von der Schule abgehen
Scotland	Schottland
Scottish 4 T	schottisch
Scout: Girl Scout *(AE)* 10 A 1	Pfadfinderin *(in den USA)*
scream 6 T	Schrei; Aufschrei
sea	Meer
sea lion 8 A 1	Seelöwe
season	Jahreszeit; Saison
second	Sekunde

(to) **see**	sehen
I see. 4 T	Ich verstehe. Ach so!
Let me see, … 1 Ex 8	Warte mal! Laß mich mal überlegen!
Let's see. 4 T	Wollen mal sehen.
See you soon.	Tschüs. Bis bald.
seen → (to) **see**	
(to) **sell**	verkaufen
(to) **send** 9 A 3	schicken, senden
sent → (to) **send**	
sentence	Satz
September	September
set 5 A 5	Satz *(Tennis usw.)*
several 6 A 1	mehrere; verschiedene
shall 8 S	(tun) werden
shan't = shall not 8 S	nicht (tun) werden
(to) share (with)	(sich) teilen (mit)
she	sie
shelf; *pl.* shelves	Bord, Brett; Regal
shell 10 T	Muschel(schale)
(to) shine	scheinen *(Sonne)*
ship 9 A 3	Schiff
shirt 7 A 1	(Ober-)Hemd
shoe 3 A 1	Schuh
shone → (to) shine	
shop	Laden, Geschäft
pet shop	Tierhandlung
repair shop	Reparaturwerkstatt für Fahrräder
shop assistant	Verkäufer, Verkäuferin
short	kurz
shorts *(pl.)* 7 A 1	Shorts, kurze Hose(n)
(to) **shout** 2 A 10	(laut) rufen, schreien
(to) **show** 3 A 3	zeigen
shower 4 A 3	Dusche, Brause; (Regen-)Schauer
(to) **have a shower** 4 A 3	(sich) duschen
(to) **shut**	schließen, zumachen
sight	Sehenswürdigkeit
(to) see the sights	sich die Sehenswürdigkeiten ansehen
sight 9 A 3	*hier:* Anblick
sign 2 27	Zeichen; (Hinweis-)Schild
road sign 2 27	Verkehrszeichen
silly	albern, dumm, blöd
(to) sing	singen
singer	Sänger/in
(to) **sink** 9 A 3	sinken, untergehen; versenken
sir	*höfliche Anrede für einen Mann*
Dear Sir or Madam, … 8 110	Sehr geehrte Damen und Herren, …
sister	Schwester
(to) **sit**	sitzen
(to) **sit down**	sich setzen
site: camp site	Campingplatz, Zeltplatz
size 7 A 3	Größe
What size do you take? 7 A 3	Welche Größe hast du/haben Sie?
skiing 5 A 2	Skilaufen, Skifahren
skirt 7 A 1	Rock
skyscraper	Wolkenkratzer
(to) **sleep**	schlafen
slept → (to) **sleep**	
slow 5 A 3	langsam
small	klein
smelly 1 A 4	stinkend
They're smelly. 1 A 4	Sie stinken.
smuggler 9 A 3	Schmuggler/in
so	darum, deshalb; also
so	so
so that 10 A 1	damit, so daß
I don't think so.	Das glaube/finde ich nicht.
I think so.	Ich glaube (ja).
sock 7 A 1	Socke, Strumpf
sofa	Sofa
sold → (to) **sell**	
some	einige, ein paar; etwas
some more 1 Ex 2	noch einige/etwas
somebody 3 S	jemand
something 3 A 13	etwas
sometimes	manchmal
somewhere 3 S	irgendwo(hin)
son 6 T	Sohn
song	Lied
soon	bald
sore 4 A 12	wund, rauh, entzündet
a sore throat 4 A 12	Halsschmerzen, Halsweh
sorry: (I'm) sorry.	Entschuldigung! Tut mir leid!
Sorry?	Wie bitte?
Sorry I'm late.	Entschuldigen Sie, daß ich zu spät komme.
sound	Laut, Ton; Klang
soup 3 A 13	Suppe
south (of) 6 A 1	südlich (von); Süd-; (nach) Süden
southern 10 129	südlich, Süd-
southernmost 10 129	südlichste(r, s)
souvenir	(Reise-)Andenken, Souvenir
space 10 128	(Welt-)Raum; Platz
spaghetti *(sing.)* 3 T	Spaghetti
Spain	Spanien
Spanish 10 128	spanisch; Spanier/in; Spanisch
(to) **speak** (to)	sprechen (mit)
Amy Connor **speaking.** 10 A 3	(Hier) Amy Connor. *(am Telefon)*
special 2 A 2	besondere(r, s); Sonder-
(to) **spell**	buchstabieren, schreiben
spelt → (to) **spell**	
(to) **spend** (money on)	(Geld) ausgeben (für)
(to) **spend** 10 128	*(Zeit)* verbringen
spent → (to) **spend**	
spoke → (to) **speak**	
spoken → (to) **speak**	
spoon 3 A 2	Löffel
sport	Sport, Sportart
(to) **do sports** 5 A 2	Sport treiben
spring	Frühling, Frühjahr
in (the) spring	im Frühling/Frühjahr
square	Platz *(in einer Stadt)*
stadium	Stadion
stairs *(pl.)*	Treppe(nstufen)
stamp	(Brief-)Marke
(to) **stand**	stehen
(to) **stand up** 4 A 1	aufstehen; aufrecht stehen
star 6 A 10	Stern
(to) **start**	anfangen (mit), beginnen; starten
starter 2 A 5	Starter/in
state	Staat
station	Bahnhof
police station	Polizeiwache, Polizeirevier
statue	Statue
(to) **stay**	bleiben; übernachten, wohnen
steering wheel 8 T	Steuer(rad), Lenkrad
stereo	Stereo, Stereo-
still	(immer) noch
still	trotzdem, dennoch
(a) **stomach ache** 4 A 12	Magenschmerzen, Bauchschmerzen
stone 3 Ex 6	Stein
stood → (to) **stand**	
stop: bus stop 8 Ex 4	Bushaltestelle
(to) **stop**	aufhören; anhalten, stoppen
storm 9 A 6	Sturm; Gewitter
story	Geschichte, Erzählung
strange 6 A 10	seltsam, sonderbar; fremd
street	Straße
in Sandfield **Street**	in der Sandfieldstraße
in the street	auf der Straße
strong	stark; kräftig
style 7 Ex 5	Stil, Mode; Art, Weise
suburb 10 A 1	Vorstadt, Vorort, Randbezirk
successful 5 A 8	erfolgreich
suddenly 2 A 11	plötzlich
sugar 3 A 11	Zucker

(to) suit 7 A 3	jm. stehen
summer	Sommer
in (the) summer	im Sommer
sun	Sonne
Sunday	Sonntag
sung → (to) sing	
sunk → (to) **sink**	
sunshine 10 128	Sonne(nschein)
super	phantastisch, toll; Super-
supermarket 1 T	Supermarkt
(to) **suppose** 8 A 10	annehmen, vermuten
sure	sicher, gewiß
swam → (to) **swim**	
sweets	Süßigkeiten, Bonbons
(to) **swim**	schwimmen
swimming 5 A 2	Schwimmen
swimming-pool	Schwimmbad; Schwimmbecken
swum → (to) **swim**	

T

table	Tisch
table-tennis	Tischtennis
(to) **take**	(mit)nehmen; (hin)bringen, (weg)bringen
(to) **take part** (in) 5 A 8	teilnehmen (an), mitmachen (bei)
(to) **take photos/ pictures**	fotografieren, Fotos/ Bilder machen
(to) take the dog for a walk	mit dem Hund raus-gehen
What size do you take? 7 A 3	Welche Größe hast du/haben Sie?
taken → (to) **take**	
(to) **talk** (to)	sprechen, reden (mit)
tall	groß; hoch
taught → (to) **teach**	
tea	Tee
(to) have tea 3 A 9	Abendbrot essen, zu Abend essen
(to) **make tea**	Tee kochen
(to) **teach** Intro 2	unterrichten, lehren, beibringen
teacher	Lehrer, Lehrerin
technology 10 129	Technologie, Technik
(tele)phone	Telefon
(to) answer the (tele)phone 8 110	ans Telefon gehen
(to) **be on the (tele)phone**	am Telefon sein, gerade telefonieren
(tele)phone call 8 110	Anruf, Telefon-gespräch
(to) **(tele)phone**	anrufen
television = **TV**	Fernsehen, Fernseher
on TV	im Fernsehen
(to) **watch TV**	fernsehen
(to) **tell**	sagen, nennen; erzählen, berichten
(to) **tell the way**	den Weg beschreiben
a **temperature** 4 A 12	Fieber, (erhöhte) Temperatur
tent	Zelt
terrible	schrecklich, furchtbar
test 4 T	Test, Klassenarbeit
(to) **do a test** 4 T	eine Arbeit schreiben, eine Prüfung machen
(more) **than**	(mehr) als
Thank you.	Danke (schön).
Thank you very much. 1 Ex 13	Vielen Dank.
Thanks.	Danke (schön).
that	der/die/das (da), jene(r, s) (dort)
... that ...	..., daß ...
so that 10 A 1	damit, so daß
the	der, die, das; die *(Plural)*
their	ihr, ihre
theirs 8 A 5	ihre(r, s)
them	ihnen, sie
then	dann
then 2 Ex 9	zu der Zeit, damals
there	da, dort; dahin, dorthin
over there 7 Ex 13	dort drüben, da drüben
there is/are	da ist/sind, es gibt
these	diese, die (hier)
they	sie
thing	Ding, Sache
(to) **think**	meinen, finden, glau-ben, denken
I don't think so.	Das finde/glaube ich nicht.
I think so.	Ich glaube (ja.)
What do you think about ...? 4 Ex 12	Was hältst du von ...? Wie findest du ...?
(to) **think of**	denken an
thirsty 3 A 4	durstig
(to) be thirsty 3 A 4	Durst haben
this	diese(r, s), der/die/ das (hier)
This is how you do it. 1 Ex 13	So/Auf diese Weise macht man es.
this morning/ afternoon/evening	heute morgen/nach-mittag/abend
those	die/diese (da), jene (dort)
thought → (to) **think**	
threw → (to) **throw**	
throat: a sore throat 4 A 12	Halsschmerzen, Hals-weh
through	durch, hindurch
(to) **throw** (away) 7 T	(weg)werfen
thrown → (to) **throw**	
thumb 4 A 1	Daumen
Thursday	Donnerstag
ticket	Eintrittskarte; Fahr-karte, Fahrschein
ticket inspector	Kontrolleur/in
tidy 7 Ex 3	ordentlich, auf-geräumt
(to) tidy up	aufräumen
tie 7 A 1	Krawatte, Schlips
tiger	Tiger
tight 7 A 2	eng(anliegend), stramm
(from ...) till	(von ...) bis *(Zeit-angabe)*
time	Zeit
(to) have a nice time 3 Ex 4	eine schöne Zeit/ viel Spaß haben
Have a good time.	Viel Spaß! Viel Vergnügen!
What time is it?	Wie spät ist es?
time(s) 4 A 2	Mal, mal
for the first time 8 A 7	zum ersten Mal
tin	Dose, Büchse
tin mine 9 A 3	Zinnmine, Zinnberg-werk
tired	müde
to	zu, nach, in
(to) **give to** sb. 7 A 5	jm. geben
(to) **go to bed** 1 A 7	ins Bett gehen
(to) **happen to** 6 Ex 1	passieren, geschehen mit
I've **been to** ... 6 A 9	Ich bin in ... gewesen.
(to) **listen to**	(sich) anhören
next to	neben
quarter to ten	viertel vor zehn
(to) **speak to**	sprechen mit
(to) **talk to**	sprechen mit
(to) **write to**	schreiben an
to: Try **to** come.	Versuche zu kommen!
... **to** ... 7 A 8	..., um zu ...
tobacco 9 A 5	Tabak
today	heute
today's paper 7 Ex 13	die heutige Zeitung, die Zeitung von heute
together	zusammen
toilet	Toilette
told → (to) **tell**	
tomato, *pl.* tomatoes 3 A 11	Tomate
tomorrow	morgen
tomorrow morning	morgen früh
tomorrow's paper 7 Ex 13	die morgige Zeitung, die Zeitung von morgen
tonight	heute abend, heute nacht
..., **too.**	auch

too small	zu klein
took → (to) **take**	
tooth, *pl.* **teeth** 3 A 1	Zahn
top: on top (of) 9 A 3	oben, zuoberst (auf)
(to) touch	berühren, anfassen
tour: (to) go on a bus tour 10 128	eine Bus(rund)fahrt machen
(to) go on a guided tour 9 A 3	eine Führung (mit)machen
tourist	Tourist/in
towards 2 A 11	auf … zu, in Richtung auf
town	Stadt
in town 5 A 1	in der (Innen-)Stadt
toy; toys 7 A 5	Spielzeug; Spielsachen
track 2 A 4	(Renn-)Bahn, Rennstrecke, Piste
tradition 10 A 3	Tradition
traffic 2 Ex 13	Verkehr
traffic lights *(pl.)* 2 Ex 13	(Verkehrs-)Ampel
train	(Eisenbahn-)Zug
by train	mit dem Zug
(to) train 5 A 8	trainieren, ausbilden
training 10 128	Ausbildung, Schulung; Training
travel 10 128	(das) Reisen
space travel 10 128	Raumfahrt
(to) **travel**	reisen, fahren
tree	Baum
trick 2 A 1	Kunststück; Trick
(to) play a trick (on) 3 Ex 1	(jm.) einen Streich spielen
trip: (to) **go on a trip** 6 A 2	eine Reise/Fahrt machen, einen Ausflug machen
trouble: (to) **get into trouble** 9 A 10	in Schwierigkeiten geraten, Probleme bekommen
trousers *(pl.)* 7 A 1	(lange) Hose, Hosen
true	wahr
(to) **try**	versuchen, probieren
(to) try on 7 A 4	anprobieren
Tuesday	Dienstag
tunnel 9 A 3	Tunnel; Bergwerksstollen
turn: It's your turn.	Du bist an der Reihe.
(to) **turn**	abbiegen, einbiegen
TV = television	Fernsehen, Fernseher
on TV	im Fernsehen
(to) **watch TV**	fernsehen
two by two 8 A 2	zu zweit, paarweise
typical (of) 9 A 3	typisch (für)
tyre 2 A 3	Reifen

U

uncle	Onkel
under	unter
Underground	Untergrundbahn, U-Bahn
by Underground	mit der U-Bahn
underlined 5 Ex 11	unterstrichen
(to) **understand**	verstehen, begreifen
understood → (to) **understand**	
underwater 10 129	Unterwasser-; unter Wasser
unhappy 7 Ex 3	unglücklich, traurig
uniform	Uniform
unit	Lektion; Einheit
united	vereinigt
the **U.S.A.** *(sing.)* = the **United States of America**	die Vereinigten Staaten von Amerika
(to) unload 6 A 2	ausladen, abladen
unlucky day 2 Ex 2	Unglückstag
untidy 7 Ex 3	unordentlich, unaufgeräumt
until 10 A 1	bis
up 9 T	herauf, hinauf
(to) **get up**	aufstehen
(to) **put up** 6 A 5	aufbauen, aufstellen; aufhängen, anbringen
(to) stand up 4 A 1	*(von einem Platz)* aufstehen; aufrecht stehen
upstairs	oben *(im Haus)*; nach oben
us	uns
(to) **use**	benutzen, gebrauchen, verwenden
usual 8 Ex 10	üblich, gewöhnlich
usually	normalerweise, gewöhnlich

V

vacation *(AE)* 10 A 2	Ferien, Urlaub
very	sehr
(to like) **very much** 5 A 1	sehr (gern mögen)
village	Dorf
virus 4 T	Virus, Krankheitserreger
visit: on a **visit to** …	bei einem Besuch in …
(to) **visit**	besuchen, besichtigen
visitor 10 128	Besucher/in, Gast

W

waffle 10 A 3	Waffel
waggon 9 T	Pferdewagen, Planwagen
(to) **wait** (for)	warten (auf)
Wait a minute. 4 T	Einen Augenblick! Moment mal!
Wales	Wales
walk: (to) take the dog for a walk	mit dem Hund rausgehen, mit dem Hund spazierengehen
(to) **walk**	(zu Fuß) gehen, laufen
(to) go **walking** 10 A 1	wandern
wall	Wand; Mauer
(to) **want**	(haben) wollen
(to) **want to**	(tun) wollen, mögen
wanted 8 110	gesucht
wardrobe 7 A 1	Kleiderschrank
warm	warm
was 2 A 5 → (to) **be**	war
wash: (to) **have a wash** 4 A 3	sich waschen
(to) **wash**	(sich) waschen
(to) wash the dishes	(das Geschirr) spülen, abwaschen
watch	(Armband-) Uhr
My watch is wrong.	Meine Uhr geht falsch.
(to) **watch**	ansehen, beobachten; zuschauen
(to) **watch TV**	fernsehen
water	Wasser
way	Weg
in the way	im Weg
on my way (to)	unterwegs (nach)
(to) **tell the way**	den Weg beschreiben
way 3 A 1	Art und Weise
This is **the way** you do it. 3 A 1	So/Auf diese Weise macht man es.
in different **ways** 3 A 1	auf verschiedene Weise(n)
we	wir
weak 5 A 3	schwach
(to) **wear**	*(Kleidung)* tragen, anhaben
weather 1 Ex 13	Wetter
wedding 10 A 3	Hochzeit
Wednesday	Mittwoch
week	Woche
weekend: at the weekend	am Wochenende
weightlifting 5 A 2	Gewichtheben
welcome: You're welcome.	Bitte (sehr). Nichts zu danken.
Well, …	Nun, …; Also, …
Well! 7 T	Na so was! Du meine Güte! Wirklich?
well *(adj.)* 4 A 13	wohlauf, gesund

well: She played **well.** *(adv.)* 5 A 6	Sie spielte gut.
went → (to) **go**	
were 2 A 5 → (to) **be**	warst, waren, wart
west (of)	westlich (von); West-; (nach) Westen
wet	naß; feucht
What?	Was?
What ...?	Was für ein(e) ...?, Welche(r, s) ...?
What a question! 4 Ex 3	Was für eine Frage!
What colour is ...?	Welche Farbe hat ...?
What date is it (today)?	Der Wievielte ist heute?
What do you call ...? 10 128	Wie nennt man ...?
What is it?	Was ist denn (los)?
What's it **like?** 2 Ex 15	Wie ist es? Wie sieht es aus?
What's wrong with Kevin? 4 A 12	Was fehlt Kevin? Was hat Kevin?
What time is it?	Wie spät ist es?
wheel 2 A 3	Rad *(am Fahrrad, Auto usw.)*
steering wheel 8 T	Steuer(rad), Lenkrad
wheelchair 5 A 8	Rollstuhl
When?	Wann?
when	wenn
when 2 T	als
Where?	Wo? Wohin?
Where are you from?	Wo kommst du her?
Which? 4 A 9	Welche(r, s)?
Which of you? 4 A 9	Wer von euch?
while 9 A 7	während
white	weiß
Who?	Wer?
Whose? 4 A 8	Wessen?
Whose is it? 4 A 8	Wem gehört es?
Why?	Warum? Weshalb?
Why not ...?	Warum nicht ...? Könnten wir nicht ...?
wife, *pl.* **wives**	(Ehe-)Frau
wild 8 T	wild; ausgelassen; stürmisch
will 8 A 8	(tun) werden
(to) **win** 4 A 5	gewinnen
wind 9 A 7	Wind
window	Fenster, Schaufenster
winter	Winter
in (the) winter	im Winter
with	mit; bei
with the girls	bei den Mädchen
without 2 A 2	ohne
wolf, *pl.* wolves 8 T	Wolf
woman, *pl.* **women**	Frau
won → (to) **win**	
won't = **will not** 8 A 8	nicht (tun) werden
wood 6 A 5	Holz
wood(s) 1 A 1	Wald
word	Wort
wore → (to) **wear**	
work	Arbeit
at work	bei der Arbeit
(to) **go to work**	zur Arbeit gehen
(to) **work**	arbeiten
(to) **work** 9 A 3	in Betrieb sein, funktionieren
world	Welt
in the world	auf der Welt
worn → (to) **wear**	
(to) **worry** (about) 6 Ex 2	sich Sorgen machen (wegen)
Don't worry. 6 Ex 2	Mach dir keine Sorgen! Ist schon gut!
worried (about) 6 Ex 3	besorgt (um), beunruhigt (wegen)
worse (than) 4 A 6	schlechter (als); schlimmer als
(the) **worst** 4 A 6	(der/die/das) schlechteste, schlimmste; am schlechtesten, schlimmsten
worth 7 A 8	wert
would: I'd like	ich möchte (haben)
I'd like to	ich möchte (tun)
I'd love (to) 6 Ex 11	ich hätte (liebend) gern; ich würde sehr gern (tun)
wreck 9 A 3	Wrack
wrecker 9 A 6	Strandräuber
(to) **write** (to)	schreiben (an)
(to) **write down** 3 A 10	aufschreiben
written → (to) **write**	
wrong	falsch
(to) **be wrong** 1 A 6	unrecht haben
My watch is wrong.	Meine Uhr geht falsch.
What's wrong with Kevin? 4 A 12	Was fehlt Kevin? Was hat Kevin?
wrote → (to) **write**	

Y

year	Jahr
yellow	gelb
yes	ja
yesterday 2 A 7	gestern
yesterday's lesson 7 Ex 13	die gestrige Stunde, die Stunde gestern
the day before yesterday 7 Ex 13	vorgestern
... yet? 6 A 7	... schon ...?
not ... yet 6 A 6	noch nicht
yoghurt 3 A 4	Joghurt
you	du, ihr, Sie; dir, euch, Ihnen; dich, Sie, euch; man
you know	weißt du, nämlich
young	jung
your	dein(e); Ihr(e); euer, eure
yours 8 A 5	deine(r, s); Ihre(r, s); eure(r, s)
Yours, ...	Dein(e) ...; Ihr(e) ...; Euer/Eure ... *(am Briefende)*
youth club	Jugendclub, Jugendzentrum
youth hostel	Jugendherberge
Yugoslavia	Jugoslawien

Z

zebra 8 A 1	Zebra
zoo 8 A 4	Zoo

Irregular verbs

Infinitive	Simple past	Past participle	
(to) be	(I) was, (you) were	(I've/she has) been	sein
beat	beat	beaten	schlagen, besiegen
become	became	become	werden
begin	began	begun	beginnen, anfangen
blow	blew [uː]	blown [əʊ]	blasen, wehen
break [eɪ]	broke [əʊ]	broken [əʊ]	(zer)brechen; kaputtmachen
bring	brought [ɔː]	brought [ɔː]	(mit)bringen, (her)bringen
buy	bought [ɔː]	bought [ɔː]	kaufen
catch	caught [ɔː]	caught [ɔː]	fangen, erwischen
choose [uː]	chose [əʊ]	chosen [əʊ]	(aus)wählen, aussuchen
come	came	come	kommen
cut [ʌ]	cut [ʌ]	cut [ʌ]	schneiden
do [uː]	did	done [ʌ]	tun, machen
draw	drew [uː]	drawn	zeichnen
drink	drank	drunk	trinken
drive	drove	driven [ɪ]	(Auto) fahren
eat	ate [e, eɪ]	eaten	essen
fall	fell	fallen	fallen
feed	fed	fed	füttern
feel	felt	felt	(sich) fühlen
find (out)	found (out) [aʊ]	found (out) [aʊ]	(heraus)finden
fly	flew [uː]	flown [əʊ]	fliegen
get	got	got	bekommen; gelangen, (hin)kommen
get up	got up	got up	aufstehen
give	gave	given	geben; schenken
go	went	gone [ɒ]	gehen; fahren
go by	went by	gone by	vergehen *(Zeit)*
go on	went on	gone on	weitermachen
grow	grew [uː]	grown [əʊ]	wachsen
have (got)	had	had	haben
hear [ɪə]	heard [ɜː]	heard [ɜː]	hören
hide [aɪ]	hid [ɪ]	hidden [ɪ]	(sich) verstecken
hit [ɪ]	hit	hit	schlagen, treffen
know [əʊ]	knew [juː]	known [əʊ]	kennen; wissen
leave	left	left	weggehen, verlassen; (zurück)lassen
let	let	let	(zu)lassen
lie [aɪ]	lay [eɪ]	lain [eɪ]	liegen
lose [uː]	lost [ɒ]	lost [ɒ]	verlieren
make	made	made	machen, bauen
mean [iː]	meant [e]	meant [e]	bedeuten; meinen
meet	met	met	(sich) treffen, kennenlernen
overtake	overtook [ʊ]	overtaken	überholen
pay (for) [eɪ]	paid (for) [eɪ]	paid (for) [eɪ]	(be)zahlen
put [ʊ]	put [ʊ]	put [ʊ]	stellen, legen, setzen
put in	put in	put in	einsetzen
put on	put on	put on	*(Kleidung)* anziehen
put up	put up	put up	aufbauen, aufstellen; aufhängen
read [iː]	read [e]	read [e]	(vor)lesen
ride [aɪ]	rode	ridden [ɪ]	reiten; (rad)fahren
ring	rang	rung	klingeln, läuten; anrufen
run	ran	run	rennen, laufen
say	said [e]	said [e]	sagen
see	saw	seen	sehen

Infinitive	**Simple past**	**Past participle**	
sell	sold	sold	verkaufen
send	sent	sent	schicken, senden
shine	shone [ɒ]	shone [ɒ]	scheinen *(Sonne)*
show [əʊ]	showed [əʊ]	shown [əʊ]	zeigen
shut [ʌ]	shut [ʌ]	shut [ʌ]	schließen, zumachen
sing	sang	sung	singen
sink	sank	sunk	sinken; versenken
sit (down)	sat (down)	sat (down)	sitzen; sich setzen
sleep	slept [e]	slept [e]	schlafen
speak	spoke	spoken	sprechen
spell	spelt	spelt	buchstabieren, schreiben
spend	spent	spent	*(Geld)* ausgeben; *(Zeit)* verbringen
stand (up)	stood (up) [ʊ]	stood (up) [ʊ]	(auf)stehen
swim	swam	swum	schwimmen
take	took [ʊ]	taken	(mit)nehmen; (hin-, weg)bringen
teach	taught [ɔː]	taught [ɔː]	unterrichten, lehren
tell	told	told	sagen, nennen; erzählen, berichten
think	thought [ɔː]	thought [ɔː]	meinen, denken
throw (away) [əʊ]	threw (away) [uː]	thrown (away) [əʊ]	(weg)werfen
understand	understood [ʊ]	understood [ʊ]	verstehen, begreifen
wear [eə]	wore [ɔː]	worn [ɔː]	*(Kleidung)* tragen, anhaben
win	won [ʌ]	won [ʌ]	gewinnen
write (down)	wrote (down)	written (down)	(auf)schreiben

"Somewhere with no irregular verbs."

Answers to the questions on page 52

1. The red line is as long as the black line.
2. The white ball is as big as the black ball.
3. You can jump higher than a house. A house cannot jump!
4. No cat. Because no cat has got more than two ears!
5. Short(**er**).

Bildquellen:

Anthony Verlag, Starnberg (S. 120 Bild 2); Barnaby's Picture Library, London (S. 56 oben, S. 57 Bilder 1, 6, S. 71, S. 115 oben, S. 117, S. 129 Bild 1); BBC Hulton Picture Library, London (S. 116 Mitte); British Tourist Authority, London (S. 7 Bild 7); Camera Press, London (S. 83 Mitte/rechts, S. 128 Bild 2); J. Allan Cash, London (S. 8 rechts, S. 27 Bild 5, S. 57 Bilder 2-5, 7, S. 83 oben links/unten links, S. 115 Mitte/unten, S. 129 Bild 3); David Dore, Guildford (S. 6, S. 27 Bilder 6, 7, S. 32, S. 56 Mitte/unten); Michael Ferguson, Berlin (S. 7 Bilder 1-3, 5-7, S. 8 oben links); Angelika Fischer, Berlin (S. 39); J. Horner, Cambridge (S. 67); Jarrold Colour Publications, Norwich (S. 102 unten, S. 103); Judges Postcards Ltd., Hastings (S. 7 Bild 4); Tim Leighton-Boyce, London (S. 17/18); The Lions of Longleat Safari Park, Warminster (S. 102 oben); Magnum Photos, Hamburg (S. 129 Bild 4); The Observer, London (S. 60); Orlando Chamber of Commerce, Orlando, Florida (S. 128 Bild 1); Günter Peters, Berlin (S. 101); Punch Publications Ltd., London (S. 182); Christfried Tschepe, Berlin (S. 83 oben rechts/unten rechts); John Walmsley, Biggleswade (S. 27 Bilder 3, 4, S. 57 Bild 8); Raymond Williams, Berlin (S. 87).
Einband: Ingeborg Ullrich, Berlin.